THE GRAND FLEET

Admiral Sir John Jellicoe

◢ships su[…]

Engadine - seaplane carrier

23 LIGHT CRUISERS

8 ARMOURED CRUISERS

4 FAST BATTLESHIPS

5th Battle Sqdn.: Barham, Valiant, Warspite, Malaya

9 BATTLE CRUISERS

1st Sqdn.: Lion, Princess Royal, Queen Mary ◢, Tiger

2nd Sqdn.: New Zealand, Indefatigable ◢

3rd Sqdn.: Invincible ◢, Inflexible, Indomitable

24 DREADNOUGHTS

1st Battle Sqdn.:
- 6th Div.: Marlborough, Revenge, Hercules, Agincourt
- 5th Div.: Colossus, Collingwood, Neptune, St. Vincent

4th Battle Sqdn.:
- 3rd Div.: Iron Duke, Royal Oak, Superb, Canada
- 4th Div.: Benbow, Bellerophon, Téméraire, Vanguard

2nd Battle Sqdn.:
- 1st Div.: King George V., Ajax, Centurion, Erin
- 2nd Div.: Orion, Monarch, Conqueror, Thunderer

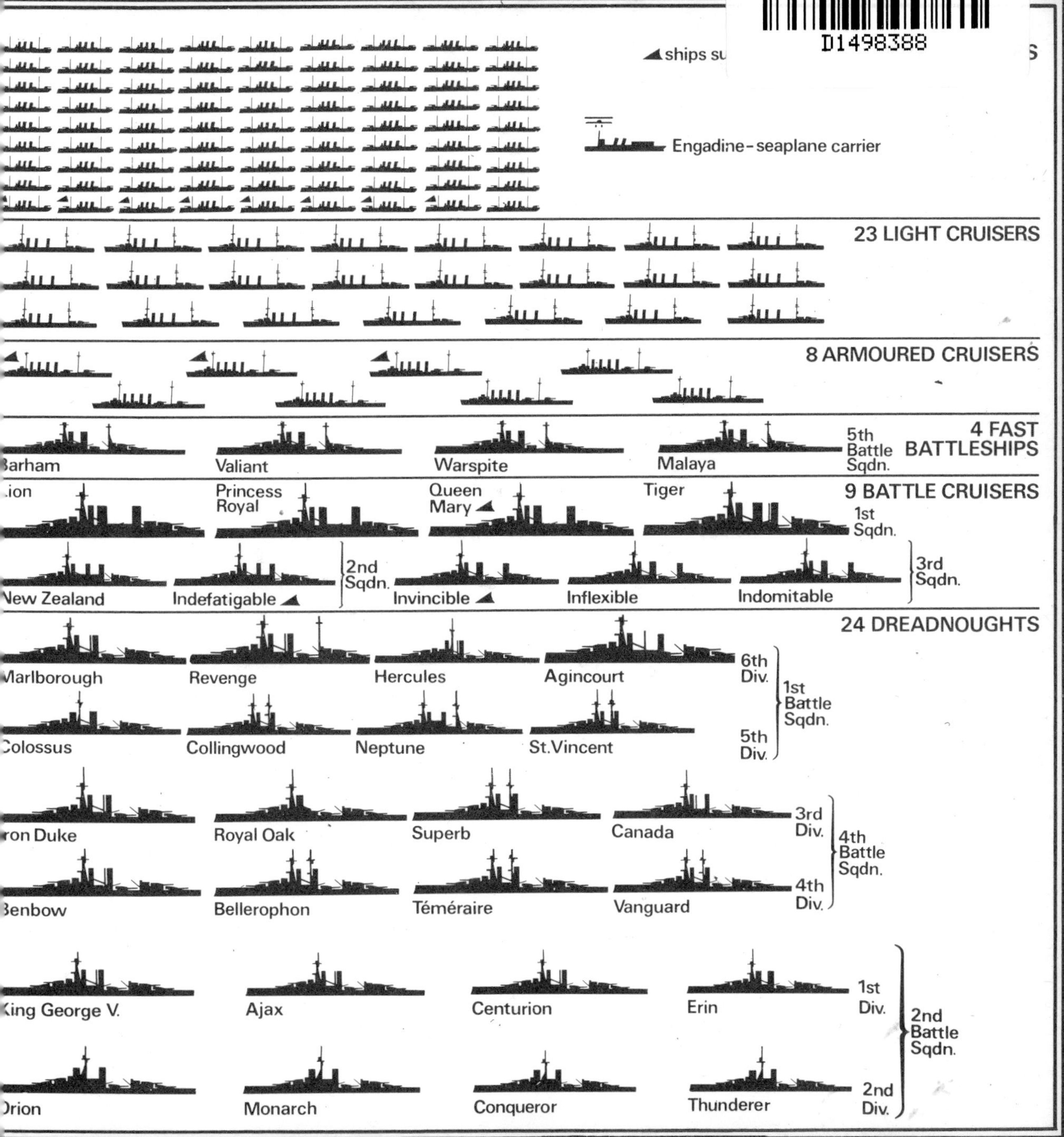

JUTLAND 1916

JUTLAND

John Costello
and Terry Hughes

Holt, Rinehart and Winston
New York

Library of Congress Cataloging in Publication Data
Costello, John.
Jutland 1916.
Bibliography: p.
Includes index.
1. Jutland, Battle of, 1916. I. Hughes, Terry, joint author. II. Title.
D582.J8C63 1977 940.4'56 76-15599
ISBN 0-03-018466-5

First published in the United States in 1977.

Designer: David Eldred

Printed in Great Britain
10 9 8 7 6 5 4 3 2 1

CONTENTS

ACKNOWLEDGMENTS

Photographs and illustrations are supplied by or reproduced by kind permission of the following:

Bilderdienst Süddeutscher Verlag: pages 2 (left), 2–3, 3, 12, 14–15, 18–19, 23 (top), 24, 24–5, 26–7, 32–3, 39, 40–1, 52, 53, 70–1, 79, 81 (top), 88–9, 90, 90–1, 95 (bottom), 98–9, 99, 100, 103, 107, 113 (top), 118–19, 120–1, 122–3, 137, 140, 161, 162, 178–9, 182, 183, 185 (bottom), 190–1, 191 (top), 199 (right), 203, 207 (top), 212, 226;

Bundesarchiv: pages 17, 70, 80–1, 95 (top), 150–1, 186–7, 192–3, 216;

Daily Mail War Album: pages 67 (inset), 74, 88 (inset), 153 (inset);

Fujiphotos: pages 30, 31;

Lt-Cdr Hoyle: pages 94 (bottom), 109 (top);

Illustrated London News: pages 96, 96–7, 148;

Imperial War Museum: pages 10, 34–5, 35, 66, 86–7, 94 (top), 94–5, 108–9, 110, 124–5, 130–1, 132–3, 134–5, 135, 138, 144–5, 164–5, 165 (inset), 168–9, 169, 194–5, 201 (top), 210–11, 214–15, 222–3;

Miss Margery Jinkin: pages 60, 93;

J. G. Moore: page 91;

Nautic Presentations Ltd: pages 2 (right), 11, 13, 37, 38, 42, 54 (left & right), 55, 56, 57, 66 (inset), 69 (inset), 102, 106, 126, 130 (top), 139 (inset), 149, 156 (inset), 166 (inset), 170, 172 (inset), 178 (top left & top right), 179 (top), 199 (inset), 225, 231;

Public Record Office, London: pages 116 (left), 139, 142–3, 146–7, 174–5, 176, 217, 220–1;

Roger Viollet: pages 22–3;

Radio Times Hulton Picture Library: pages 8–9, 18, 29, 36, 43, 44–5, 47 (left & right), 48, 49, 62, 68, 116 (right);

W. P. Trotter: pages 1, 20–1, 46–7, 50–1, 54 (bottom), 58–9, 61, 63, 64–5, 67, 68–9, 72–3, 75, 76–7, 80 (top), 82, 82–3, 84–5, 105, 111, 112–13, 114–15, 115 (top), 128–9, 129 (top), 143 (top), 152–3, 154–5, 156, 158–9, 165, 166–7, 172, 173, 175 (top), 180–1, 185 (top), 196–7, 198–9, 200–1, 204, 206–7, 208–9, 209 (top), 218–19, 220 (top), 229;

Ullstein: page 188.

Picture research by J. G. Moore.

Acknowledgment is made for permission to quote from the following:

The World Crisis, W. S. Churchill;
From the Dreadnought to Scapa Flow, Arthur J. Marder;
Scapa Flow 1919, Admiral Ruge;
Kiel and Jutland, G. Von Hase;
The Life and Letters of David Beatty, W. S. Chalmers;
The Grand Fleet 1914–16, Admiral Jellicoe;
Germany's High Seas Fleet, Admiral Scheer;
My Memoirs, Grand Admiral Tirpitz;
The Private War of Seamon Stumpf, Richard Stumpf.

All possible care has been taken in tracing the ownership of copyright material used in this book and in making acknowledgement for its use. If any owner has not been acknowledged the publishers apologize and will be glad of the opportunity to rectify the error.

PREFACE

The Battle of Jutland took place over two generations ago, but today it still holds a fascination, which is attributable not just to its huge scale, or even to the magnitude of the stakes involved. As the culmination of a great naval arms race that began before the turn of the century, embracing the technological and industrial might of Europe's greatest powers, Jutland holds intriguing parallels for our own times – which have also witnessed a colossal arms race between two power blocks.

From the moment that the last shot was fired at Jutland, the argument and debate began about who were the victors. The controversy over the true significance of Jutland is still being argued. Over the years many books have been written about Jutland, in particular, Professor Arthur Marder's monumental study, *From Dreadnought to Scapa Flow*, which surpasses all other works in its brilliant analysis and objective appraisal of the naval war.

In producing this new account, however, we have sought to put the battle into a contemporary perspective and to follow the course of the action from eyewitness accounts drawn from the British and German reports, memoranda and published material. (For the sake of clarity, we have standardized all references to time during the action to the British time then in operation, which was two hours ahead of German.) In recounting the action we have been fortunate in receiving the assistance of survivors who have supplied us with valuable first-hand memories of one of the most important days of their lives. Foremost amongst those whom we would like to extend our thanks are: Cmdr. H. Burrows, Cmdr. Betts, E. L. Edds, J. Cockburn, Lt. Cmdr. Hoyle, Lt. Bickmore.

It has been our intention to produce not just an illustrated account but a visual record and we are especially indebted to Wilfred Pym Trotter both for his advice and permission to include material from his extensive and unique picture archive. Miss Margery Jinkin has also kindly provided documents and photographs from Admiral Jinkin's archive. We have been fortunate in the assistance of the staff of the Imperial War Museum, Bundersarchiv and Suddeutscher Verlag photographic archives in locating a wealth of visual material.

We are grateful for the helpful advice and suggestions given by Professor Jürgen Rohwer of Bibliothek für Zeitgeschichte, Stuttgart, Professor Berghahn of Warwick University, Dr Paul Kennedy of East Anglia and Admiral Wegener of Kiel. We are particularly indebted for the exhaustive research carried out in the German Archives by Dr Paul Winzen of Cologne, and to Stephen Hartley and Alan Goodger for their work in the British Archives. The staff of the Admiralty Library, RUSI Library and the Public Records Office also provided generous help.

Assembling such a considerable mass of documentary material into this book would not have been possible without the dedicated assistance of Fiona Parker and Ursula Kelf on the translation and typing of the manuscript; Jonathan Moore who organized the picture research; Peter White who designed the maps and most important of all Ann Wilson of Weidenfeld who edited the book and David Eldred who designed it. The project would not have been realised without the encouragement and guidance we have received from Rear Admiral Morgan Giles, the support given by Mr Read and the understanding and effort of Jackie Baldick.

John Costello
Terry Hughes
London 1976

CHA

The 15,000-ton 'Majestics' – the world's most powerful battleships – had pride of place at the Diamond Jubilee review of the Royal Navy, 26 June 1897.

LENGE TO BRITANNIA

June 1897 was a month of great festivity for the British people. Throughout the Empire, from the cotton towns of Lancashire to the frontier settlements of Africa and the hill stations of India, there were parades and parties to mark the Diamond Jubilee of Queen Victoria, whose reign witnessed the creation of the greatest Empire the world had ever seen. On Saturday, 26 June, all attention was focused on the city of Portsmouth where, after celebrating the unity of the Empire, the triumph of their institutions and the strength of their economy, the British prepared to pay tribute to their Navy.

On the waters of Spithead, between Portsmouth and the low hills of the Isle of Wight, 173 British warships manned by 35,000 men concentrated for a Royal Review by HRH the Prince of Wales. The ships were anchored in five long lines covering some thirty square miles of sea, making a brilliant sight for the thousands of spectators crowding along the shores and beaches of Southsea and the Isle of Wight. Each ship, with its black hull, white superstructure and buff funnels had its full company drawn up on deck, awaiting the Royal Yacht. There were warships of every description; rakish four-funnelled cruisers, turtleback destroyers and flotillas of torpedoboats, but pride of place went to the fifty battleships, the heart of the fleet.

Spirits were high and there was an air of excitement. 'The day was fine, the atmosphere fairly clear, there was enough breeze to blow out the bunting and to stir the surface of the water, and as all the ships - foreign as well as British - were dressed rainbow fashion, the enormously long avenues of gala vessels looked extremely brilliant.'

Two faces of Britannia (right) The Navy's prestige was at the heart of the Empire – 'Jack Tar's' sterling character was a hallmark of quality; (below) at the other end of the scale, Vice-Admiral Sir John Fisher, C-in-C Mediterranean Fleet – the pivot of Britain's naval power – exports the Victorian lifestyle aboard his flagship HMS *Renown*.

Even after all the imperial parades and pageants, the people were 'surprised to see the magnitude and perfection of the great machine which we have of late created'. *The Times* significantly pointed out: 'We have done all this without withdrawing a single ship from a foreign station . . . There are two factors in the celebration which transcend all others in their significance as symbols of imperial unity. One is the revered personality of the Queen, the other the superb condition of Her Majesty's Fleet.'

The Navy had a special place in the affection of Victorian England. It was a clear reminder that the security of Britain herself depended on the seas and that while the fleet remained strong 'Britons never shall be slaves'. But it symbolized far more. Its image of dependability and stern competence mirrored those attributes of the Victorian character which the British people liked to project throughout the world. The Navy was loved and admired, the Royal Family identified themselves closely with it and industry proudly used its image to market its products, whether tobacco or the latest designs of marine engines. The music halls played sketches showing how the brave bluejackets dealt with foreign tyrants. English mothers dutifully dressed their children in sailor suits. Nor was this deep respect for the Navy confined to England. Throughout the British Empire Her Majesty's subjects depended on the Navy: 'the fleet over the horizon' was always there to protect the subject, his family and his property wherever they might be.

The British Fleet fulfilled a world role beyond the maintenance of the Empire and the security of the homeland. According to the influential journal, the *Fortnightly Review*: 'The maintenance of the British Fleet in all its traditional power is not merely a matter of importance to the people of the British Empire but it is the cornerstone on which rests the preservation of the *status quo* in Europe and in more distant parts of the world.'

One contemporary naval officer 'looked on the Navy more as a world police force than as a war-like institution. We considered that our job was to safeguard law and order throughout the world – safeguard civilization, put out fires on shore, and act as a guide, philosopher and friend to the merchant ships of all nations.'

The Royal Navy's 330 ships and 92,000 men were deployed as a 'far-flung battle line' throughout the world, maintaining a purely British interpretation of justice which the 'lesser breeds' had to accept. Yet in spite of its size and worldwide distribution, the British Navy's power was based on moral strength rather than the weight of its shot. The mere appearance of a British ship 'showing the flag' could make a tremendous difference in a faraway trouble spot. Suddenly off the coast of some distant colony or half-civilized shore an immaculate warship would appear flying the white ensign. Her officers would be unruffled, her crew calm and highly disciplined. The ship itself, with holystoned decks made bright by constant scrubbing, gleaming paintwork and sparkling brass, would produce an overwhelming impression of competence and good order.

But Britain had allowed herself to be lulled into a sense of complacency about her superb Navy, which still operated in the style and tradition of Nelson's day. Character was all; the science and material end of war took second place. At the end of the nineteenth century the strategic disposition of the Royal Navy

'Admiral of the Atlantic' (below) The role in which the Kaiser romantically cast himself portrayed by German artists; (right) an aspiring marine painter himself, Germany's 'Supreme War Lord' exhibited seascapes and sketched numerous designs for new battleships on the backs of menus and Imperial papers.

fleets was still based on the rationale of the days of wooden walls, reflecting Britain's distrust of her hereditary enemies, France and Russia. Most of the important units were outside home waters. The main fleet was based on Alexandria and Malta in the Mediterranean, where it could protect the route to India through the Suez Canal.

The Royal Navy might be omnipresent, yet towards the end of the nineteenth century, as the new 'Majestic' class battleships evidenced, Britain was growing anxious about the permanence of her sea supremacy. British naval policy was based on the 'Two-Power Standard', defined by Lord Goschen, the First Lord of the Admiralty in 1898, as 'the principle that we must be superior in power and equal in numbers to the fleets of any other two countries'. The Two-Power Standard, plus a little extra, continued to be the guiding yardstick for the British Government. In the 1880s there had been a sudden anxiety that Britain was falling behind other powers and the Naval Defence Act of 1889 had established a large battleship building programme. The British Government believed it could always rely on the pre-eminence of British shipbuilding and that Britain could build her ships faster than anybody else in the world. By 1898 Britain was to have 29 first class (i.e. less than 15 years old) battleships with 12 under construction. Other ships like the fast cruisers were required for trade protection, scouting and many other operational requirements at sea, but the essence of sea supremacy was judged to reside in a battle fleet of the heaviest and most powerful ships that could be concentrated against an enemy.

Apart from France and Russia, Britain's traditional enemies, the United States, Japan and Germany were all waking up to the importance of sea power. Technological advances in naval construction particularly favoured the new industrial nations. As the 'Majestic' demonstrated, the modern battleship was 'a box of machinery'.

After 1883 the United States had consistently pursued a policy of naval expansion, laying down four battleships starting with the *Maine*. American ships gave a very good account of themselves in the 1898 war against Spain. The United States was also vigorously upholding the Monroe Doctrine by which she sought to establish exclusive rights as the dominant power in the Americas.

Japan was a different matter. Her Navy was virtually subcontracted to Britain. It had started in the 1850s after Queen Victoria had presented the Mikado with a paddle steamer. The Admiralty had sent officers to train the Japanese in sea warfare and many orders were placed with British yards. Imperial Japanese warships were brilliantly and devastatingly used in the 1895 war against China.

Nearer home, 'a cloud no bigger than a man's hand' had arisen across the North Sea, where Kaiser Wilhelm II was determined to turn Germany into a naval power. British public opinion did not take Germany seriously as a sea power. Yet in 1888 *The Times* reported from Germany:

> At this very moment there is no navy which is better officered or better manned than the German. The officers are, almost without exception, men of high scientific attainments, first rate seamen and magnificent disciplinarians. The men are models of smartness, and, although the majority of them are inland born, they are in all respects as good sailors as our own bluejackets.

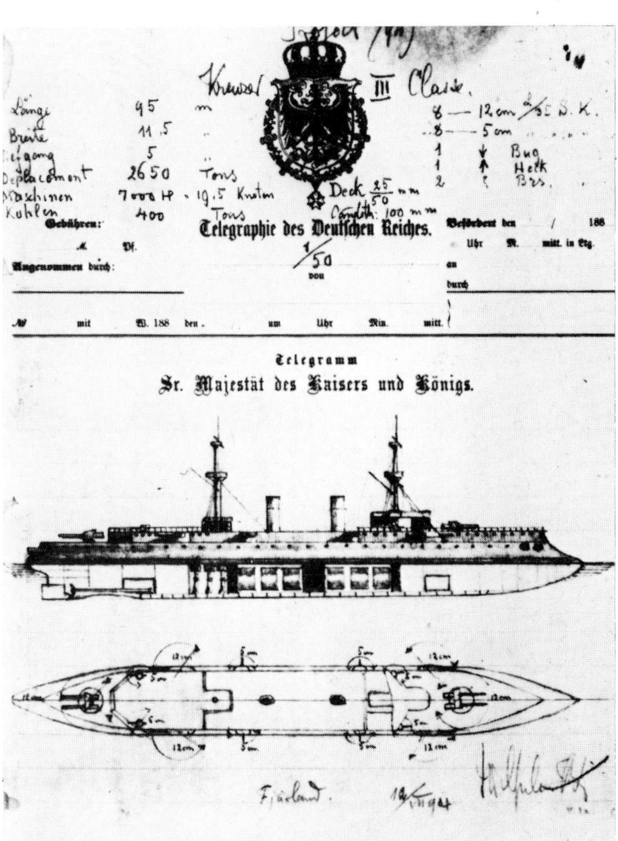

The German Reich had a very long way to go before it could present a display of naval might comparable to Britain's, but the Kaiser was ambitious.

In the very same month of June 1897 when Britain's naval might assembled for the Jubilee Review, secret plans were being drawn up in Imperial Germany to challenge Britain's mastery of the seas. Kaiser Wilhelm II was a passionate advocate of sea power. A grandson of Queen Victoria, the Kaiser had attended many British naval occasions and was proud to be a full Admiral of the Fleet in the Royal Navy. He had learned from Britain's example that world power could be achieved through the effective use of sea power. Admiral Mahan's famous book, *The Influence of Sea Power on History*, made a profound impression on him and his intellectual enthusiasm was supported by a boyish zeal for everything associated with naval matters. He delighted in wearing naval uniforms, appearing at a performance of Richard Wagner's *Flying Dutchman* as an officer of the Imperial Navy, and he sketched designs of battleships in the margins of state papers. He even tried his hand at marine painting.

Germany already possessed the strongest army in the world, but the Kaiser was dedicated to the creation of an equally powerful and prestigious navy. Germany had been a unified state for only 17 years when Wilhelm succeeded to the Emperor's throne in 1888. His new German State was an amalgam of different interests. By force of arms Prussia had incorporated into the Reich no less than four kingdoms (Bavaria, Württemburg, Mecklenburg-Schwerin and Prussia), six duchies, six principalities and three free cities (Hamburg, Bremen and Lübeck). The Emperor's powers were ill-defined and he acted as a *primus inter pares.* Such constitutional authority as existed came from the associated governments of the Reich which met as the Federal Council, the Bundesrat. There was a popular assembly, the Reichstag, but it had little control over the Kaiser. Germany did not possess a national anthem and some state politicians even objected to the use of the term 'Germany' at all. The main instruments of state power – the Army and Navy – were under the total control of the Kaiser, who enjoyed the title 'Supreme War Lord'.

But the unification of Germany had begun to release powerful forces creating new pressures within this cumbersome framework. Germany was industrializing at a rapid pace, her population was soaring and she sought 'a place in the sun' and world power by the acquisition of a colonial empire. Between 1871 and 1914 Germany annexed one million square miles of territory and 13 million people were taken under

The genesis of Germany's naval challenge (below) The Kaiser, accompanied by Empress Augusta Viktoria and the Court, launches an Imperial warship. On the first day of the twentieth century he pledged: 'As my grandfather did for the army, so I will for my navy, carry on unerringly and in similar manner the work of reorganization so that it may also stand on an equality with my armed forces on land, and so that through it, the German Empire may also be in a position abroad to attain that place which it has not yet reached.'

imperial protection. But everywhere Germany turned she was confronted by the interests of other nations, particularly those of Britain. The Kaiser realized that to establish his overseas empire he needed a strong fleet.

The notion of a large navy was important to the Germans for another reason. Under the terms of the 1871 Constitution the Navy was made an imperial institution. As such it became the natural focus for the growing nationalistic elements in German society such as the Pan-German Movement and the German Colonial Society. But although the Kaiser threw his prestige and influence behind the Navy there was considerable political opposition to any plans for a large fleet. According to Tirpitz, who was to play a key role in creating Germany's Navy, 'certain conservative circles distrusted the idea of a fleet. It was not considered to be in keeping with the Prussian tradition; it competed in some degree with the Army and seemed too closely related to industry and commerce in view

of the agricultural distress of that time and the great economic conflicts of the parties.' Individual members of the extreme right even voted against the creation of the 'horrible fleet', but overwhelming support for the Navy was to be found among the liberal bourgeoisie.

Progress towards the establishment of a large Imperial Navy was slow and dilatory, until the last day of 1895 when an event took place in the remote colonial settlements of South Africa which forced the issue of Germany's naval programme. On 31 December 1895, 800 men raided the Boer Republic of the Transvaal. They were led by Dr Jameson, an employee of Cecil Rhodes, the leading British imperialist. A highly sensitive political situation had been developing for some time between the British settlers, who had flocked into the Transvaal following the discovery of gold, and the Boer Government of President Kruger. Germany too had interests in the area, and President Kruger sought to involve Germany as his protector.

The Boers had little trouble in suppressing the

Germany's drive for *Weltmacht* was expressed by economist Gustav Schmoller: 'If we do not participate in the Grand Power struggles of the world, we have no future.' In 1898 the theory was seen in practice when the cruiser SMS *Deutschland* anchored with a powerful squadron at Port Arthur in Manchuria to make Germany's presence felt during the confrontation between the Great Powers over China.

freelance invader, but the Kaiser was beside himself with fury and discerned a British plot to gain control of the troublesome Boers. He realized that, with the British Navy effectively dominating the seas, there was little real help that Germany could send to this colony of German sympathizers but he did ostentatiously telegraph his moral support to Kruger. He then insisted that the Reichstag should immediately approve the construction of a fleet large enough to give Germany the power to influence events overseas. His Chancellor warned that there was 'not a trace of enthusiasm' for a large navy in Germany, to which the Kaiser replied by calling for the education and instruction of his subjects in what he termed 'the development of our sea interests'. Chancellor Hohenlohe was proved right; the Reichstag, deeply suspicious of the Kaiser's schemes for an unlimited fleet, duly cut his estimates. The Secretary of the Imperial Naval Office, Admiral Hollmann, was sacked and the Kaiser turned to a new man to push his plans to fruition – Alfried von Tirpitz.

In 1897 Tirpitz was recalled from the Far East where he was commander of Germany's naval base at Tsingtao. The new Secretary of the Imperial Naval Office was to become the architect not only of the German Navy, but also a major influence on the Kaiser's thinking and on imperial foreign policy. It was to be Tirpitz's plan, as it gradually unfolded from 1897 to the eve of the Great War, which drove Britain into deep hostility towards Germany, swinging her to the side of France and Russia and contributing to her involvement in the First World War. His policy of threatening a North Sea confrontation between British and German battle fleets led ultimately to Jutland.

Tirpitz shared Wilhelm II's ambivalence towards England. Although he spoke English fluently, was well-read in English literature and sent his daughters to Cheltenham Ladies' College to be properly educated, Tirpitz resented the patronizing attitude of the English. On a visit to Gibraltar in the cruiser *Friedrich Karl* in 1873 he recalled that an Englishwoman had been amazed to see German bluejackets: '"Don't they look just like sailors!" she said. When I asked her how else they should look she replied in a most decided tone: "But you are not a sea-going nation."' He blamed 'selfish England's colonial and economic policy' for keeping Germany excluded from the riches of empire, and this, 'combined with our hemmed-in and dangerous continental position, strengthened me in my conviction that no time was to be lost in beginning the attempt to constitute ourselves as a sea power.'

Building up a strong navy was seen by Tirpitz as the answer to Germany's strategic ambition, and he believed other powers would be tempted into alliances with Germany once she could pose a serious threat to British sea power. Britannia could not be everywhere at once watching every naval power. Alternatively, Britain might deem it in her interest to conclude a deal with Germany to their mutual advantage around the world. To those nervous staff officers who asked what Britain would do while this large and threatening fleet was being built on the other side of the North Sea, a mere 300 miles from London, Tirpitz calmly replied that there would be a 'danger zone' through which Germany had to pass before her fleet became strong enough to deter a pre-emptive attack.

If Germany were to challenge Britain at sea, Tirpitz knew that this could only be resolved by a major industrial contest, in which Britain, because of her adherence to the Two-Power Standard, would have to build two ships to every one vessel laid down by Germany. It was debatable how long the British voter and taxpayer would tolerate such heavy demands, should Germany mount a sustained battleship programme at such a rate that Britain would be forced into a huge ship-building programme.

The blueprint for Germany's naval challenge was contained in a top secret memorandum of June 1897, in which Tirpitz submitted his detailed plan for the creation of the new German Navy to the Kaiser. Tirpitz was perfectly certain of Germany's strategic requirement:

> For Germany the most dangerous naval enemy at the present time is England. It is also the enemy against which we most urgently require a certain measure of naval force as a political factor.
>
> Commerce raiding and transatlantic war against England is so hopeless, because of the shortage of

bases on our side and the superfluity on England's side, that we must ignore this type of war against England in our plans for the constitution of our fleet.

Our fleet must be so constructed that it can unfold its greatest military potential between Heligoland and the Thames.

The emphasis was to be on battleships which 'must be designed for action in the line. This demands above all flexibility of the line, heavy guns, and armour thick enough to prevent hits from penetrating.' But even with the fast pace of Germany's industrial expansion, he concluded, 'we cannot create in the near future, that is roughly up to 1905, more than two full squadrons of eight battleships each.'

In a law placed before the Reichstag, Tirpitz set out the numbers of ships required by 1905 to build the battle fleet aimed at the heart of Britain: 19 battleships (2 as reserve); 8 armoured coastal ships; 12 large cruisers (3 overseas reserve); 30 small cruisers (3 overseas reserve); 12 torpedoboat divisions. The overseas fleet would be: 3 large cruisers; 9 small cruisers and 4 gunboats, backed by a reserve of 3 large and 3 small cruisers. The Emperor enthusiastically approved the plan which now had to be carried through the Reichstag. But there was considerable doubt on the part of the Chancellor, and the political parties who still deeply distrusted the Emperor's schemes to build a great navy.

Outside the confines of the Reichstag and the Kaiser's court, Tirpitz showed a mastery of the political situation. He realized that the Navy could be converted into a major national issue in Germany, a focus of pride and ambition for the new nation. In order to achieve this he threw his Ministry into the first modern political public relations campaign. Its success created a role for the Navy in German society.

Under the command of one of his handpicked and 'fiery' young officers, Captain August von Herringen, Tirpitz set up a special News and Parliamentary Unit inside the Admiralty. Its purpose was to 'influence the Press and public opinion decisively in favour of the imperial naval plans'. This would completely outflank the Reichstag and act as a powerful stimulus to German nationalism and unity. Academics and intellectuals were pressed into speaking at meetings called all over Germany in support of a large navy. Business-

Architect of the *Riskflotte* (left) Vice-Admiral Alfried von Tirpitz, Germany's leading advocate of seapower: 'A State which has oceanic, or in equivalent terms world interests, must be able to uphold them and make its power felt beyond its territorial waters. National world commerce, world industry, and to a certain extent, fishing on the high seas, world intercourse and colonies are impossible without a fleet capable of taking the offensive.' By the time of the launching of the SMS *Wittelsbach* in 1890 (below) the Kaiser's fleet to challenge British sea supremacy was becoming a reality.

men and industrialists were also prime targets for the cause. Meetings and dinners were held in chambers of trade and industrialist clubs, with special attention devoted to the old Hanseatic towns like Hamburg and Bremen as well as the rapidly developing Ruhr. The pro-navy movement quickly attracted the support of the influential Pan-German Movement. The German Colonial Society also threw its weight behind the campaign, its members making 173 lectures and distributing 140,000 pamphlets in 1897. Pro-naval opinion was channelled into the German Navy League (*Flottenverein*), which rapidly attracted members and published its own regular magazine, *Die Flotte*.

The German nation, under the impact of this skilfully handled campaign, was soon thinking of itself as a naval power. The first Navy Law passed the Reichstag. The naval race had begun.

RUTHLESS, RELI

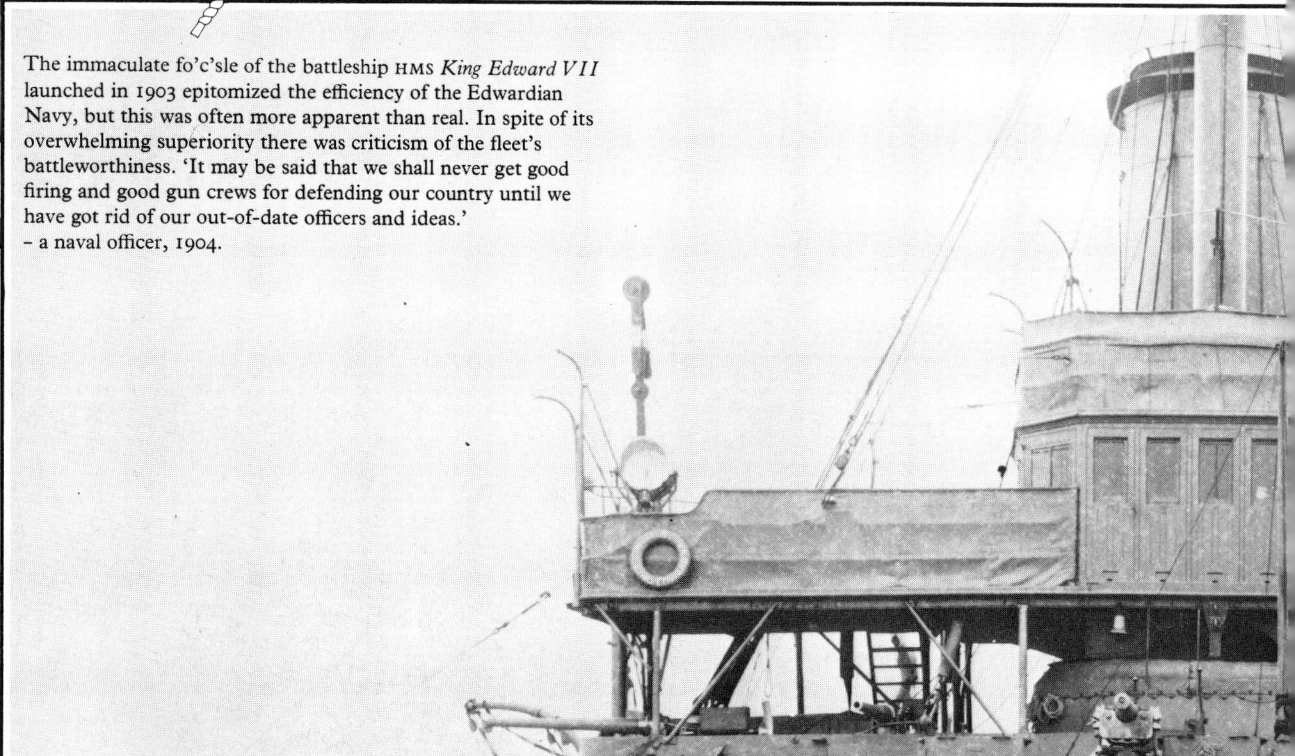

The immaculate fo'c'sle of the battleship HMS *King Edward VII* launched in 1903 epitomized the efficiency of the Edwardian Navy, but this was often more apparent than real. In spite of its overwhelming superiority there was criticism of the fleet's battleworthiness. 'It may be said that we shall never get good firing and good gun crews for defending our country until we have got rid of our out-of-date officers and ideas.'
– a naval officer, 1904.

TLESS, REMORSELESS

Tirpitz regarded the passage of the first Navy Law as the beginning of a vast industrial and military process which would give Germany a fleet capable of challenging the Royal Navy. Less than two years after the law passed the Reichstag, he published the text of a formidable new measure to increase the size of the German Fleet. Britain had provided him with an unsurpassable opportunity to ask for a far-reaching Reichstag commitment to a big navy by becoming embroiled in war against the two small Boer Republics in October 1899.

There was an immediate revulsion of feeling in Europe: a mighty empire and the British Navy had mobilized against a few thousand European settlers fighting bravely to defend their homes. The international Press violently attacked Britain, and Germany far outdid the other powers in her vehement anglophobia.

The *Flottenverein*, now with over a quarter of a million members, which had so effectively stirred up German public opinion in support of Tirpitz's 1898 Navy Law, seized the opportunity to call for a massive increase in the naval programme. Its magazine, *Die Flotte*, poured out arguments of every kind to press the case for German sea power.

This gave Tirpitz a perfect opportunity to commit the Reichstag to a hugely increased shipbuilding programme. The cost of the battleships approved in 1898 had already far exceeded the Reichstag's provision and 'a still more important reason in favour of the speeding up of the supplementary bill was of a technical and administrative nature. We had to try and

Crisis in South Africa President Paul Kruger and General Botha (below centre) led the Boers against the British Empire on the outbreak of war in October 1899. Britain's military operations infuriated European public opinion. Germany was particularly hostile but powerless in the face of British sea power. The Kaiser spoke of 'Germany's bitter need of a strong fleet'. His new Chancellor, Prince von Bülow (right) with yachting cap strolling with the Kaiser aboard the Imperial Yacht *Hohenzollern*, had counselled, 'Germany cannot yet meet England at sea'.

build as nearly as possible an equal number of ships each year; our military object and the means at our disposal suggested three big ships a year.'

With the sudden surge of activity in the shipyards of Danzig, Kiel and Hamburg resulting from the imperial contracts awarded under the 1898 Law, Tirpitz could see the need to raise the schedule of production to a steady and growing output if a battle fleet were to be created capable of challenging the Royal Navy. The Emperor, as eagerly receptive to Tirpitz's opportunism as ever, told his Chancellor, von Bülow, 'I am not in a position to go beyond the strictest neutrality and I must first get myself a fleet. In twenty years time when the fleet is ready I can use another language.'

In January 1900 Tirpitz published his draft Navy

Attacking the Two-Power Standard Tirpitz's new navy flexed its muscles with large-scale amphibious exercises on the Schleswig-Holstein coast (below). This began to stir fears in Britain that her historic dominance of the seas was under threat; but displays of German naval strength backed by vigorous public relations and ships' visits (right) brought enthusiastic public support for a rapidly growing Imperial Fleet.

Law, which extended the building programme by fifteen years to 1920 and raised the total number of ships to be constructed to 38 battleships with powerful supporting cruiser squadrons and torpedoboat flotillas. Britain at this time boasted 47 battleships, but how many could she have by 1920? The British Government began to sense the challenge.

There was strong political opposition to the Bill inside Germany with the Social Democrats holding large meetings in Berlin and the Catholic Centre Party demanding a cut in the programme. However, Tirpitz was so confident that anti-British sentiment in Germany would ensure the passage of his new Bill, aided by the public relations campaign of the Imperial Naval Office's experts, that he publicly spelt out the full implications of the *Riskflotte* strategy which had been kept completely secret in 1897. In the preamble to the Bill, Tirpitz wrote, 'Germany must have a fleet of such strength that even for the mightiest naval power, a war with her would involve such high risks as to jeopardize its own supremacy.'

When the Law passed the Reichstag in June 1900, strategists in the British Admiralty became alarmed. Commentators saw the new Law as a direct attack on the Two-Power Standard, but public opinion in Britain did not take the German threat seriously. Britain still had far larger ship-building capacity and

'We did not want to put railings round ourselves, but wanted to have a fleet recognized as belonging to the German people.'
– *Tirpitz*.

the Royal Navy outnumbered the German Navy by nearly three to one in battleships alone. Secure behind the steel walls of the fleet the British still stood in splendid isolation, eschewing all alliances and entanglements. Yet, if the British people slept safely in their beds, confident in the power of their fleet to defend them against invasion by Russians, French and Germans, they were unaware of the true strength of the Royal Navy. It was more apparent than real.

The Naval Defence Act had authorized a major new battleship construction programme; yet Britain deployed only one first-class fleet of ten battleships based in the Mediterranean. As the *Fortnightly Review* warned: 'Our other forces were on a sliding scale of inefficiency, ranging from the inadequately manned Channel Squadron down to the unmanned and largely neglected ships in reserve in the home ports.' These ships cluttered the creeks and backwaters of Portsmouth and Devonport, many of them far too old ever to be of use in battle.

This state of affairs was reflected around the world. The quality and fighting ability of British squadrons varied immensely, from the capital ships of the China Seas Battle Fleet to the river gunboats of West Africa. Defending homewaters there was only one squadron, comprising seven battleships and four cruisers, but no destroyers or torpedoboats. The Navy clung tenaciously to the principle that supposedly enshrined Nelson's tradition – it was the 'man who counted and not the material'. Many officers believed that innovation in ships and gunnery would undermine the efficiency of the service.

The British Government grew more concerned about the state of the Navy as it became clear that Germany was determined to create a serious naval challenge to Britain's security.

The SMS *Karl der Grosse*, a battleship of the *Riskflotte*, passing through the Kiel Canal.

'Our future is on the water.'
– *The Kaiser, 1910.*

'It is not absolutely necessary that the German Fleet should be as strong as that of the greatest sea power, because generally the greatest sea power will not be in a position to concentrate all its forces against us. But even if it should succeed in confronting us in superior force, the enemy would be considerably weakened in overcoming the resistance of a strong German Fleet that, notwithstanding a victory gained, the enemy's supremacy would not at first be secured any longer by a sufficient fleet.'
– *Tirpitz on the* Riskflotte *strategy.*

Lord Selborne, First Lord of the Admiralty, addressed a sombre note to the Cabinet in November 1901:

> The naval policy of Germany is definite and persistent. The Emperor seems determined that the power of Germany shall be used all the world over to push German commerce possessions and interests. Of necessity it follows that the German naval strength must be raised so as to compare more advantageously than at present with ours.

Improvements were also being made to the North Sea base of Wilhelmshaven and the Kiel Canal which would permit the transfer of heavy warships from the Baltic shipyards and bases to the North Sea. Selborne issued a warning to the Cabinet.

> The more the composition of the new German Fleet is examined the clearer it becomes that it is designed for a possible conflict with the British Fleet. It cannot be designed for the purpose of playing a leading part in a future war between Germany and France and Russia. The issue of such a war can only be decided by armies and on land.

Balfour's Conservative Government was now thoroughly alarmed about the Empire's vulnerability. The Germans represented a new and pointed threat as their Navy Laws indicated, but the French and the Russians were also unfriendly and Britain now embarked upon a search for allies to reduce tensions in remote parts of the world, thus enabling the Navy to concentrate in the North Sea.

Appropriately Britain's first ally was another sea power, Japan. In 1902 an alliance between the two nations minimized the dangers to Britain's colonial possessions in the Far East and China and made the British China Squadron available for redeployment elsewhere.

Britain also moved towards an agreement with France. With the assistance of the Francophile Edward VII, the outstanding questions of difference between the two nations were resolved, and in 1904 the *Entente Cordiale* was concluded. Within two years Tirpitz's plan had begun to crumble, and in Winston Churchill's words:

> England, and all that she stood for, had left her isolation and had reappeared in Europe on the opposite side to Germany. For the first time since 1870 Germany had to take into consideration a Power outside her system which was in no way amenable to threats and was not unable if need be to encounter her singlehanded.

The British Government also turned its attention to setting in motion a long overdue reform of the Navy. Fortunately for Britain one of the most extraordinary and gifted characters in her long naval history was at hand to answer the German naval threat. Admiral Sir John Arbuthnot Fisher was sixty-one when he joined the Admiralty in 1902 as Second Sea Lord and his energy and drive were already legend in the service. He was to put his stamp on the Navy, so that when the final reckoning came at Jutland its invincibility would be certain.

The Second Sea Lord's philosophy towards the Herculean task of reforming the most traditional service in the world was encapsulated in his words: 'I see my way clear *to a very great reduction* WITH INCREASED EFFICIENCY! That sounds nice and will I think come true. But the reform will require the 3 "R"s: *R*uthless, **R**elentless, ***R***emorseless.' Such an aggressive approach made Fisher a feared man in many quarters. Those who crossed him were often pilloried and persecuted, their careers suffering as a result.

As Second Sea Lord with responsibility for training all personnel, Fisher instinctively saw that the root of the problem of modernizing the Navy was a drastic reform of the methods of educating and training naval officers. It was a mammoth task. The state of naval officer training was summed up by one contemporary critic as 'a botch'.

In 1902 the 'Selborne Memorandum', named after the First Lord of the Admiralty, presented the Admiral's solution. In the first years, after entry at the age of 12½, all future officers would be trained according

'Jacky' Fisher – the revolutionary at the Admiralty. In the eight years between 1902 and his retirement in 1910 he was responsible for a total transformation of the organization and efficiency of the Royal Navy, enabling it to meet Tirpitz's challenge. Born in Ceylon, Fisher attracted the nickname 'the Oriental' as much for his shrewdness as for his place of birth. His success was also attributable to his flair for public relations and close friendship with King Edward VII.

to a common syllabus which would include engineering and mechanics as well as navigation and seamanship. When they reached the age of 22 the young officers could then specialize in the engineering, executive or marine branches of the service.

Fisher's proposals stirred a hornet's nest of opposition inside the Navy. They struck at one of the most cherished beliefs of the Navy, that character counted far more than expertise. There was a fear that the Admiralty had yielded to current social and political pressures in changing the status of specialists like engineer officers. Yet Fisher was just beginning.

In 1904 Fisher was appointed First Sea Lord and began an essential reshaping of Britain's strategic posture in the face of Tirpitz's long-term threat. This was fostered by the international tension generated by the Russo-Japanese war which led to anxious moments in the Admiralty when Europe was threatened with involvement. There was a revival of invasion scare-mongering in certain sections of the Press, and writers like Erskine Childers, whose book, *The Riddle of the Sands*, outlined a supposed secret German plan to seize the Frisian Islands, hardly calmed the public mood. Nor did the events of the night of 22 October 1904 when the Russian Baltic Fleet, despatched by the Tsar to reinforce his embattled forces in the Far East, opened fire on British fishing trawlers on the Dogger Bank, believing them to be Japanese torpedoboats.

The crisis had a major effect on Fisher's plans. It enabled him to hasten the redistribution of British naval power against a North Sea threat. At the time there were nine fleets and squadrons placed around the world; Fisher proposed to concentrate them into the 'five strategic keys that lock up the world' – Singapore, the Cape, Alexandria, Gibraltar and Dover.

The Home Fleet, which until then had consisted of older battleships, was renamed the Channel Fleet and was increased from eight to twelve battleships with four ships switched from the Mediterreanean. For the first time since Nelson, the Mediterranean ceased to be the pivot of British sea power; only eight battleships were maintained there. This greatly strengthened battle fleet now patrolled a large area, covering the western approaches and Ireland, with its pivot on

Dover. The former Channel Fleet was renamed the Atlantic Fleet and based on Gibraltar. Its eight first-class battleships could be used to reinforce either the Mediterranean or the Channel Fleet.

Fisher now cut down drastically on the waste and inefficiency in the service. Over 150 old ships were struck off the active list, many of them being sold for scrap. Their trained crews were released to increase the Navy's efficiency and the taxpayer saved considerable sums of money. With the newly-formed ties with France and Japan and a steadily improving navy, the Balfour Government began to feel more confident of its security.

In May 1905 an event took place which showed the new and frightening power of a modern navy to affect national fortunes. The lesson was not lost on Britain. After an eight-month voyage of 18,000 miles, in a desperate effort to re-establish her military fortunes against Japan, the Russian Baltic Fleet finally met Admiral Togo's Imperial Japanese ships in the straits of Tsushima. Five powerful Russian battleships supported by a second division of seven older battleships faced the Imperial Japanese Navy's Battle Squadron of four battleships and eight heavy cruisers. It was the greatest naval confrontation since Trafalgar and its outcome was eagerly analysed by naval tacticians in all maritime countries.

For the first time a larger number of armoured ships and heavy guns were deployed in a major sea battle which tested the battle fleets' tactics and the ability of

Death of a Fleet In May 1905 Admiral Togo's battle fleet, led by the battleships *Fuji*, *Asai* and *Shikishma* (below – opening fire), annihilated the Russian Fleet. Early in the action the two divisions of Russian battleships became separated and Togo (right) used his superior speed to 'cross the T' – he cut across the head of the enemy battleline blazing away with all his armament, whilst the Russians found their gunnery masked. For the first time a large number of heavy guns were employed in a major sea battle, and the battle of Tsushima was to lead to a reappraisal of naval thinking.

warships to withstand shellfire. It was an unequal contest; although Togo had fewer capital ships, the Russians, after the ordeal of their long voyage, were a poor match for the Japanese. Outmanoeuvred and outfought the Russians were disastrously defeated. When the battle was over no less than twenty out of thirty Tsarist ships had been sunk, six surrendered and six were interned. Four thousand, eight hundred and thirty Russians lost their lives and their Admiral was a prisoner of the triumphant Togo.

Tsushima presaged the new tactics of naval warfare applicable to the new generation of battleships. It temporarily eliminated Russia as a sea power and made it impossible for her to be taken seriously into account in Britain's Two-Power Standard calculations. Tsushima also affected Germany's attitude. Since Russia could not support France if Germany threatened her, it now seemed possible for Germany to smash the new British diplomatic alignments which had come into being to contain the Reich. In 1905 the German Chancellor, von Bülow, deliberately provoked a crisis in Morocco, but the *Entente* held firm, with Britain prepared to support France. The Germans now grew anxious that the British might launch a preventive war against their growing fleet.

Admiral Sir John Fisher, newly elevated to First Sea Lord, was cast in an aggressive mould. He was fond of saying 'if you rub it in both at home and abroad that you are ready for instant war with every unit of your strength in the first line, and intend to be first in and hit your enemy in the belly and kick him when he is down and boil your prisoners in oil (if you take any!) and torture his women and children, then people will keep clear of you.' It is small wonder that Fisher's pronouncements were given wide circulation in Germany where he was portrayed as an archetypal English demon.

In late 1905 the Germans took the precaution of summoning home their foreign cruisers and of cancelling all naval leave over Christmas. They were perhaps wise. Fisher had already suggested to Edward VII that 'we should "Copenhagen" the German Fleet at Kiel *à la* Nelson'.

Fears of a 'Copenhagen' and the heightened international tension presented Tirpitz with an opportunity to increase further the size of the German Fleet by six heavy cruisers and a substantial number of destroyers. Significantly a large sum of money was to be spent on submarine research.

As the tensions eased, Germany had become isolated and humiliated. She was faced with increasing encirclement brought about as a direct result of Tirpitz's *Riskflotte*. Moreover, the fighting efficiency of the British Fleet had been immeasurably strengthened as a result of the Fisher reforms. The fleet had been redeployed and a new Reserve Fleet manned by nucleus crews, ready to sail at short notice, had been established by Fisher.

Meanwhile in No. 15 Dock at Portsmouth a revolutionary battleship was nearing completion in conditions of greatest secrecy. In a dramatic bid that would transform the naval scene overnight, Britain was about to raise the stakes in defence of her sea supremacy. The industrial race was to start in earnest, gaining a tempo of its own and leading finally to the clash of the battle fleets.

PENSIONS

The Imperial Fleet returning to Kiel harbour after manoeuvres had become as familiar and popular a spectacle for German citizens as the Royal Navy reviews were for the British.

OR DREADNOUGHTS?

It was drizzling in Portsmouth on the morning of 10 February 1906. Crowds of distinguished guests who had arrived from London sheltered from a sudden downpour as they crossed the great naval dockyard, but in spite of the weather the Royal Marine band cheerfully played a medley of tunes, and 'the sun shone fitfully between the scudding clouds'. The visitors climbed the wide launching platform which extended several hundred feet across the stem of the new ship. From their high vantage point they looked down on the 526-ft-long armoured hull of 11-inch steel, and the four cavernous wells in the $2\frac{1}{2}$-inch-thick armoured deck awaiting the insertion of the gun turrets.

Below the platform, a sea of faces looked up at the King. To the Portsmouth citizenry the ship looked impressive: 'the lower part . . . was painted reddish brown, the upper being of a greyish blue colour and her lofty sides towered so high as to reduce the spectators to pygmies in comparison with her gigantic proportions.'

Prominent on the platform, Admiral Sir John Fisher watched the proceedings, savouring his brilliant political and naval coup: a complete breakthrough in warship design. The new battleship before him outclassed all its predecessors and left Britain's rivals far behind. The revolutionary combination of gun power, speed and armour embodied in the new vessel had been the product of Fisher's personal vision and his determination. The best brains in the shipbuilding industry had been summoned by the First Sea Lord to sit on a Committee of Designs with some of the

The Dreadnought revolution Dockyard paddle tugs take Britain's new battleship in tow after the launching in Portsmouth harbour on 10 February 1906 (below). The Dreadnought (right) made every other battleship in the world obsolete, and silenced criticism when at the 1907 secret gunnery trials she landed 75 per cent more weight of shell on target than any other battleship in the fleet.

brightest officers from the 'Fishpond', the Admiral's personally selected circle of talent.

More than six detailed designs had been examined before the specifications were settled. At the time of the Committee's deliberations, Tsushima and accelerating naval technology meant that a new British design philosophy had to be developed. Britain now needed new heavy battleships, capable of annihilating a rival battle fleet in a massive gunnery duel. As Japanese campaigns had demonstrated, the torpedo was a deadly threat to a capital ship, doubly so because it could be launched from fast-moving flotillas of small torpedoboats which were difficult for a big ship to outmanoeuvre. The range at which battleships engaged in gunnery duels had been greatly extended, so that by 1904 it was already nearly four miles. This put a new perspective on battleship actions and according to the Committee of Designs' Report 'The advantage therefore at long range lies with the ship which carries the greatest number of guns of the largest type, but additional advantage is gained by having a uniform armament.'

Hustled by Fisher, the Committee finally settled on the design for a new type of battleship in March 1905. It was to have a displacement of nearly 18,000 tons and its hitting power was to be concentrated in ten 12-inch

The battlecruisers 'Swift battleships in disguise', according to Fisher. HMS *Invincible* (below left) was launched in April 1907; at 25 knots it was faster than a Dreadnought, and with eight 12-inch guns it had almost the same hitting power. But its six inches of armour, only half that of the Dreadnought, gave it much less protection against enemy shells.

guns, enabling the ship to fire a broadside of 6,800 lbs – over 30 per cent greater than the biggest battleships afloat. The world had never seen such a powerful fighting ship and, with characteristic flair, Fisher decided she should be named the *Dreadnought*. It was a name that was to identify a new generation of warships.

The brilliance of the ship did not stop at the design of its armament; it was also built according to Fisher's favourite maxim that 'speed is armour'. The new Parsons steam turbines, used on the fastest transatlantic liners, were to be installed in the battleship, their 23,000 shaft horse power giving the *Dreadnought* a margin of two knots over any other heavy ship in service or on the stocks.

Once the plans had been made, no time could be wasted. Already there had been speculation in naval circles about the new generation of battleships. The United States Navy had received Congressional approval for laying down new ships which exploited the 'big-gun' principle, and the Germans could not be far behind. If Britain, with her great fleet of capital ships, forged ahead into a new generation of battleships she would be taking serious risks which had to be carefully weighed. This was eloquently stated by Admiral of the Fleet, Sir Frederick Richards, a former Sea Lord, who pointed out that once the *Dreadnought* was in service the existing British Battle Fleet would be 'morally scrapped and labelled obsolete at the moment when it was at the zenith of its efficiency and equal not to two but all the navies of the world combined.' But Fisher and the Board of Admiralty were convinced that the risks had to be accepted.

The keel plate of the new ship was laid in Portsmouth Dockyard on 2 October 1905; four months later, after feverish activity carried out in the greatest secrecy at high speed, the *Dreadnought* was ready for launching.

On the wet February forenoon the King stepped forward to resounding cheers. A frequent visitor to the Kaiser's regattas at Kiel, he appreciated the great step Britain was taking in order to seize the initiative. Standing on the platform, which was draped in union flags, the King named the great hull *Dreadnought* to a roar of enthusiasm from the crowd below. As the band broke bravely into *Rule Britannia* the great hull gathered speed and slid down into the waters of Ports-

mouth Harbour where her large white ensign flew proudly within sight of Nelson's *Victory*. It took only another eight months for the new battleship to be completed, bringing her to trials in a record twelve months with the Admiralty watching anxiously for any signs that other powers might follow Britain's lead.

Dreadnought was impressive, but Sir William White, the former Director of Naval Construction, sided with Fisher's critics, suggesting that Britain was putting all her 'naval eggs into one or two vast, costly, majestic, but vulnerable baskets'. He believed that a large number of small battleships would have done just as well. Far from abandoning the 'Dreadnought' design, however, Fisher developed it into a credo, and extended the principle of the big-gun ship beyond the role of the battleship to that of the cruiser. Fisher's theory was that new 'Invincibles' with the guns but not the armour of a Dreadnought would form a special fast battlecruiser fleet of their own with the capacity for high speed and hitting power.

Fisher watched carefully for Germany's reactions. In one respect he was extremely successful; not only did Tirpitz delay all construction, but he was misled by Fisher into believing that the Invincibles would be armed only with 8-inch guns. As a result the first German battlecruiser, the *Blücher*, was only 15,000 tons displacement, carrying relatively small 8-inch guns against the Invincibles' 12-inch batteries. The dilemma that the new Dreadnoughts posed to the British Government was whether the nation would accept the economic sacrifices necessary to rebuild from scratch her former naval superiority with a fleet of the new warships strong enough to match anything that Germany might build. The new Liberal Government of Sir Henry Campbell-Bannerman, which replaced the Conservative administration of Balfour in early 1906 to the 'resounding acclamations of liberals, peace-lovers, anti-Jingoes and anti-militarists', viewed the Dreadnought revolution with mixed feelings. At first the Government accepted the policy of the outgoing Conservatives as expressed in the Cawdor Memorandum of 1905, that four large armoured ships (Dreadnoughts) should be built in Britain every year in order to maintain naval supremacy over the next two strongest fleets, with an allowance for contingencies. But the Liberal Press complained noisily about the

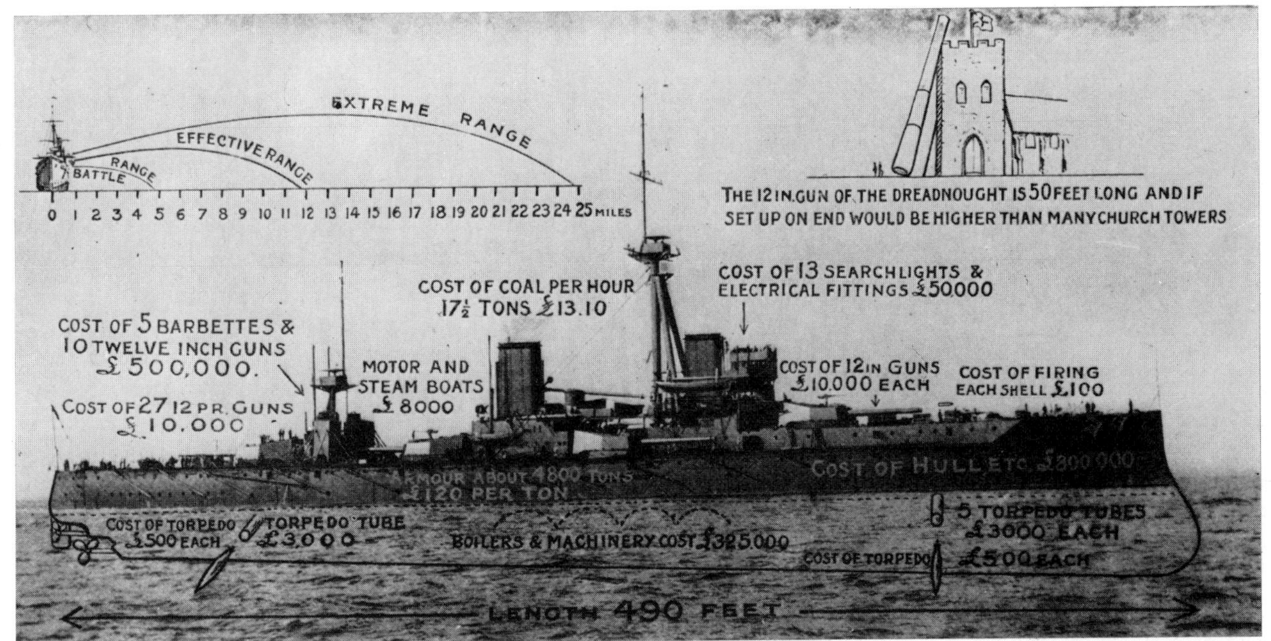

The cost of the Dreadnoughts The increased cost of the new ships, summarized in a contemporary diagram (below right), presented the Liberal Government with a painful choice between paying for social reforms or sea supremacy. Between 1905 and 1914 naval estimates increased from £36 million to £51 million.

Der Wahre Jacob.]

A Speech Illustrated.

"We Germans are a nation that rejoices in bearing arms and in the game of war. Hence we gladly endure the burden of our armaments, knowing as we do that we must preserve and maintain that peace in which alone our workers can thrive . . ."

Lustige Blätter.]

The Launching of the Ship.

EDWARD VII. : "I christen you '*The Last Shilling.*'"

(Lord Rosebery and Earl Grey have said that England would spend her last shilling in building *Dreadnoughts* if necessary.)

monstrously rising costs of armaments. In the eyes of *The Manchester Guardian*, the £$2\frac{1}{2}$ million cost of each Dreadnought would 'eat up the economies of Navy reforms and bring about a period of greater strain in the rivalry of international arms'. The Prime Minister himself favoured a move in the direction of unilateral arms restraint by Britain.

The new radical MPs and their Labour Party allies did not disagree with British supremacy in principle but the only way in which they could achieve a reduction in spending was by restraining Germany or by questioning the margin the Admiralty thought it necessary to maintain.

The radicals found an ally in Fisher who had always been enthusiastic for economy, believing that it was closely linked with efficiency. Fisher's Dreadnought philosophy saw no incompatibility between the reduction of naval expenditure and the increase in the fighting capabilities of the fleet. He liked to refer to his reform programme in typically robust terms: 'The country will acclaim it, the Navy will growl at first! (They always do growl at first!) But we shall be thirty per cent more fit to fight and we shall be ready for *instant* war!'

The Dreadnought was an important success for Britain in one respect – Tirpitz had been taken by surprise over the new generation of battleships in spite of advance intelligence gleaned from Portsmouth dockyard. He ordered a hurried review of construction plans in 1906 and halted work on the *Nassau* for nine months so that her design could be recast. As a result no German Dreadnoughts were laid down until 1907.

Fisher had persuaded his fellow Sea Lords that it was politically unwise to insist on the full Cawdor scheme for building up a Dreadnought fleet, and the delays caused whilst the Germans recast their plans gave Britain time to make a gesture of restraint in the naval race.

The opportunity for the British initiative towards a reduction of arms occurred in 1906 when Tsarist Russia proposed a reassembly of the 1899 Hague Peace Conference to discuss ways of finding peaceful solutions to international disputes. The receptivity of the British Government had been made clear in the House of Commons by Sir Edward Grey, the Foreign Secretary, who said, 'I do not believe that at any time has the conscious public opinion in the various European countries set more strongly in the direction of peace than at the present time, and yet the burden of military and naval expenditure goes on increasing. We are all waiting on each other.' Edward VII thought the whole thing was 'humbug'; and the Kaiser let it be known that he would decline to be represented if disarmament was on the Conference agenda.

Campbell-Bannerman still hoped that something could be achieved. In July the British Dreadnought and Invincible programme was cut from four ships to three; even then the third ship would only be laid down in the event of unsatisfactory results at the Hague Conference. There was an outcry from naval opinion and the Conservative Press angrily complained: 'The

Cartoons (left) from *Review of Reviews*, 1909.

Tirpitz's move Diplomatic attempts were made at the Hague Conference in 1907 to halt the European arms race, but Tirpitz (below – in conference with the Kaiser and Admiral von Holtzendorff) maintained that 'British irritation will grow when they see that we are following their lead in battlecruisers at once, all the more so, since our battlecruisers will be somewhat larger than the *Invincible*.'

advent of a Liberal Government has in ten months done more damage to the nation than we might expect from conflict with a European Power.' The First Sea Lord was dubbed the tool of 'a cheese-paring Cobdenite Cabinet'.

These reproaches did not worry Fisher, who had continued with his usual skill to become the darling of the radicals. He reassured the sceptics that 'our present margin of superiority over Germany (our only possible foe for years) is so great as to render it absurd to talk of anything endangering our naval supremacy, even if we stopped building altogether!'

When it came to the point the Liberal Party was only superficially united on the issue of cutting the Navy and in August 1907 the Foreign Secretary warned his own radical back benches:

> Of course I remain as impressed as I have ever been with what is almost the pathetic helplessness of mankind under the burden of armaments . . . The difficulty in regard to one nation stepping out in advance of the others is this, that while there is a chance that their courageous action may lead to reform, there is also the chance that it may lead to martyrdom.

Germany was convinced that Britain was acting cynically in her own interest. As German Foreign Secretary Marschall put it: 'Freedom, humanity, and civilization . . . These three catchwords are not the common property of all nations. They are the monopoly of England.' So the first major attempt to halt the Anglo-German naval race was doomed to failure and it came as no surprise in the autumn of 1907 when the Hague Conference broke up without any serious discussion of disarmament. It was a sad watershed, with the hopes of the seriously ill Liberal Prime Minister dashed by the total intransigence of the Germans.

Fisher was convinced that Britain was in no danger of martyrdom. Speaking at the Guildhall at the Lord Mayor's Banquet in November 1907 he ebulliently claimed, that the fleet was '*nulli secundus*, as they say, whether it is ships or officers or men, [cheers] . . . So I turn to all of you, and I turn to my countrymen and I say – sleep quiet in your beds [laughter and cheers].'

Fisher had every reason to be confident. The Royal Navy had never been stronger. Fisher informed the King that Britain possessed 'seven Dreadnoughts and three Invincibles (in my opinion better than Dreadnoughts), total ten Dreadnoughts built and building, while Germany in March last had not begun one!' Yet Britain's sea supremacy would remain secure only so long as she possessed the determination to outbuild Germany in the new and decisive Dreadnought class.

Now that Britain appeared to have overwhelming sea supremacy, a threat to the British position emerged from the radical wing of the new Liberal Government which sought to divert money away from armaments into badly needed social reforms. The radical case was buttressed by British diplomacy which by 1908 had skilfully woven a web around Germany to contain her

dynamic ambitions. In 1907 the Anglo-French *Entente* became the Triple *Entente* on the conclusion of a pact between Britain and Russia but the strong diplomatic ring of Britain, France and Russia had a serious effect on Anglo-German naval competition. Tirpitz redoubled his efforts to build a *Riskflotte* capable of challenging Britain. The feeling of encirclement stirred deep fears in the German mind. For the Secretary of the Imperial Naval Office the danger zone for the *Riskflotte* seemed to be prolonged. Apart from encirclement the fear of a 'Copenhagen' was particularly strong in 1907 and a panic swept Kiel on the rumour that 'Fisher was on his way'.

Tirpitz now had one very clear objective. 'The aim which I had to keep in view . . . for technical and organizing reasons as well as reasons of political finance, was to build as steadily as possible. It proved to be most advantageous if we could lay down three big ships every year.' In 1907 Tirpitz put this plan into effect by placing a new Navy Law before the Reichstag. This cut the life of all the Imperial Navy battleships from twenty-five to twenty years and had a profound effect on British naval circles, since the new German Navy would be far stronger than the Admiralty had calculated.

There was great alarm in sections of the British Press about the new Law. The *Daily Mail* believed that Germany would 'build a fleet which shall fulfil the hopes and desires of the Pan-Germans and be mightier than the mightiest navy in the world.' W. T. Stead, a well-known public commentator who had campaigned for universal disarmament, now began to call for two British keels to be laid for every one laid in Germany.

The new Naval Law was to prove a test of British nerve and brought the naval issue to the very forefront of British politics. The social reformers in the Liberal Party were on the alert to prevent the Government being stampeded into heavy spending on naval construction by Tirpitz's new Law, and Herbert Asquith, the Chancellor of the Exchequer, appeased radical opinion by ordering the Navy estimates to be cut.

The Admiralty also conceded to radical pressure and decided to ask for only two capital ships in the 1908–9 estimates. This was a gift from Mars to the Jingo coteries and members of the 'blue funk school'. The 'big navy' party were furious, and believed unjustifiable risks were being accepted in the face of the new German programme. The *Daily Mail* pointed to the true issue: 'Is Britain going to surrender her maritime supremacy to provide old age pensions?'

In spite of the radical clamour, the Liberal Government, led now by Asquith during Prime Minister Campbell-Bannerman's illness, steered a middle course. In the debate on the estimates in March, Asquith reassured the House: 'We should provide not only for a sufficient number of ships but for such a date for laying down those ships so that at the end of 1911, the superiority of Germany . . . would not be an actual fact.'

When he became Prime Minister in April 1908, Asquith soon realized the full extent of his unequivocal commitment to maintain British sea supremacy. Embarrassing evidence began to appear that the

Failure of *detente* A royal salute welcoming King Edward VII on his visit to Kiel Week in 1908 (below) symbolized the close ties between the English and German thrones. Attempts by Edward to persuade his nephew the Kaiser to slow down the pace of German naval construction failed. Wilhelm's view was: 'I have no desire for a good relationship with England at the price of the development of Germany's navy.'

Government had totally underrated the German challenge.

German industry under the stimulus of the 1908 Navy Law was developing an impressive capacity for warship construction. The number of shipyards had risen from 39 in 1897 to 47 ten years later, with more than 50,000 men employed. Behind these yards stood the great engineering and armaments complexes like Krupp which had steadily increased its output of high grade armour-plate and naval guns. The three imperial shipyards accounted for approximately one-third of naval construction; the battleships were built at Wilhelmshaven, whilst Kiel, the biggest of the imperial yards, constructed cruisers. Danzig was responsible for destroyers, torpedoboats and light craft. The national yards were only part of the shipbuilding capacity. By 1908 Tirpitz's policy had been highly successful in bringing into being a large number of commercial shipyards, which now built two-thirds of the new fleet. The key companies were the Krupp Germania yard at Kiel, Vulcan of Stettin on the Baltic and Blohm and Voss at Hamburg.

Britain had for many years relied on the fact that she could outbuild any rival not only in numbers but also in speed. It took two years to build a British battleship, and it had been estimated that the Germans took perhaps thirty-two or thirty-six months. But in 1908 the Admiralty uncovered disturbing evidence which led them to believe that the Germans were accelerating and on the point of taking a decisive lead. A great deal of material had already been collected for future building programmes. Visitors to the Krupp works at Essen reported counting as many as 100 heavy guns stockpiled for use. This huge engineering complex had also raised a substantial loan on the market, £2 million of which had been earmarked for expanding the Germania works at Kiel. The Admiralty estimated that output in the all important area of gun-mountings was twice that of the three British factories combined.

A slump in merchant ship building during 1908 acted as an added pressure to the British shipbuilding companies, with warship construction on the Clyde falling from 50,000 tons to 5,000. The *Daily Mail* urged the Government to act, and wrote: 'If the Government is not composed of stony-hearted pedants, the shipbuilding vote should be given out now . . . 80 per cent of the cost of a British battleship goes in wages to the British worker.'

It was industrial pressure of this kind that forced Tirpitz to allow two ships from the German 1909 programme to be laid down by Schichau in October 1908, even before any funds had been voted by the Reichstag.

Rear-Admiral John Jellicoe, Fisher's Controller of the Navy, spotted Tirpitz's manoeuvre. Jellicoe's keen analytical mind noticed that published figures showed a far greater sum was being spent on German construction in 1908 than in 1907. Armed with Jellicoe's analysis, McKenna, the First Lord of the Admiralty now became deeply concerned. Soon Britain might lose her lead in the important Dreadnought class. To forestall such a disaster, he resolved to request a large

programme first for six, then for eight capital ships in the 1909 estimates. On 3 January 1909, McKenna wrote to the Prime Minister:

> I am anxious to avoid alarmist language, but I cannot resist the following conclusions which it is my duty to submit to you.
>
> 1. Germany is anticipating the shipbuilding programme laid down by the Law of 1907.
> 2. She is doing so secretly.
> 3. She will certainly have 13 big ships in commission in the spring of 1912.
> 4. She will probably have 21 big ships in commission in the spring of 1912.
> 5. German capacity to build Dreadnoughts is at this moment equal to ours.
>
> The last conclusion is the most alarming, and if justified would give the public a rude awakening should it become known.

Asquith was prepared to accept the McKenna case, which was backed by Grey and Haldane, but he met resistance in his Cabinet from Lloyd George, Chancellor of the Exchequer, and Churchill, Home Secretary. According to Churchill the whole question was the result of 'windy agitations of ignorant, interested and excited hotheads into wasting the public money on armaments upon a scale not designed merely for purposes of material defence, but being a part of a showy, sensational, aggressive and Jingo policy, which is supposed to gain popularity from certain unthinking sections of the community.' Churchill was supported by the skilful arguments of Lloyd George who painted an alarming picture of Liberal defections should the Government increase warship construction.

A breach in the Cabinet appeared to be unavoidable but Asquith devised a typically astute compromise to resolve the problem. Four ships would be laid down immediately, and there would be a contingency allowance for a further four to be laid down not later than April 1910 should the situation warrant it. McKenna and the Admiralty had to accept this solution or the Liberal Government would have fallen apart. As Churchill remarked: 'The Admiralty had demanded six ships: the economists four: and we finally compromised on eight.'

It was an intensely dramatic scene in the House of Commons when the First Lord stood up on 16 March 1909 to announce the estimates. Members were taken aback at his statement.

> The difficulty in which the Government finds itself placed at this moment is that we do not know, as we thought we did, the rate at which German construction is taking place . . . and we have to take stock of a new situation, in which we reckon that not nine but thirteen ships may be completed in 1911, and in 1912 such further ships, if any, as may be begun in the course of the next financial year or laid down in 1910.

The news shocked the House, and after statements by Balfour and the Prime Minister there was a stunned silence. The situation seemed far too grave for anybody to open their mouths for several minutes. One radical described the effect on the dissident wing of the Liberal Party: 'Our men scattered like sheep.'

The naval estimates became an immediate political issue. A vociferous section of public opinion expressed alarm that the Government was not starting all eight extra ships immediately. Encouraged by naval circles, they began to call for the complete programme at once. The Conservative and naval Press whipped up the public temper in what became a remarkable exhibition of *hysteria navalis*: 'We want eight and we won't wait' was a popular catch-phrase invented by Tory MP George Wyndham. The *Daily Mail* believed that panic was spreading in English cities and *The Observer* insisted 'the Eight, the whole Eight and nothing but the Eight'. The Press was suddenly full of stories of strange airships hovering over English towns and once again there was talk of invasion, with exercises in which troops were rushed to the coast by the motorcars of the Automobile Association.

The excitement affected the whole Empire and a significant contribution was the offer of two capital ships by Australia and New Zealand, which was grate-

Radicalism v Imperialism The sustained German naval challenge created severe pressures inside the Liberal Government when the First Lord of the Admiralty, Reginald McKenna, demanded the building of eight Dreadnoughts in the 1909 estimates. Prime Minister Asquith narrowly averted a Cabinet split by compromising with the Chancellor of the Exchequer, David Lloyd George and the Home Secretary, Winston Churchill (picture below).

fully accepted by the Government.

On 29 March the Opposition moved a vote of censure on the Government. The debate was dominated by Sir Edward Grey. In a long and brilliant speech, he held out the hope of an agreement with Germany, but whilst deploring the arms race he maintained that Britain would have to insist on her maritime supremacy.

> There is no comparison between the importance of the German Navy to Germany, and the importance of our navy to us. Our Navy is to us what their Army is to them. To have a strong Navy would increase their prestige, their diplomatic influence, their power of protecting their commerce; but as regards us – it is not a matter of life and death to them that it is to us.

The Navy's case was reinforced by the news that the strategic situation in the Mediterranean was changing with the announcement by the Austrian and Italian Governments that they were to start building Dreadnoughts. Later in the year the Government agreed that work could go ahead on the four extra ships. At the same time Fisher pulled another coup, by ordering the ships to be equipped with a new heavy calibre 13.5-inch gun which was bigger than any German weapon.

The Germans did not increase their building programme or accelerate their construction tempo, so that 1912 was to pass without the feared loss of sea supremacy. But the crisis had stirred deep emotions on both sides, and mutual distrust and animosity henceforth prevented any real attempts to halt the naval race.

HE NARROW MARGIN

Super-Dreadnought HMS *Queen Elizabeth* was launched at Portsmouth on 16 October 1913 and heralded a new generation of advanced battleships. Displacing 27,500 tons the Queen Elizabeth class was as fast as a battlecruiser; their eight 15-inch guns were the most powerful in the world and their 13-inch armour the thickest.

A deceptive calm settled over Anglo-German relations in 1910. When it was seen that Germany was not accelerating her construction programme but was maintaining her scheduled output of capital ships, there were radical calls for a reduction in the estimates. The Prime Minister, however, accepted the need for five Dreadnoughts to be laid down in 1910–11, but was soon to discover that the Admiralty possessed no effective plans for the use of this ever growing British Fleet in the event of war.

The awakening came in 1911. Germany had despatched a gunboat, the *Panther* to the Moroccan town of Agadir, ostensibly to protect German lives and interests during a rising against the Sultan. The *Entente* powers were extremely sceptical of Germany's claims, particularly as there seemed to be few Germans in Agadir, and it seemed as if the Germans were out to embarrass the *Entente*. The British Cabinet realized that, as before, they would have to stand by France whatever the outcome.

David Lloyd George, the Chancellor of the Exchequer, speaking at the Mansion House on 21 July, warned Germany:

> If a situation were to be forced upon us in which peace could only be preserved by the surrender of the great and beneficent position Britain has won by centuries of heroism and achievement, by allowing Britain to be treated where her interests were vitally affected as if she were of no account in the Cabinet of Nations, then I say emphatically that peace at that price would be a humiliation intolerable for a great country like ours to endure.

The Germans were shocked by this display of British nerve and demanded an explanation of Lloyd George's comments. Churchill and Lloyd George were summoned by Sir Edward Grey to his room in the House of Commons where he was anxiously waiting for McKenna: 'I have just received a communication from the German Ambassador so stiff that the fleet might be attacked at any moment.' War seemed to be only hours away when the British Cabinet was horrified to discover that no war plans existed for the deployment of the Navy.

Fisher, who retired in 1910, had always resisted the creation of a 'thinking department' for the Navy and this had been one of the criticisms levelled at him by his numerous enemies, who had been successful in persuading Asquith to appoint a Committee of Inquiry into the state of the Navy. Its findings had led indirectly to the First Sea Lord's downfall but this was primarily engineered by Fisher's arch enemy Lord Charles Beresford, Commander-in-Chief of the Channel Fleet, whose immediate objective on retiring from his command in March 1909 was to bring about the departure of Fisher. He complained to the Prime Minister that 'the Service is very sore and irritated throughout, not so much upon what is done as upon the way in

Summer crisis 1911 The Royal Navy's great strength, which massed at the Coronation review (below), was found to be dangerously dispersed at the peak of the Agadir crisis later that summer. The lack of an overall naval war plan was attributed to the dictatorial manner in which Fisher (below left) had run the Admiralty. A naval inquiry had preceded Fisher's retirement, examining the charges of maladministration and primarily engineered by Lord Charles Beresford (below right).

which things are done.' The row between Fisher and 'Charlie B' had become an embarrassment to the political establishment.

An Imperial Maritime League was set up with the sole purpose of getting rid of Fisher. At the other end of the political spectrum the radical journal, *Concord*, enjoyed the spectacle and decided that 'Naval Jingoism is a kind of rabies; having united to bite the public, these gentlemen are now breaking up into droves and rending each other.' When the Committee reported, it was obviously disturbed about the lack of a naval war staff. This had caused the Army great frustration as it had been busily trying to plan the possible despatch of an expeditionary force to France should war break out.

The Admiralty strongly believed that the Navy would win any future war on its own, and that there was no need for the Army to become involved except to be landed on the Baltic coast by a British fleet in order to threaten Berlin. This scheme was rejected as wildly impractical by the Army planners, to whom Fisher had scathingly replied that 'the Army is a projectile to be fired by the Navy'.

The view at the Admiralty had not changed after the departure of Fisher and now in the middle of a very dangerous crisis the Navy still appeared to be woefully unprepared for war. Although there were rumours that the German High Seas Fleet was raising steam in Wilhelmshaven for a strike across the North Sea, the British forces were still scattered between Cromarty in Scotland and Berehaven on the south-west coast of Ireland. Reservists were being paid off from ships returning from exercises, and Churchill was astounded to discover that the First Sea Lord, Sir Arthur Wilson, Fisher's successor, had gone on a fishing trip to Scotland.

Worse was to follow when at a specially summoned conference of defence chiefs on 23 August, Wilson failed to make a positive contribution after the Army had outlined the most detailed plans for moving an expeditionary force into France. This was the last straw for Haldane, the Secretary for War. He lobbied Asquith for a change at the Admiralty, and Asquith decided to move McKenna and bring in the young lion, Winston Churchill, as First Lord.

The last bid to stop the race The British Cabinet despatched Lord Haldane (below) to Berlin to negotiate a naval agreement with the Kaiser. Germany's terms proved unacceptable, adding crucial importance to the work of the First Lord of the Admiralty, Winston Churchill (left).

The thirty-six-year-old Home Secretary moved to the Admiralty in October with a brief to set up a war staff and galvanize the Department into action. Wilson was the first to go. He was succeeded for a short time by Sir Francis Bridgeman, who was then supplanted by Prince Louis of Battenberg. This able strategist and tactician, 'child of the Royal Navy', immediately began the task of planning Britain's Fleet actions in the event of a war with Germany.

Fortunately, the dangerous Agadir crisis petered out, leaving the *Entente* intact, but the Asquith Government faced a new problem. Germany's diplomats had once again provided Tirpitz with an excuse to introduce a revised Naval Law. Under the earlier German Laws, the rate of construction was to fall to two ships in 1912, 1914 and 1916. It was Tirpitz's aim to make this three a year by building three extra battleships. It was presented to the Kaiser as a means of establishing a permanent 3:2 ratio with Britain.

The British, however, would not accept the new German ratio, which would mean an increase in the size of the German Fleet and abandonment of the Two-Power Standard. The British Government, anxious to stop a further escalation, despatched the German-speaking Secretary of War, Richard Haldane, to attempt the negotiations of a settlement. Haldane had a series of meetings with Chancellor Bethmann Hollweg, Tirpitz and the Emperor. The deal offered by Germany was straightforward: if Britain consented to remaining neutral in any war in which Germany could become involved where the Reich was not the aggressor, then the new Navy Law would not be introduced. The negotiations went through twists and turns, with the Chancellor trying hard to reach an agreement. Haldane stuck closely to his brief: 'There could be no agreement without a shipbuilding understanding. It would be bones without flesh . . . the world would laugh at such an agreement, and our people would think we had been fooled.'

The British Government tried to appease the German appetite for world power by offering to allow Germany to annex large parts of Africa, but this foundered on a failure to agree on naval limitation. Ironically, the very day on which Haldane sat down with the Emperor in Berlin, Churchill spoke defiantly in Glasgow, where he delivered a strong riposte:

> 'The purposes of British naval power are essentially defensive. We have no thoughts and we have never had any thoughts of aggression, and we attribute no such thoughts to other great powers. There is however this difference between the British naval power and the naval power of the great and friendly Empire – and I trust it may long remain the great and friendly Empire – of Germany. The British Navy is to us a necessity and from some points of view, the German Navy is to them more in the nature of a luxury. Our naval power involves British existence. It is existence to us; it is expansion to them . . .'

On his return from Berlin Haldane brought back the final draft of the German Naval Law of 1912. The worst fears of the Cabinet were confirmed. Britain would have to achieve a building rate of five capital ships annually for three years to maintain a 60 per cent supremacy in Dreadnoughts and battlecruisers over the Germans. British ships would have to be withdrawn

The Eagle at Spithead Germany's new battlecruiser, the 20,000-ton SMS *Von Der Tann*, puts in an impressive appearance at the 1911 Coronation review. In the same year Tirpitz proposed to step up the construction of German capital ships to establish a permanent 3:2 ratio with Britain.

'The purpose and aim of our naval policy is political independence from England . . . to accomplish this purpose and this aim, we must diminish the military distance between England and ourselves, not increase it. If we do not succeed, then our whole naval policy of the last 14 years has been in vain.'
– *Tirpitz, 1911.*

from the Mediterranean for deployment in home waters, thrusting Britain closer to France.

The British defence commitment and contributions to its support steadily widened to include the Empire. Already Australia and New Zealand had supplied funds for capital ships, and they were joined by Malaya. The issue was also put before a more reluctant Canadian Parliament, who eventually agreed to supply funds for a battleship.

Churchill saw the growing German menace and this now motivated his intense activity in preparing the Fleet for war. His mentor was Fisher, who in retirement struck up an intense and lively correspondence with Churchill, bombarding him with closely-typed sheets of paper on all aspects of policy.

Churchill pressed forward with plans to convert the fleet to oil, which added a margin in speed and radius of action over coal-burning ships. The decision was a momentous one since it made British defences dependent on oil supplies in faraway lands which she might find difficulty in controlling.

The First Sea Lord was aware of the formidable reputation of the Germans in gunnery, and with the support of Sir John Jellicoe, who became Second Sea Lord, Churchill pressed for the adoption of the director system of gunnery control, developed by Admiral Sir Percy Scott. This method enabled all guns on a ship to be aimed and fired simultaneously from a spotting position high above the bridge, away from the smoke and cordite fumes which obscured vision.

The British Government continued to try and modify the naval arms race, but Churchill gave a clear warning of what his attitude would be when he introduced the 1912 estimates. If Germany added two ships Britain would add four; if she added three Britain would add six.

Churchill however made a firm offer of a 'naval holiday': 'any retardation or reduction in German construction will within certain limits be followed here . . . by large and fully proportional reductions.' At the same time, the Royal Navy was concentrated in home waters; the French holding the Mediterranean.

As the final showdown with Germany approached, the Royal Navy was a very different service in 1914 from Victoria's navy which had imposed the *pax Britannica* only two decades before. The feverish naval race with Germany had produced a revolution in warship construction and dramatic changes in the attitudes and organization of the two rival navies. The ships of both sides had been revolutionized in all classes, with massive increases in firepower following the adoption of the all-big-gun principle.

In front line strength Britain had 18 Dreadnoughts in service with 14 being built and 9 battlecruisers at sea, with one under construction. Germany had 13 modern battleships, with 6 being built, plus 7 battlecruisers built or being built. Britain could also deploy a vast pre-Dreadnought strength of 25 battleships, in very good fighting order, against Germany's 18 older battleships.

The caste-conscious navy The Imperial Navy inherited the rigid disciplinary attitudes of the Prussian Army. Petty Officers (*Deckoffizieren*) celebrating at a mess party before the war (left) found promotion to the officer corps difficult. The lower deck had the toughest jobs like coaling ship (right) and very little chance of promotion, but nevertheless were a very highly trained and efficient force.

Both navies had been equipped with new bases, dockyards and shore facilities during the naval race. The Royal Navy no longer sailed the world in stately fashion but was concentrated in the cold waters of the North Sea, ready to apply its strategy of distant blockade by closing the Norway–Orkneys gap. Scapa Flow, the largest natural anchorage in the British Isles, was considered as the future home of the Grand Fleet because its remoteness and difficult currents offered some defence against U-boat and surface attack. However in 1914 there was little at Scapa except seagulls and cormorants, and there were no facilities for making life bearable for the thousands of sailors who would have to live there if war broke out. Other bases were also being hastily developed at Cromarty and Rosyth, whilst the east-coast ports of Harwich and Sheerness had assumed a new importance as the centres for cruiser and destroyer operations.

Britain lacked a system of bases along her east coast with sufficient dockyard and repair facilities for the heavy capital ships. Successive governments had been unprepared to vote the necessary funds for such unglamorous expenditure, and there was even a shortage of facilities in the established bases of Portsmouth, Chatham and Devonport.

Germany had rapidly built up her North Sea base of Wilhelmshaven. Although the Kiel Canal could not handle the largest ships from Germany's main Baltic base of Kiel until 1914, large units of the High Seas Fleet were already mustered in Wilhelmshaven and new facilities had been built at Brunsbüttel at the northern entrance of the canal. In contrast to the British at Scapa Flow and the Scottish bases where the crews had to live on board ship, the Germans at Wilhelmshaven and Kiel could easily go ashore for exercise or drill. Many of the ships' crews could live in barracks and there were well served officers' clubs. The German sailors preferred to be based at Kiel, which had not grown up 'utilitarian, sober and austere' like Wilhelmshaven, but offered plenty of amusement and entertainment with cinemas and concert halls.

Everybody in Britain and Germany was conscious that any clash between the two fleets would be determined not purely on grounds of equipment but on leadership and the quality of the men. Here the two navies mirrored their own societies, and the tensions within them. In 1910 Admiral Mahan had annoyed the British Press by doubting Britain's will to win the naval confrontation with Germany. The American historian admired German efficiency and had said, 'insular democracies are lax and inefficient in preparation for war and in natural consequence their wars have been long and expensive. But wars in future cannot be long, though they may be expensive of much besides their immediate cost; expensive in advantages lost and indemnities exacted.'

Britain certainly had been undergoing major social changes and a loosening of the class structure. Lloyd George's budgets, parliamentary crises, and the pressure of industrial strikes had started a major process of liberalizing British society. This attitude was reinforced by the Navy's need to recruit the best-trained manpower to service the new technologies incorporated into modern warships. There was a need for engineers, artificers, radio operators and electricians; even the demands on the ordinary seaman had increased so that he now required above-average skills to man the big guns and master the complexities of signalling and torpedoes.

The seaman of 1914 was no longer the barefoot tar of *HMS Pinafore*. Reform of lower deck conditions by Fisher removed some of the harsher forms of punishment, and in 1912 Churchill increased the fleet's wages. Life however was still hard.

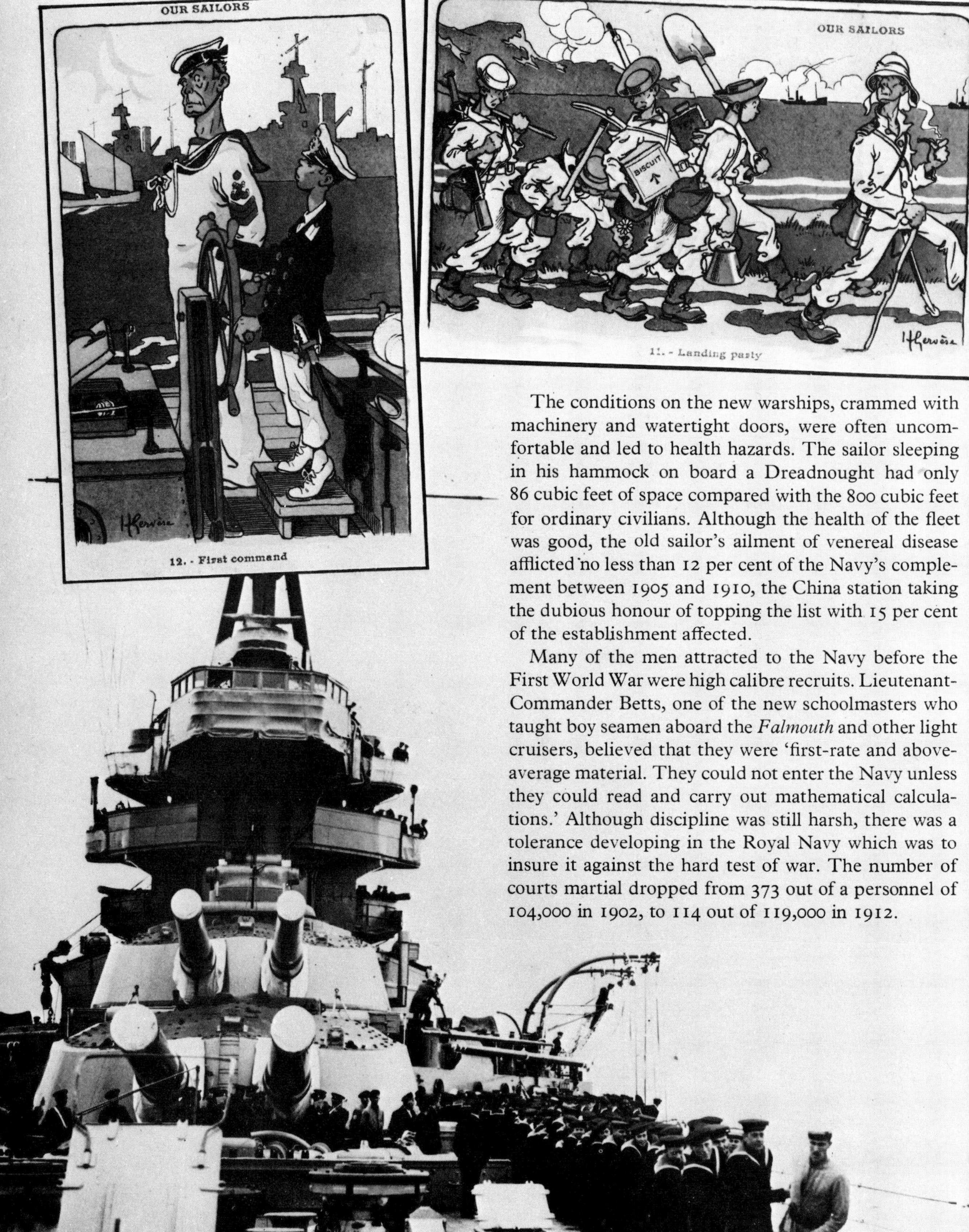

12. - First command

11. - Landing party

The conditions on the new warships, crammed with machinery and watertight doors, were often uncomfortable and led to health hazards. The sailor sleeping in his hammock on board a Dreadnought had only 86 cubic feet of space compared with the 800 cubic feet for ordinary civilians. Although the health of the fleet was good, the old sailor's ailment of venereal disease afflicted no less than 12 per cent of the Navy's complement between 1905 and 1910, the China station taking the dubious honour of topping the list with 15 per cent of the establishment affected.

Many of the men attracted to the Navy before the First World War were high calibre recruits. Lieutenant-Commander Betts, one of the new schoolmasters who taught boy seamen aboard the *Falmouth* and other light cruisers, believed that they were 'first-rate and above-average material. They could not enter the Navy unless they could read and carry out mathematical calculations.' Although discipline was still harsh, there was a tolerance developing in the Royal Navy which was to insure it against the hard test of war. The number of courts martial dropped from 373 out of a personnel of 104,000 in 1902, to 114 out of 119,000 in 1912.

Naval routine The reality – boat drill to the music of the Marine band aboard the battleship HMS *Marlborough* (below left) – and as the cartoonist saw it on seaside postcards (left).

Discipline was firm and some punishments were still very severe. Death was the penalty for striking an officer and boy seamen could still be birched. The junior officers traditionally exercised their authority over the midshipmen and cadets with beatings in the gunroom.

The German Navy was very different from the Royal Navy. It was a newly created force with a history extending back only as far as the 1850s. It had drawn heavily on the traditions of the Prussian Army and the notion that the German officer was the most elite member of society. Like the Royal Navy, the Imperial Navy also had to contain the pressures for social and technical change being experienced in the Reich itself. Far from presenting a picture of tolerance, the German Navy was moving in the opposite direction with a strong disciplinary code and a new officer corps which suffered all the indignity of the parvenu alongside the established Prussian army officers.

The German Navy was technically extremely efficient and needed to attract technicians as much as the Royal Navy did. Unlike the British, however, the German Navy was conscripted. This was very different from the all-regular British Navy where men served for an initial twelve years, usually from boyhood, and often went on for another ten. In Germany skilled men were often drawn away from good jobs in the Ruhr and other industrial centres only to become frustrated with naval discipline. Many of them were deeply opposed to the social and political values of the officer corps and on the bigger ships where there were several separate messes serving markedly different food for the various grades, these feelings were aggravated.

The German naval officers were recruited primarily from the upper and middle classes, but there was considerable social prejudice. Even in the middle of the War the Inspector of the Education Department of the Navy rejected a candidate because the family was 'composed largely of lower-class people (inn-keeper and manual labourer, carpenter and awning-maker, dentist and confectioner). In addition the [financial] means for the career were insufficient.' As one historian of the German officer corps noted, 'the bourgeois cadet who entered the naval officer corps was only too eager to adopt the manners, outlook and often the accompanying arrogance of the Prussian nobility, particularly of the Prussian Officer Corps.' Many of them 'looked down on their poorer fellows in the same way that the aristocrat looked down on the bourgeois, but with much less accustomed restraint.'

The executive officers also regarded themselves as a cut above the engineer officers, echoing the attitudes inside the Royal Navy. The German deck officers, who corresponded to the British warrant officers, supervised the military functions of the ship and they particularly resented the closed caste of the executive officers.

Much of the efficiency of the German officer corps stemmed from the strict training given to the executive officer cadets during their $3\frac{1}{2}$-year training course. They were given a course in which they spent $1\frac{1}{2}$ months on infantry training, $10\frac{1}{2}$ months on practical navigation and engine tending, 12 months on professional sciences with the emphasis on engineering, followed by 6 months special training in gunnery, torpedoes and weapons. Their last year was spent at sea, and was heavily biased towards the sea sciences.

The Royal Navy's officers were trained according to a completely different tradition. The emphasis was on practical training at sea, based on complicated and carefully balanced rules which had been built up empirically over centuries as a result of the hard experience of officers and men living and fighting in close proximity at sea. Fisher's reforms of officer cadet training were designed to remove the weaknesses of a system that, at its worst, encouraged little attention either to professional duties concerned with modern warfare or new strategic and tactical problems presented by Dreadnoughts and submarines.

WILLS'S CIGARETTES.
NORTH DAKOTA

WILLS'S CIGARETTES.
PETROPAVLOVSK

WILLS'S CIGARETTES.
RIVIDAVIA

WILLS'S CIGARETTES.
INDEFATIGABLE

WILLS'S CIGARETTES.

WILLS'S CIGARETTES.
SOUTH CAROLINA

WILLS'S CIGARETTES.
ARKANSAS

WILLS'S CIGARETTES.
BLUCHER

WILLS'S CIGARETTES.

WILLS'S CIGARETTES.
MINAS GERAES

WILLS'S CIGARETTES.
NASSAU

WILLS'S CIGARETTES.
DANTE ALIGHIERI

WILLS'S CIGARETTES.
LORD NELSON

WILLS'S CIGARETTES.
INVINCIBLE

WILLS'S CIGARETTES.

WILLS'S CIGARETTES.

WILLS'S CIGARETTES.

WILLS'S CIGARETTES.
WESTFALEN

WILLS'S CIGARETTES.

WILLS'S CIGARETTES.

WILLS'S CIGARETTES.

Men and Materials The massive revolution in naval technology had penetrated the public mind so that the tobacco manufacturers could use 'The World's Dreadnoughts' as selling aids (left). The majority of young 'bluejackets' could not remember the unchallenged supremacy of Victoria's navy. With war approaching most faced the bleak prospect of years away from home and family, and sentimental postcards expressed their duty (below).

Fisher abolished the crude system of entry whereby a naval cadet was thought fit to be an officer if he came from the right family, could recite the Lord's Prayer and could jump naked over a chair. His attempts to bring about an integrated training scheme for officers entering the service at 12½ years old still met with determined resistance by the Navy's old guard, and to a lesser extent there was a deep prejudice against engineer officers which the Admiralty sought to dispel. Fisher was aware that the Navy's officers, who should have been drawn from the most intelligent sections of the community, were still provided by the privileged upper-middle classes. It required an income of £700 a year to send a boy into the Royal Navy as a cadet, and in 1905 there were only about 300,000 people in Britain with such an income. This was very disappointing to an ardent reformer like Fisher who believed in the meritocracy, and it affected particularly the able long-service petty officers and seamen for whom there was no chance of promotion to the gilded ranks of the wardroom.

Fisher and Churchill both tried to break down these attitudes to some extent. In 1912 Churchill introduced a system whereby promising petty officers and warrant officers could be promoted to commissioned rank. However even when war broke out, there was still a deep dissatisfaction about promotion prospects, especially when Royal Navy Volunteer Reserve officers and other 'outsiders', rather than the veteran warrant officers and men who had fought their way up, were offered promotion if they would undertake the command of new torpedoboats and other ships. Fisher campaigned against the prejudice towards the officers from the lower deck: 'When they make a sailor a lieutenant, they stow him away in some small vessel so that he shan't mess with the blue-bloods. King Edward said I was a socialist. So I am!'

In spite of Fisher's ruthless purges, senior naval officers still embodied the traditions of the days of sail and Nelson's navy. However at the lower levels the midshipmen and junior officers were products of a far more liberal system of selection than that of the Germans and were being drawn from a widening social background. Furthermore the democratic parliamentary system, believed to be so inefficient by naval professionals like Admiral Mahan, was an important safety valve capable of rectifying the worst abuses.

Now on the eve of war, after last minute hopes of an agreement with Germany had foundered, the two great fleets were at a high pitch of battle-readiness. All that was needed was a small, unforeseen spark to ignite the highly explosive situation. The British Fleet stood ready to sail for its distant and inhospitable bases where it could immediately apply the blockade strategy. This strategy, which was not even finalized until the outbreak of war, would prove disastrous for Tirpitz's plan of wearing down the British forces until a final confrontation could take place on equal terms. When that final clash came, however, it would lead to the biggest sea battle of all fought in the classic pattern of a gunnery duel, which tested men and material to their limit.

Mobilization The British Fleet, led by the flagship HMS *Iron Duke*, concentrated at Spithead for review before annual manoeuvres on 18 July 1917. 'The greatest assemblage of naval power ever witnessed in the history of the world', according to First Lord of the Admiralty Winston Churchill, served as a reminder of Britain's determination to maintain command of the seas during the summer crisis of 1914.

SALVOES IN ANGER

The saluting guns of Royal Navy battleships boomed across the waters of Kiel Bay on the 23 June 1914, announcing the arrival of a powerful British naval squadron for the annual regatta week. This goodwill visit was viewed by some German naval officers with the utmost suspicion: 'England is ready to strike; war is imminent, and the object of the naval unit is spying.'

No attempt was spared to impress the visitors, both with the German battleships and the hospitality of many official luncheons and dinners. Whilst the seamen were taken by special trains to sample the pleasures of Hamburg and Berlin, officers ploughed through caviar, *geflügelpastete*, and *heligolander Hummer mit mayonnaise*. Selections from Wagner were played as they ate, interspersed with sentimental Anglo-Saxon melodies like *Home, Sweet Home*. Senior German naval dignitaries made long speeches flattering their guests and expressing incredulity at the Press rumours which suggested the possibility of war between the two nations. 'I read it with horror,' said the Captain of the battleship *Pommern* at one of these functions, 'to us such a war would be a civil war'.

The awkward official theatricality of the occasion reached its highlight with the dramatic arrival of the Kaiser, resplendent in his uniform as Admiral of the Atlantic, on a platform high above the bridge of the Imperial Yacht. Wild cheering arose as the *Hohenzollern*'s prow snapped the silk ribbons stretched across the new locks. The newly deepened and widened Kiel Canal was now open so the biggest battleships in the German Fleet had a short cut to the North Sea.

Two days later, on the afternoon of 28 June, the sailing regattas and the celebrations were stopped

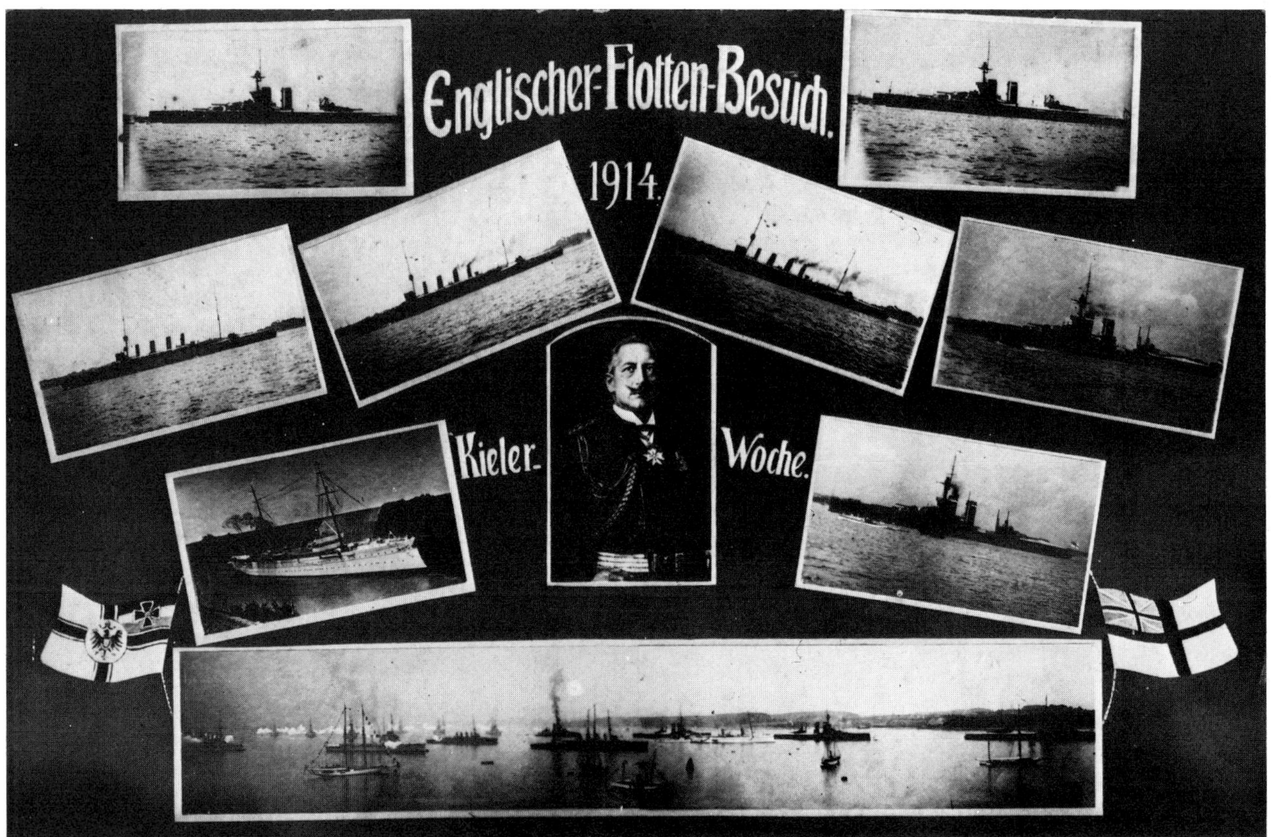

'The lights are going out all over Europe' In the last weeks of peace, relations between the Royal Navy and the Imperial Fleet were outwardly cordial. A souvenir issued to officers and men during the British 2nd Battle Squadron's visit to Kiel Week (below left) displayed a benevolent portrait of the Kaiser surrounded by the British ships, the Imperial Yacht *Hohenzollern* and a panorama of Kiel harbour. On the eve of war the Royal Navy treated the British public to a dazzling spectacle of searchlights and fireworks (below right).

abruptly. News that the heir of the Austro-Hungarian throne had been assassinated in Sarajevo was telegraphed to every ship. A despatch boat raced out into the harbour to take the news to the Emperor who had set off with his party for a day's racing in the *Meteor*. By the time he returned, moody and silent, ensigns of the fleet were already being dropped in response to his order, 'Flags at half-mast, Austrian Flag at the mainmast for the murder of the Austrian heir.'

The following day the Kiel festivities were hurried to an abrupt end. The Kaiser rushed back to a crisis-torn Berlin as the British ships prepared to raise anchor for home. The tension was visibly increasing. Zeppelins circled ominously above and from every bridge over the canal photographers took detailed pictures of the ships as they passed below.

Three weeks later, the European crisis was still simmering when almost the entire Royal Navy marshalled itself in long, grey lines for review by King George V. For the last time in peace the historic waters of Spithead presented what the First Lord, Winston Churchill, described as 'incomparably the greatest assemblage of naval power ever witnessed in the history of the world'. For two days whilst at anchor, the combined First, Second and Third Fleets were a blaze of entertainment, parties and fireworks. On 19 July the King himself in the Royal Yacht, *Victoria and Albert*, took up position at the head of his ships to lead the squadrons into the Channel for exercises. Fifty three battleships headed the procession of over 400 ships including 20 new Dreadnoughts and 9 new battlecruisers, the Navy's total Dreadnought strength except for the 3 battlecruisers on station in the Mediterranean and the *Australia* based in the South

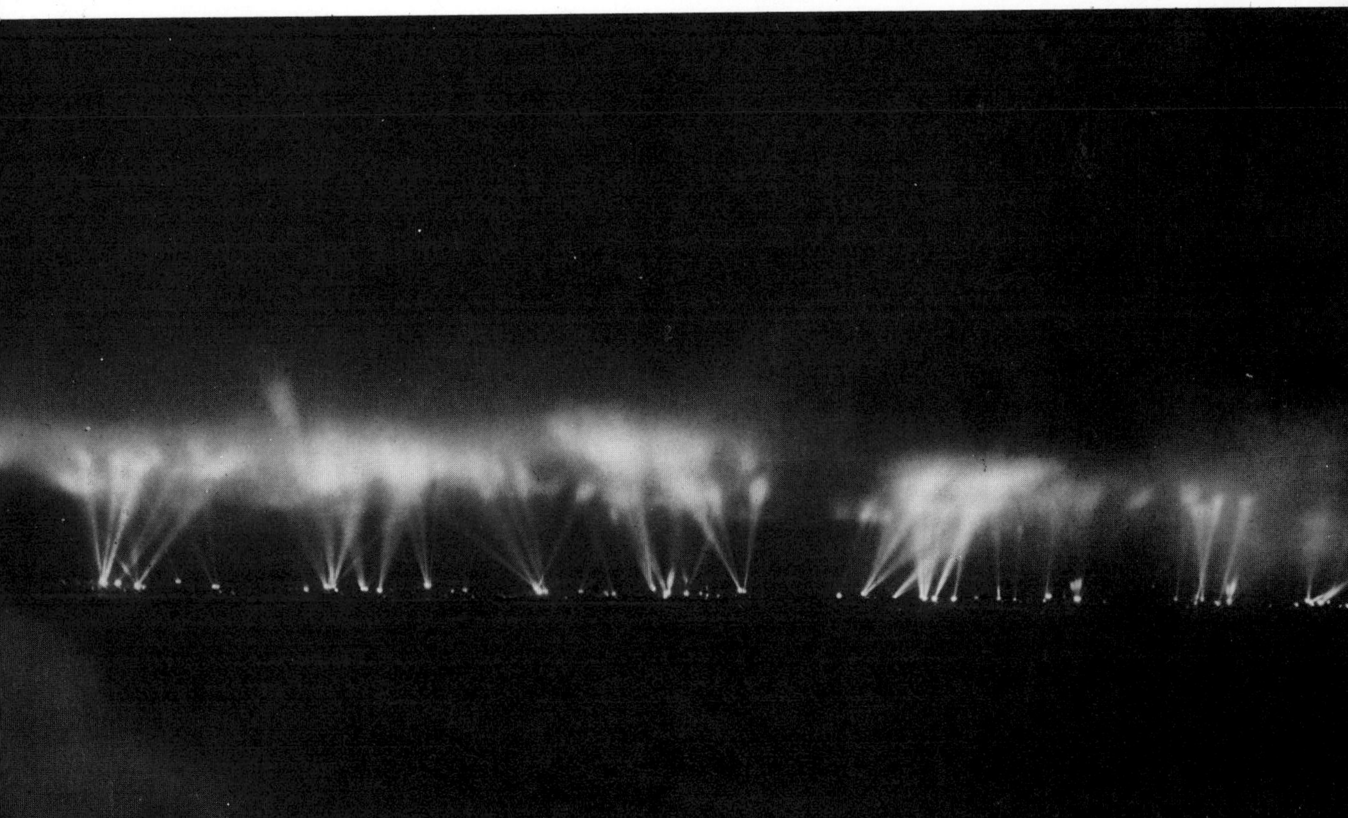

Keeping a step ahead As Britain and Germany moved towards war, the major preoccupation of Winston Churchill and the First Sea Lord, Prince Louis of Battenberg (left), was to trap the German battlecruiser *Goeben* and its consort the armoured cruiser *Breslau* (right) before they could attack Allied sea routes in the Mediterranean. As a result of a 'tragedy of errors' the British failed to stop the enemy, and German forces reached Constantinople where they were to influence Turkey's attitude towards the Allies.

Pacific. This concentration of naval might in the northern waters was a show of strength to impress and warn Germany and her allies.

The ships had hardly returned to Portsmouth on 23 July when the Austrian Government delivered its ultimatum to Serbia. Churchill wrote hurriedly to his wife, 'Europe is trembling on the verge of a general war, the Austrian ultimatum to Serbia being the most insolent document of its kind ever devised.'

On Sunday morning the First Sea Lord, Prince Louis of Battenberg learned that Austria had rejected Serbia's conciliatory reply to the ultimatum. Aware that this situation was bringing war closer, Prince Louis took a crucial personal decision to halt the imminent disbandment of the mobilized Fleet. The reservists already preparing to go home were ordered to remain on duty. His telegram – 'Admiralty to C-in-C Home Fleets. Decipher. No ships of the First Fleet or Flotillas are to leave Portland until further orders. Acknowledge.' – stopped all dispersal. The Royal Navy was on instant readiness for war.

However much Asquith and most of his cabinet might wish to remain mere 'spectators', the European situation dragged them forwards to its climax. On 28 July Austria declared war on Serbia. Russia mobilized to support the Serbs, and Churchill obtained Asquith's approval to move the Fleet into the North Sea as a precautionary measure. During the hours of darkness the 18-mile line of British Dreadnoughts steamed through the Channel, clearing Dover at midnight with their crews on stand-by and guns at the ready. War routine was observed in every ship.

The British Cabinet waited to see how Germany would react. Would the *Riskflotte* strategy be put to the test? In Berlin, Tirpitz energetically tried to persuade the Chancellor, Bethmann Hollweg, to put the Navy on immediate war footing by concentrating all ships on the North Sea ports and urged that the war should be opened with a landing by a naval corps on Britain's east coast. This found no favour with the all-powerful German generals whose 'dry land' thinking demanded an attack on Russia and execution of the Schlieffen Plan to sweep through Belgium and overwhelm France. The Chancellor also hoped to avoid a direct clash of arms with Britain in the coming conflict, regarding her as 'a bulldog which must not be irritated'.

On 1 August the European states hesitated on the brink of war. The High Seas Fleet was ordered to concentrate at Wilhelmshaven and the Jade anchorage to be ready for action in the North Sea; the British Grand Fleet was on the alert in its North Sea base, and only 450 miles now separated the greatest concentrations of naval power ever assembled; 34 Dreadnought battleships, 10 battlecruisers, 28 pre-Dreadnought battleships together with over 30 cruisers, 50 submarines and nearly 150 destroyers. The stage was now set for the naval war. That night the diplomatic crisis in Europe came to a head. Churchill awaited developments in his room at the Admiralty. He wrote, 'We sat down at a card table and began a game of bridge. The cards had just been dealt when another red, Foreign Office box came in. I opened it and read "War declared by Germany on Russia."'

On 3 August Germany invaded Luxembourg; the invasion of Belgium was imminent. The British Government at last realized they would soon be dragged into the war through their commitment to Belgium. It was vital that the Admiralty should act

quickly if the British and French forces were to move against the German battlecruiser *Goeben*, on the loose in the Mediterranean. Churchill telegraphed to Admiral Sir John Jellicoe, who had been sent to Scapa Flow two days earlier, that he was to take over as Commander-in-Chief of the Grand Fleet.

On Monday morning 3 August the Germans issued their ultimatum to Belgium, and started preparing to move their troops over the border. Britain solemnly warned Germany to halt the invasion of Belgium within twenty-four hours. Lord Kitchener, Britain's most distinguished soldier, was recalled from Dover, where he was embarking for Egypt, and made Secretary of State for War.

In the Mediterranean events were moving towards the first naval action of the war. The *Goeben*, shadowed by the battlecruisers *Indomitable* and *Indefatigable*, sailed to attack the coast of French North Africa. Churchill, anxious that the quarry should not escape, wanted to intercept her before nightfall. The Cabinet were hostile, still hoping for last-minute peace moves; but, as Asquith recorded, 'Winston, who has got on all his war-paint, is longing for a fight in the early hours of the morning to result in the sinking of the *Goeben*.'

In the final hours, anxious crowds of Londoners gathered in front of Buckingham Palace. At Scapa Flow, tension was running high and there were several false alarms; the crews of the great warships were convinced that the next forty-eight hours would see a great fleet action. The German Fleet was in harbour, but under steam and ready to weigh anchor at any moment. At 11 o'clock the signal flashed out from the wireless masts high above the Admiralty House building in Whitehall to British ships around the world: 'Commence hostilities with Germany . . .' But while the Grand Fleet at Scapa Flow were awaiting action in the North Sea, the Royal Navy lost its first opportunity of decisive action against the *Goeben* in the Mediterranean.

As Prince Louis of Battenberg had feared, after bombarding the Algerian coast, the *Goeben* and her consort, the heavy cruiser *Breslau*, gave the British battlecruisers the slip during the night while sailing back to Messina to coal. Concern for Italian neutrality prevented the British battlecruisers attacking immediately when the *Goeben* sailed again on 6 August. Hugging the Italian coast she gave her pursuers the slip by heading into the Adriatic before making a course

Fleets over the horizon For the first months of the war both Germany and Britain were reluctant to risk their main fleets. The Grand Fleet was concentrated at Scapa Flow (below) where it could blockade Germany, whilst the Kaiser preferred to keep his fleet safe in port as a bargaining counter at the anticipated early peace conference.

for Turkey. Throughout that night the *Goeben* was shadowed by a squadron of British armoured cruisers under Rear-Admiral Troubridge. But, painfully aware of a recent Admiralty telegram that warned against 'being brought to action against superior forces', Troubridge decided after much anguish that his sixteen ships were no match for the two German vessels. The opportunity of bringing the Germans to battle was lost; the British Mediterranean Fleet's battleships were too far away and confused signals led to a combination of fatal errors which allowed the *Goeben* to reach Constantinople in triumph, without a salvo being fired.

At home enthusiasm was running high amongst the crews when at 8.30 am on the first day of the War, Jellicoe led the Grand Fleet out of Scapa Flow to make the first of many routine sweeps. The Grand Fleet was fulfilling the Naval War Plan that dictated the distant blockade of Germany and the bottling up of the High Seas Fleet. The principal 'stopper' in the strategy was the Grand Fleet, with the exit into the Atlantic covered by the northern patrol of the 10th Cruiser Squadron, a line of warships extending east and north from the Shetlands.

The Channel Fleet, based in Portland and consisting of the older pre-Dreadnoughts of the 5th, 7th and 8th Battle Squadrons, controlled the Straits of Dover, together with the destroyers of the 6th Patrol Flotilla – the famous 'Dover Patrol'. On the east coast, at Harwich, an advance unit of the Grand Fleet, was stationed under Commodore Tyrwhitt, whose destroyers and cruisers closely patrolled the waters adjacent to the German Bight.

Grand Admiral Tirpitz believed that attacks by the High Seas Fleet could break the North Sea blockade. 'Battleships alone could save us,' he argued, against the Army General Staff who had thrust his fleet into the background and who were trying to undertake the impossible task of 'defeating England before the walls of Paris'.

But his arguments carried little weight. Nominal operational command was exercised by the cautious

Admiral von Pohl, the *Oberkommando de Marine.* The Naval Staff (*Admiralstab*) was nominally responsible for strategy, but it was staffed by senior officers of no great ability, and the overall direction of the naval war was effectively left in the hands of the Emperor himself. Tirpitz was an 'adviser' but the overall strategy of the Fleet was dominated by the views of the all-powerful Army General Staff. Britain's 'distant blockade' strategy had already thrown the Imperial Navy's plans into confusion since their War Orders and Tirpitz's predictions had anticipated a close blockade of the German coast.

For the Germans aggressive schemes meant putting their fleet at risk, and both the Kaiser and his Chancellor were convinced that Paris would soon fall and that an undamaged fleet would be an important asset at the peace table. On 12 August, a decision was made to keep the fleet 'in being' and intact in the Jade anchorage.

The immediate result of this weak strategy was that no attempt was to be made by the Imperial Navy to interfere with the vital transportation of the British Expeditionary Army across the Channel to the Continent. It was not necessary to risk battleships, argued the Generals: 'We shall arrest them.' Tirpitz was furious:

> It was simply nonsense to pack up the fleet in cotton wool. The fleet 'in being' has some meaning for England, for her fleet thus achieves its purpose of commanding the seas. But the principle is meaningless for Germany, whose object must be to keep the seas free for herself. Besides, we cannot allow the war to develop into a war of exhaustion, but must attempt to shorten matters.

In Britain there was similar frustration as the British public looked to the Grand Fleet for action. Churchill put forward plans for a wide range of offensive actions against the Heligoland base, a landing in the Baltic, raiding up the Elbe – anything to stir the High Seas Fleet into action. Experienced naval advisers pointed

'Singeing the Kaiser's moustache' Britain took the initiative in August when the light cruisers and destroyers of the Harwich forces commanded by Commodore Tyrwhitt (left) raided the Heligoland Bight. They were supported by Beatty with five battlecruisers including *Invincible* (right). The Germans lost three light cruisers and a destroyer; the British escaped with damage to one light cruiser.

out the risks entailed in such bold thrusts and on a strategic analysis the fleet had so far been brilliantly successful in applying the blockade strategy without any serious naval engagement. But England expected and wanted the big naval battle.

So did the officers and men of the Grand Fleet. As the weeks passed their initial enthusiasm waned and they grew bored with routine and monotonous patrolling in the cold northern waters. The Commander of the battlecruiser squadron, Vice-Admiral Sir David Beatty, wrote home: 'For thirty years I have been waiting for this day, and have as fine a command as one could wish for and can do nothing. Three weeks of war and haven't seen the enemy.'

The initiative was finally seized by the aggressive Commodore Keyes who was in charge of the Submarine Flotillas based at Harwich. He proposed a plan involving Tyrwhitt's Harwich force, with his submarines, to lure and attack the German cruiser patrols in the Bight at dawn on 28 August.

The actual conduct of the operation revealed a weakness in co-ordination and communication that could have been disastrous. After first refusing Tyrwhitt the support of any heavy ships, the Admiralty consented to the two battlecruisers then stationed in the Humber taking part. At the last minute the Admiralty changed the plan and agreed to Beatty's two battlecruisers and the 1st Light Cruiser Squadron of Commodore Goodenough joining the operation. Incredibly, the news of this was not transmitted to the ships of Tyrwhitt and Keyes, which were already at sea.

The action was ill co-ordinated and confused because the three British squadrons all acted independently in dangerous, enemy-held waters. The Germans were alerted by the excessive use of wireless telegraphy by the light cruisers and despatched a heavy force of their own fast cruisers to reinforce the destroyer flotilla that had been attacked off Heligoland. Caught in a 'hornet's nest', Tyrwhitt's light cruiser, *Arethusa*, was soon badly hit and on fire. Realizing that Goodenough's cruiser force might not be strong enough to save Tyrwhitt in the face of German reinforcements, Beatty, standing 25 miles off the enemy island of Heligoland, had a difficult decision to make. Taking account of the danger from mines and torpedoes he raced to Tyrwhitt's rescue despite his worry 'if I lose one of these valuable ships the country will not forgive me'.

Beatty's gamble paid off and it turned the British flop into a German rout as the big guns of the battlecruisers shot two of the German cruisers, *Mainz* and *Köln*, to pieces, left the *Ariadne* sinking, and scattered the rest. Beatty prudently retired, shepherding the damaged *Arethusa*. The German battlecruiser squadron was penned up for an hour in the Jade anchorage, unable to cross a river sandbar until high tide. When it arrived on the scene all it found was the wreck of the *Ariadne* and a few survivors. The High Seas Fleet had lost a destroyer, three cruisers and over a thousand men, killed, wounded and taken prisoner (one of them Tirpitz's son).

The British attack brought home to the more

cautious German Admirals, and to the Kaiser himself, the risk to their fleet of any action. Instructions were sent to the High Seas Fleet Commander, Admiral von Ingenohl, restricting him still further.

In the face of the German refusal to send their fleet out to battle Churchill gave vent to his feelings before a 15,000-strong recruiting rally at Liverpool on 21 September. He told a cheering audience: 'Although we hope the Navy will have a chance of settling the question of the German Fleet, yet if they do not come out and fight in time of war they will be dug out like rats in a hole.' Such strong language delighted the public, but upset the Admiralty establishment and the King, who sent him note of complaint.

Unfortunately, Churchill's rhetoric rang hollow when the following day a single U-boat torpedoed and sank three British armoured cruisers, *Aboukir*, *Cressy* and *Hogue*, with the loss of 1,459 officers and men.

The Admiralty tried to put a brave face on the sinking of the old ships, which ought not to have been patrolling in circumstances that invited an easy attack. In Berlin the Kaiser was reported to be 'in seventh heaven', and Weddigen, Commander of the victorious *U9*, and his crew were fêted as national heroes.

This demonstration of the growing U-boat threat was rated very seriously by Jellicoe. Submarines had, contrary to all predictions, penetrated as far north as Scapa Flow, forcing the C-in-C into a series of panic evacuations of the fleet to the security of Loch Ewe on Scotland's west coast; and then to Lough Swilly on the northern Irish coast. This meant even longer passages for the fleet in order to get to the North Sea. But adequate anti-submarine defences at the fleet anchorages were progressing very slowly and there was a desperate shortage of minesweepers – just six were available in the early months of the War. Moreover, the

The first defeat since Trafalgar Fisher (left), who replaced Prince Louis of Battenberg as First Sea Lord in October 1914, was immediately confronted with a naval disaster when Rear Admiral Sir Christopher Cradock's (inset) weak South American squadron was destroyed by von Spee's cruisers in the 'most rotten show imaginable'. Cradock's flagship *Good Hope* (below) and the cruiser *Monmouth* were both sunk with all hands.

very personal way in which he was running the naval war, coupled with the lack of the expected quick victory at sea, brought Churchill much criticism. Matters came to a head in the last week of October; Antwerp had fallen and his 'adventure' of defending the city with a naval brigade had backfired in a public outcry of 'Churchill must go'. A shake-up was demanded at the Admiralty. The Press campaign fastened unfairly on the First Sea Lord, Prince Louis of Battenberg because of his German origins. In spite of staunch defence by his colleagues, certain sections of the Press and anonymous letter-writers pursued him mercilessly.

In the face of mounting clamour, the Cabinet took the easy course and asked for Battenberg's resignation. There were some who wanted to see the First Lord go too, but Churchill rode out the storm and in a masterly

move brought back the veteran 'Jackie' Fisher to replace Battenberg. It was a controversial appointment but popular with the British public. Seventy-four years old, but still vigorous, Fisher had been waiting on the sidelines since war began, anxious to direct the fleet he had created.

Many felt that the combination of Fisher's intolerance and Churchill's aggressive energy would be too powerful for the Navy to live with; the veteran Admiral left people with the feeling of having been 'run over by a motor bus without suffering actual physical injury'. But Churchill believed he could handle him. He wrote: 'Our compact was that neither did anything of importance without the other. On this basis, as I worked till about 12.30 am and he began at 4 am – the Admiralty ran twenty-four hours a day.'

But whilst the new First Sea Lord was busily

Fisher's revenge Fisher acted decisively to restore the Royal Navy's prestige; the battlecruisers *Invincible* (right) and *Inflexible* were ordered across the South Atlantic where they trapped von Spee's squadron off the Falkland Islands. Of the German cruisers portrayed on a souvenir postcard, only the *Dresden* escaped the British guns in the decisive action of 8 December 1914. 'It was not victory but annihilation', was Fisher's jubilant verdict.

gingering up the organization and bullying the shipyards into a massive new construction programme for 600 ships, the Germans sank a Dreadnought and two cruisers in their most successful week of the naval war.

On 27 October one of Britain's most powerful Dreadnoughts, the *Audacious*, foundered after striking a mine off Ireland. Since she sank in full sight of the liner, *Olympic*, photographs appeared two weeks later in the *Philadelphia Public Ledger*, and prevented Churchill concealing the disaster.

Worse was to come. The following week the Germans achieved their one major naval victory of the war at the battle of Coronel. Admiral von Spee's commerce raiding squadron had been hunted across the Pacific, but his powerful modern cruisers, *Scharnhorst* and *Gneisenau*, in company with the light cruisers *Nürnberg*, *Leipzig* and *Dresden* had evaded all the Navy's attempts to bring them to action. On the afternoon of 1 November, in Chilean waters, Admiral Sir Christopher Cradock finally contacted von Spee's ships, and headed into attack with his weaker force, consisting of the armoured cruisers *Good Hope* and *Monmouth*, the light cruiser *Glasgow* and the armed merchantman *Otranto*. It was a gallant but disastrous decision. Outgunned and outmanoeuvred by von Spee, Cradock's ships were picked off as they lay silhouetted against the setting sun. The *Good Hope* and *Monmouth* were sunk with the loss of over 1500 officers and men. The *Otranto* and *Glasgow* managed to escape into the gathering darkness.

When the news of Coronel reached Britain on 4 November, the effect was stunning. It was the first British naval defeat since Trafalgar.

In Germany there was jubilation amongst the High Seas Fleet. 'This news filled us in the fleet with pride and confidence', wrote Vice-Admiral Scheer. In Valparaiso the large German contingent welcomed the triumphant von Spee with flowers.

Fisher and Churchill were painfully aware of how Britain's prestige had been damaged and within an hour of receiving the news they were planning von Spee's defeat. The moment had come to justify Fisher's brilliant conception of 1906 – the battlecruiser. A powerful force consisting of the *Invincible* and *Inflexible* was detached from the Grand Fleet – regardless of the risk in reducing the British forces in the

North Sea – and in six hours they were steaming to Plymouth to store for the trip to South America with Admiral Sturdee in command.

A month later the British battlecruisers had just arrived at the Falkland Island base when, in the middle of coaling on the 8 December, two unidentified warships were spotted from the south. They turned out to be the *Gneisenau* and *Nürnberg* scouting for von Spee's squadron. When the German lookouts realized that the tripod masts they had spotted were British battlecruisers, the two cruisers fled to rejoin von Spee, hotly pursued by Sturdee's battlecruisers, four heavy cruisers, two light cruisers and an armed merchant cruiser.

Escape was impossible and with their superior speed the British ships overhauled von Spee's squadron. Ordering his light cruisers to scatter, he gallantly took on the heavy battlecruisers with the *Scharnhorst* and *Gneisenau.* The result was never in doubt. Overwhelmed by the heavy gunfire, the Germans stubbornly refused to surrender and were pounded into the water whilst the British light cruisers hunted down the rest of the force and the German colliers. Only the *Dresden* escaped – only to be sunk in March by the *Glasgow* at Juan Fernandez island.

The victory at the Falklands avenged the defeat at Coronel and raised British morale. As Beatty commented: 'It has done us all a tremendous amount of good getting the news, and I hope it will put a stop to a lot of the unpleasant remarks one can detect in a certain portion of the Press that the British Navy has been an expensive luxury and is not doing its job.'

Underwater menace In 1914 the mine and the submarine profoundly influenced British strategy. After the major setback of the loss of the new Dreadnought *Audacious* (sunk after hitting a mine off the coast of Northern Ireland), Jellicoe laid great stress on the danger of these underwater weapons in the deployment and use of the Grand Fleet.

LOST CHANCES

The weeks between von Spee's Coronel victory and his Falklands' defeat were among the most anxious in the whole war for the British Navy. A combination of factors had cut the fighting strength of the Grand Fleet to a point of near equality with the High Seas Fleet. Had the German High Command realized this and given their C-in-C, Admiral von Ingenohl, the initiative that he wanted, the course of the War - and history - might have been transformed.

Admiral von Ingenohl knew that the Grand Fleet had been weakened by the loss of the *Audacious*, and that the *Invincible* and the *Inflexible* were in the South Atlantic. But neither he nor his hesitant superiors appreciated the extent to which their mining and submarine offensive had been successful in reducing the forces opposing them through mechanical wear and tear. They might have been deceived too by a squadron of skilfully converted steamers masquerading as Dreadnoughts which Jellicoe deployed to camouflage his shrinking fleet.

The constant routine patrolling of the Grand Fleet (in the first four months of the war it had steamed 18,805 miles) had revealed many defects in the British ships. Jellicoe was profoundly disturbed at the growing unserviceability of his Dreadnoughts and the threat posed by German submarines and mines.

'Submarine-itis' and 'mine-itis' naturally afflicted the British C-in-C more than anyone else. To Jellicoe's coolly analytical mind, these two threats demanded that he reassess his strategy. Three days after the mining of the *Audacious*, on 30 October, he set out his new tactical thinking in a historic letter which he sent to Fisher. Jellicoe believed that if the German Fleet was drawn into a battle, their inferior numbers would be compensated by submarines and minelayers deployed offensively as an integral part of their tactics. The Germans might make use of their submarines and mines in two ways. First, the submarines, led by the cruisers and destroyers might attack the Grand Fleet as it deployed. This was to be countered by his cruisers and destroyer flotillas operating well in advance to break up the attack before it developed. Second, the submarines could be deployed on the flanks or to the rear, the objective being for the enemy to lure the Grand Fleet into contact. This manoeuvre, the more dangerous, could be countered, argued Jellicoe, by a 'refusal to comply with the enemy's tactics by not moving in the invited direction'. Since this might be considered a retreat in the face of the enemy, Jellicoe wisely spelt out his tactical assessment for the approval of the Admiralty.

The Admiralty agreed with Jellicoe's new battle tactics and confirmed their 'full confidence' in the Commander-in-Chief. Well aware of the fickle nature of 'their Lordships' approval', Jellicoe decided not to risk their disapproval at some later date and lodged the correspondence at his bank.

The burden of command fell heavily on Admiral Sir John Jellicoe (left). His precise and analytical mind denied him the ruthlessness and dash of the true Nelson touch, but his understanding of human nature and 'eye for the battle' earned him a reputation in the Fleet, where he was known as 'Silent Jack'. His chief concern during the first winter was maintaining the full strength of the Grand Fleet when battleships like HMS *Marlborough* (below) began to suffer from mechanical defects from constant patrolling – by the end of 1914 the Grand Fleet had been reduced to near parity with the Germans.

Risking the Fleet In December 1914 the Kaiser reluctantly agreed to Tirpitz's argument that 'it was simply nonsense to pack up the Fleet in cotton wool'. The C-in-C, Admiral von Ingenohl (inset) received permission for a series of raids on the English coast. Anxious to avoid a confrontation with the Grand Fleet, fast battlecruisers like the SMS *Von der Tann* and *Derfflinger* (below) were sent out to bombard the weakly defended East coast ports. However, the German C-in-C intended to exceed the Kaiser's wishes by seeking to trap the British battlecruisers with the full High Seas Fleet.

Whilst Jellicoe was advocating a more cautious approach to future naval operations, von Ingenohl, supported by Tirpitz, tried to persuade the German High Command to adopt a more aggressive strategy against the numerically reduced British Fleet.

Finally, after strong pressure by Tirpitz, von Ingenohl obtained permission for a limited series of cruiser raids on the English coast.

The first victims of the new aggressive German policy in the North Sea were to be the defenceless citizens of the Norfolk town of Yarmouth. Just before dawn on 3 November they awoke to the sound of gunfire as salvoes from four German battlecruisers crashed into the streets. Urgent telephone calls flooded into the Admiralty War Room and the Grand Fleet was put on alert to counter an expected great naval operation, or even an invasion, for which the raid could be a diversionary cover. In fact the enemy squadron was covering a minelaying operation and before the Navy could take action, battlecruisers and minelayers vanished back into the mist. The reaction of the public was immediate and hostile to the Navy, the Admiralty and particularly Churchill. The Navy had failed to bring the Germans to action on the high

seas and now the British could not depend upon it for the defence of their own homes.

Fisher was convinced that the 'insult bombardment' presaged an imminent 'big naval operation', and he worried that there might be a repetition of the Yarmouth raid on a larger scale. His hunch was correct. The next German raid was planned for 15 December but this time a confident von Ingenohl decided, strictly against the terms of his orders, that the battle fleet would provide back-up cover and he hoped to decoy a part of the Grand Fleet over a freshly-laid minefield. The Yorkshire ports of Scarborough and Whitby were selected as targets because they were near the northern bases of the Grand Fleet and the chances of British heavy units being trapped were therefore increased.

Unfortunately for von Ingenohl, British Naval Intelligence had been given the German Navy's secret cypher keys recovered by the Russians from a wrecked destroyer, the *Magdeburg*. On the evening of 14 December, using this secret information, Naval Intelligence intercepted the signals and pieced together von Ingenohl's operation. An immediate warning was sent to Jellicoe.

The 1st Scouting Group, consisting of Admiral Hipper's five battlecruisers, sailed from the Jade at 3 am on the morning of 15 December. Beatty's four battlecruisers had already cleared their Scottish base of Cromarty to be joined by the 1st Light Cruiser Squadron and the six Dreadnoughts of the 2nd Battle Squadron with escorting destroyers of the 4th Flotilla. Vice-Admiral Warrender was in overall command, although his slow grasp of strategic matters and deafness did not make him the ideal leader.

The British plan was to cut the German battlecruisers off from their base by concentrating the British forces in the middle of the North Sea. Keyes and his submarines were to wait off Terschelling and Tyrwhitt's force was to guard the Yarmouth approaches. The operation began with both sides confident that they had laid a trap for each other. But the Admiralty had not discovered that von Ingenohl had sent the whole High Seas Fleet in support of Hipper.

In the pitch darkness at 5.15 am on the morning of 16 December a chance clash between one of Warrender's detached destroyers and a German destroyer of the High Seas Fleet's advance screen presented von Ingenohl, on the battleship *Friedrich der Grosse*, with the opportunity to immortalize himself as Germany's Nelson. Reports from his cruisers confirmed that the High Seas Fleet was barely ten miles from the heavy British forces. For two hours the destroyers fought an intermittent skirmish in the darkness and the British were still ignorant that they had run into the 14 Dreadnoughts, 8 pre-Dreadnoughts, two armoured cruisers and 54 destroyers of the High Seas Fleet. It was the very tactical situation German strategists had prayed for since the beginning of the War: the opportunity to trap an isolated and powerful unit of the Grand Fleet. Warrender and Beatty could have been easily overwhelmed by the German forces, and at a stroke the British would have been reduced to parity.

For a few minutes in the pre-dawn darkness von Ingenohl, on the bridge of the *Friedrich der Grosse*, held the destiny of the naval war in his hand. But he decided to play safe in accordance with the imperial attitude of not taking risks. There was no way in which the German Commander could be certain he was not up against the whole of the Grand Fleet. He gave orders for the engagement to be broken off and the High Seas Fleet retreated back across the North Sea leaving Hipper heading towards Scarborough, a hundred miles to the north-west.

Warrender and Beatty continued to their rendezvous entirely ignorant that for forty minutes they had been very close to the main German Battle Fleet.

Intercepting reports about enemy cruisers to the east at 9.05 am, Beatty sped off at high speed in pursuit of the Germans, oblivious to the fact that he was trying to cut off the whole of the High Seas Fleet! Fortunately for the survival of his battlecruisers a succession of signals at 9.54 made him aware that a heavy enemy force was bombarding Scarborough. Beatty and Warrender now both headed north to cut off Hipper's retreat.

The German battlecruisers had meanwhile split: to the north the *Moltke* and *Seydlitz* attacked the harbour defences at Hartlepool; to the south the *Von der Tann* and *Derfflinger* bombarded the defenceless ports of Whitby and Scarborough. At 9.30 am they joined up again and made for home through a gap in the minefields. Warrender and Beatty raced to the north to cover the exit on the wirelessed instructions of Jellicoe.

The two forces were steaming steadily towards each other, less than a hundred miles apart when all at once the capricious North Sea weather intervened. Good visibility and flat calm suddenly changed to squalls and driving rain. Visibility was curtailed, often to less than a mile. Changing course to avoid the wrecks and shallows of the Dogger Bank, Beatty's force became separated from Warrender's battleships at the critical moment. The British were hampered by confused signalling and bad luck, aggravated by the poor visibility. At 11.25 am the *Southampton* actually sighted and opened fire on the van of Hipper's force, until a signal from Beatty was misinterpreted causing the action to be broken off. Hipper now knew that he was being hunted and made a wide detour to the north and successfully escaped back to the Jade. 'Thus ended this heart-shaking game of blindman's-buff', wrote a bitterly disappointed Churchill.

On 15 December the German battlecruisers (below) sailed ahead to bombard Hartlepool, Whitby and Scarborough, whilst von Ingenohl followed with the High Seas Fleet ready to trap the British battlecruisers. He missed his chance to overwhelm Beatty's squadron when he refused to risk an engagement. Bad weather prevented the British making contact, and the German battlecruisers escaped. The British public was outraged by scenes of destruction (left) like that at the Grand Hotel restaurant in Scarborough, and demanded to know 'where was the Navy?'

For Beatty it was 'the blackest week of my life' as he accepted responsibility for the signalling error that had allowed the Germans to escape.

The bombardment received great attention in the German newspapers, but when the Naval High Command appreciated the great opportunity von Ingenohl had thrown away they were furious. Tirpitz wrote: 'Ingenohl had the fate of Germany in the palm of his hand. I boil with inward emotion whenever I think of it.'

In Britain the public outcry against the Navy rose to angry levels. 'Where was the Navy?' questioned the coroner at the Scarborough inquest on the 122 victims killed. It had been two hundred years since foreign guns had killed Britons on British soil. In a move to restore public confidence the Admiralty allowed Beatty to move his battlecruisers south from Cromarty to Rosyth in the Forth.

The Germans determined to keep the pressure up with more coastal raids in early 1915, hoping to rush the British into hasty retaliation. British problems were not eased by Jellicoe's anxiety about the serviceability of his ships and the diminishing strength of the Grand Fleet. Although new battleships were being commissioned it took many weeks before a major unit could be worked up into an efficient fighting force. It was also becoming increasingly difficult to find the crews of over a thousand men to man the new battleships. The mechanical deficiencies continued and on-the-spot repairs were commonplace: leaking decks and unwatertight gun casements could be tackled by the fleet engineers; but turbine, condenser and boiler defects required major dockyard repairs with ships absent for several months.

The German Fleet suffered from the same problems. On 22 January von Ingenohl noted: 'Generally speaking, allowance must be made for one battleship of each squadron, one large cruiser, one modern and one light cruiser to be in dockyard hands . . .' But once the weather eased von Ingenohl was determined to get his forces to sea again. His objectives were limited to a cruiser and destroyer operation to clear the Dogger Bank of enemy trawlers and patrols. It was believed that Beatty's battlecruisers were coaling and therefore considered unnecessary to provide the battle fleet as support when the operation was set for 24 January.

British Admiralty Intelligence again intercepted the German operational signals and warned that Hipper's

Battle at dawn On 24 January 1916 von Ingenohl sent Admiral Hipper's battlecruisers to surprise the British patrols. Warned by Intelligence, Beatty's battlecruisers (left) were already at sea. Hipper's battlecruisers *Seydlitz*, *Moltke* and *Derfflinger* were straddled (right) by heavy British shells, but inflicted enough damage on Beatty's flagship for it to drop out of the action. Beatty's second in command gave up the pursuit and finished off the crippled *Blücher*, which turned turtle and sank (below).

force would be north of the Dogger Bank at dawn on the morning of 24 January.

Since Hipper's force consisted only of the battlecruisers *Seydlitz*, *Moltke*, *Derfflinger* and the smaller *Blücher*, supported by 4 light cruisers and 18 destroyers, the Admiralty decided to despatch 5 battlecruisers under Beatty and Tyrwhitt's 3 light cruisers and 35 destroyers to intercept the Germans. As an added precaution, late that afternoon, Jellicoe was told to raise steam and sail in support of Beatty.

It was still dark when Beatty's battlecruisers arrived off the Dogger Bank at 7 am. Twenty minutes later Hipper was taken completely by surprise when Tyrwhitt's cruisers opened fire. Still uncertain about the strength of the forces engaging him, he turned his squadron for base, signalling: 'Seven enemy light cruisers and twenty-six destroyers are chasing. There are more columns of smoke behind them. Do not intend to shake off pursuit till I reach the inner German Bight.' Hipper's decision not to increase speed until the early morning light could allow the ships to be identified proved to be a grave tactical mistake. All too soon the columns of smoke turned into the five battlecruisers *Lion*, *Tiger*, *Princess Royal*, *Indomitable* and *New Zealand*, which rapidly overhauled the Germans. Limited by the *Blücher*'s maximum speed of 23 knots, Hipper knew there was no escape

As the distance between the two forces narrowed, Beatty ordered his battlecruisers to close the enemy in echelon. Soon after 9 am most of the ships were heavily engaged. At 9.08 am Hipper's plight was made clear to von Ingenohl by the signal: 'Enemy battlecruiser squadron in sight WNW and *Seydlitz* is in action with 1st Battlecruiser Squadron . . .' Von Ingenohl immediately ordered the battle fleet to raise steam for action, but this would take several hours and in response to Hipper's increasingly urgent signals the impatient C-in-C could only tell him: 'Main fleet and flotillas coming out.' This was transmitted in plain language in an attempt to deter the British but von Ingenohl added in code the revealing proviso, 'as soon as possible'.

Chewing on a cigar, the German Admiral let forth a string of Bavarian oaths as heavy shells crashed into the sea around his ships. His flagship, the *Seydlitz*, was

hit by the *Lion* and the shell plunged through the after-turret igniting its cordite. In a terrifying chain reaction, fire swept through the working chambers of the turret and leapt across into the adjacent turret where it created another holocaust. An executive officer promptly ordered the flooding of the main magazines seconds before the flames reached them; this saved the ship from destruction.

The speed at which Beatty was fighting the action caused the two slower battlecruisers, *Indomitable* and *New Zealand*, to fall behind and the *Lion* came under increasingly heavy fire. Shortly after 10 am three 12-inch shells from the *Derfflinger* struck her, one of which pierced the waterline armour and damaged the port feed-tank. Half an hour later the port engine had to be stopped; the ship was crippled, and at 10.50 am another German shell knocked out the last dynamo plunging the ship into darkness and leaving flags as the only method of signalling.

Then a submarine was reported off the starboard bow and Beatty ordered his squadron to turn away by hoisting 'Course NE'. The *Lion* was now dropping so far behind that Beatty was in danger of losing control of the battle. He then gave the order: 'Attack the rear of the enemy'. Unfortunately, his flag-lieutenant ran up this new order while the flags for the previous order were still flying, so Beatty's ships read the two together as, 'Attack the rear of the enemy bearing NE'. By a stroke of ill-luck the crippled *Blücher* was lying away to the north-east. She had fallen far astern of the main squadron and Hipper had decided to abandon her and make for the Jade at the best speed his damaged flagship could manage. So away sped four British battlecruisers to attack a battered ship while the rest of Hipper's force disappeared over the horizon.

Beatty was aghast at what he saw happening. He ordered his flag-lieutenant to hoist Nelson's signal, 'Engage the enemy more closely', only to find that the hoist had been removed from the signal book since it was last used at Trafalgar! A pathetic substitute, 'Keep nearer the enemy', was run up. But it was too late. The *Lion* was now far astern and obscured by smoke. In a hectic attempt to reverse the situation Beatty transferred to a destroyer and raced for the battlecruiser, *Princess Royal*. He boarded her just as the shattered *Blücher* turned over, her battered upper-works stained yellow-green by the lyddite of the British shells and her single surviving gun still firing defiantly. Beatty ordered the battlecruisers to turn around in pursuit of a now vanished Hipper. But as his flag-lieutenant, who had in part been responsible for the fiasco, put it, it was 'like trying to win the Derby after a bad fall at Tattenham Corner.'

The Dogger Bank left the British Navy with a victory of sorts. The enemy had fled the field and the *Blücher* had been sunk. For the public the Navy had avenged Scarborough and the newspapers made much of the fact that the Germans had been taught a lesson: 'It will be some time before they go baby-killing again.'

German reactions to Dogger Bank were mixed. The lightly-armoured and lightly-gunned hybrid battlecruiser, *Blücher*, had been lost, but her crew had put up a gallant fight against overwhelming odds in the best naval tradition. Severe damage to the *Lion* was

The unhappy victory Hailed by the British public as a spectacular victory, Beatty and Jellicoe wanted an inquiry into the Dogger Bank action. They felt that the performance of ships, gunnery, signalling and certain officers had proved wanting. HMS *Tiger*'s (left) gunnery had been 'villainous', and HMS *Lion* had been so badly damaged that she had had to be towed (below) by HMS *Indomitable*. A full inquiry was refused, as Churchill did not want anything to tarnish the naval victory.

proof of the efficiency of German gunnery, and the *Seydlitz* had withstood many hits. Eyewitnesses had initially claimed to have seen the *Tiger* sunk; and newspapers used this to good effect to claim a German victory. Tirpitz knew better: 'The effect on the Kaiser will be to have everything shut up again.'

The High Command regarded the battle as a serious defeat that left the High Seas Fleet weaker than before. Since von Ingenohl had clearly exceeded strict instructions not to risk his ships, he was summoned for a painful interview and dismissed. The Fleet's new commander was to be the Naval Chief-of-Staff, Admiral von Pohl, who had proved to be a suitably submissive subordinate. The Kaiser and his staff believed that his caution could be fully trusted. They were right. Admiral von Pohl was never to take the fleet further than the sheltered waters of the German Bight. The year of inactivity was not entirely wasted by the German Navy. A thorough analysis of the damage to the *Seydlitz* revealed the need for more protection in the turrets against cordite flash; immediate modifications were ordered to make the magazines flashproof. The British, neglecting a detailed analysis, remained ignorant of the vulnerability of the thin deck armour and turrets of their battlecruisers to this defect.

Internally the Royal Navy was not at all happy about its victory. Beatty knew that he should have produced better results. The bad gunnery performances of the *Tiger* caused disquiet in the Fleet as she was the newest of the battlecruisers and the only one fully equipped with the latest gunnery control director. The ship's poor showing related to training and manning since the action was the first time that her guns had been fired at a moving target. Her crew also comprised an unusually high proportion of deserters which affected her fighting efficiency. Fisher wanted a full-scale inquiry into the 'villainously bad' gunnery performance that had obviously been outmatched by the German battlecruisers.

These were crucial defects that a full-scale inquiry into and analysis of the conduct of the Dogger Bank battle on the lines proposed by Fisher might have revealed. Certainly the weak squadron commanders and inadequate captains might have been weeded out before Jutland. Such an examination might also have revealed the inconsistencies in Jellicoe's tactics which were based on the assumption that the Germans would employ submarines and mines integrally with the battle fleet. A really searching analysis of the damage suffered by the *Tiger* and the *Lion* might have shown the weakness in British armour protection in time to have saved valuable ships and thousands of lives later at Jutland.

Such an inquiry never took place. Churchill was determined that nothing should tarnish the spectacular success of the battle as presented to the public. Turning down Jellicoe's request that certain officers be replaced because of poor performances, Churchill noted on the official minute: 'The future and the present claim all our attention.' However, the First Lord allowed one gesture to be made to the past; Nelson's famous flag hoist, 'Engage the enemy more closely', was restored to the fleet signal book.

HMS *Agincourt*, the battleship Britain had requisitioned from the Turks and which carried more guns than any other in the Fleet (fourteen 12-inch guns, twenty 6-inch) leads a Battle Squadron home after yet another abortive sweep in the North Sea early in 1915.

THE DISTANT VIGIL

'The British Navy and the sea power which it exerts will increasingly dominate the general situation,' Churchill confided to the House of Commons on 15 February 1915.

After Dogger Bank the British popular Press were confident that the Navy was a war-winning weapon which had driven 'the second navy in the world to the mudbanks of the Elbe'. At Scapa Flow Jellicoe confidently awaited the day when the Germans would overcome their reluctance and come out to fight.

But Churchill was nursing plans for the Navy to strike an offensive blow of such brilliance that the strategic results could end the War before a 'second Trafalgar' in the North Sea. The First Lord was backing a deceptively simple plan for the Navy to force a passage through the Dardanelles with a squadron of pre-Dreadnoughts. According to Churchill this would 'cut the Turkish empire in two, paralyse its capital, unite the Balkan states against our enemies, rescue Serbia, help the Grand Duke [the Russian armies were being pressed by the Turks in the Caucasus] in the main operation of the War and, by shortening its duration, save countless lives.'

Unfortunately, this project soon hit rough water, and was bitterly contested in the Admiralty. Fisher was the leading critic fighting 'tooth and nail' against the scheme. He was concerned that a Balkan naval offensive would drain ships and men from the decisive North Sea theatre, and that his own project for landing an army on Germany's Baltic Coast would be shelved.

Overriding all criticism and with the half-hearted acquiescence of his naval staff, Churchill pressed ahead with the Dardanelles plan.

On 19 February the bombardment of the outer Dardanelles' forts began. But the brilliant strategy was soon to be frustrated as the battleships were unable to progress up the Narrows because of mines and shore batteries.

At the start Fisher had cautioned Churchill in no uncertain terms about depleting Jellicoe's margin over the High Seas Fleet: 'The Empire ceases if our Grand Fleet ceases. No risks can be taken.' In the weeks of March and April 1915 he saw his worst fears realized. Churchill tried to extract more ships to support the army which had now to be landed in an attempt to break the deadlock and this set the two men increasingly at loggerheads.

The Dardanelles adventure When Churchill presented his plan to break the strategic deadlock by smashing through the Dardanelles with a force of battleships, 'the whole atmosphere changed. Fatigue was forgotten. The War Council turned eagerly from the dreary vista of a slogging match on the Western Front to brighter prospects as they seemed in the Mediterranean. The Navy, in whom everyone had implicit confidence, and whose opportunities had so far been few and far between, was to come into the front line.' – *Lord Hankey, Secretary of the War Cabinet, 1915.*

The Dardanelles operation began on 19 February 1915 with the bombardment of the outer Turkish forts. Little progress was made by the fleet of sixteen Allied battleships, mostly pre-Dreadnoughts like HMS *Albion* (below, seen firing at Gaba Tepe). The decisive point was reached on 18 March when three Allied capital ships were sunk. The Navy's failure to force the Narrows led to the landing of Allied troops at Gallipoli in early April.

On the other side of the North Sea an equally fierce debate was raging inside the German High Command. Hemmed in by the strong British blockade and realizing that the Kaiser and his Chancellor were deliberately holding back the High Seas Fleet, a group of senior naval officers pressed for a submarine offensive against British shipping. It seemed the only way of bringing to life an offensive spirit in the German Navy. Their ideas were summarized in a memorandum to Admiral von Pohl which had been submitted the previous November: 'As England completely disregards International Law, there is not the least reason why we should exercise any restraint in our conduct of the war.'

But the Chancellor was concerned about the reaction of neutral opinion, particularly American, to an unrestricted submarine offensive. However, Admiral von Pohl, argued that the English were operating a strict surface blockade against neutrals and this was a precedent for an 'undersea' blockade. The Chief of Naval Staff saw in the submarine campaign the chance to break the British blockade without risking the ships of the cherished High Seas Fleet.

During Wilhelm's visit to Wilhelmshaven on 4 February 1915 a determined von Pohl, now C-in-C of the High Seas Fleet, 'took the Kaiser by storm' and obtained approval for the declaration of a 'War Zone' around Britain that was published the same day.

Tirpitz was furious at von Pohl's 'flourish of trumpets', the immediate result of which was to produce a stream of American diplomatic notes protesting against the proposed War Zone. The German Foreign

Undersea blockade Admiral Hugo von Pohl, German Chief of Naval Staff (inset), unleashed 22 submarines in the first U-boat offensive against Allied commerce in early 1915. Declaring a 'War Zone' around the British Isles, the Germans stated that: 'From February 18 onwards every merchant ship met within this War Zone will be destroyed, nor will it always be possible to obviate the danger with which crews and passengers are thereby threatened.' After the first sinkings the Kaiser modified the campaign under American pressure.

Minister, von Jagow, and the Chancellor tried to get the Kaiser to change his mind, denying that they had ever given their support to von Pohl's schemes. 'Thus before the campaign was born', recorded Tirpitz, 'its own parents were hurrying, panic-stricken to throttle it.' The Kaiser ordered that the declaration must be amended to make it clear that neutral ships were to be spared and that submarine commanders were to observe this strictly.

The first German submarine campaign against merchant shipping was launched on 18 February, twenty-four hours before the British began their bombardment in the Dardanelles. There were only 22 U-boats available (Tirpitz believed that 200 were needed) and in the first three months they sank only 105,000 tons of shipping. As a result Churchill confidently asserted that 'the failure of the German submarine campaign was patent to the whole world'. The Royal Navy however was uncertain about how it should counter the submarine. Ideas proposed and tried included training seagulls to perch on periscopes (to make them visible) and using small boats with crews armed with canvas bags (for dropping over periscopes) and pointed hammers (to smash through submarine hulls). These bizarre techniques were soon dropped in favour of underwater bombs – depth charges. But the most effective anti-submarine weapon proved to be diplomatic rather than military.

The international political consequences of submarine warfare, with the threat that America would be forced into the War, alarmed the German Chancellor and Foreign Ministry. Their worst fears were realized on 7 May 1915, when Lieutenant-Commander Schwieger of *U20* sent a torpedo slamming into the side of the *Lusitania* off the Irish coast.

The political consequences of Commander Schwieger's torpedo were immense. The 'outrage to humanity' was magnified by the scale of the tragedy and the British Press and Government exploited the propaganda value of a German act which had caused the death of 1,198 civilians, including 128 Americans. The Americans demanded that the Germans denounce the sinking and pay a large indemnity. The whole question of unrestricted submarine warfare was brought to a head on 19 August, when the British liner, *Arabic*, was torpedoed off Ireland by *U24*. Forty people were killed, including three Americans, and this brought more United States protests flooding into the German Foreign Ministry. The Chancellor, now thoroughly alarmed that the combination of the *Lusitania* and *Arabic* incidents would bring America rushing into the war, persuaded the Kaiser to make conciliatory moves. The *Lusitania* indemnity went to arbitration, and the U-boat commanders were re-

NOTICE!

TRAVELLERS intending to embark on the Atlantic voyage are reminded that a state of war exists between Germany and her allies and Great Britain and her allies; that the zone of war includes the waters adjacent to the British Isles; that, in accordance with formal notice given by the Imperial German Government, vessels flying the flag of Great Britain, or of any of her allies, are liable to destruction in those waters and that travellers sailing in the war zone on ships of Great Britain or her allies do so at their own risk.

IMPERIAL GERMAN EMBASSY

WASHINGTON, D. C., APRIL 22, 1915.

Death of the *Lusitania* The 32,000-ton liner *Lusitania* (below) became the most spectacular victim of the U-boat campaign when she was torpedoed by *U20* off the Irish coast on 7 May 1915 with heavy loss of life. Although the Germans issued a warning in the American press (left) and later claimed from evidence in the U-boat commander's report that the ship was carrying war materials, American public opinion was outraged by the loss of 128 American lives. Washington demanded an indemnity and a cessation of U-boat attacks on passenger ships.

'An unusual detonation followed which gave off a very large cloud of smoke, rising far above the funnel. . . . The superstructure over the point of impact and the bridge were torn asunder, fire breaks out and smoke envelops the upper bridge . . . Great confusion reigns on board. The boats are cleared away and some are lowered into the water. Many people appear to have lost their head, as a number of fully manned boats almost fall from the davit heads and strike the water bow or stern first, only to be swamped immediately. . . .'

– report of Commander Schwieger, U20

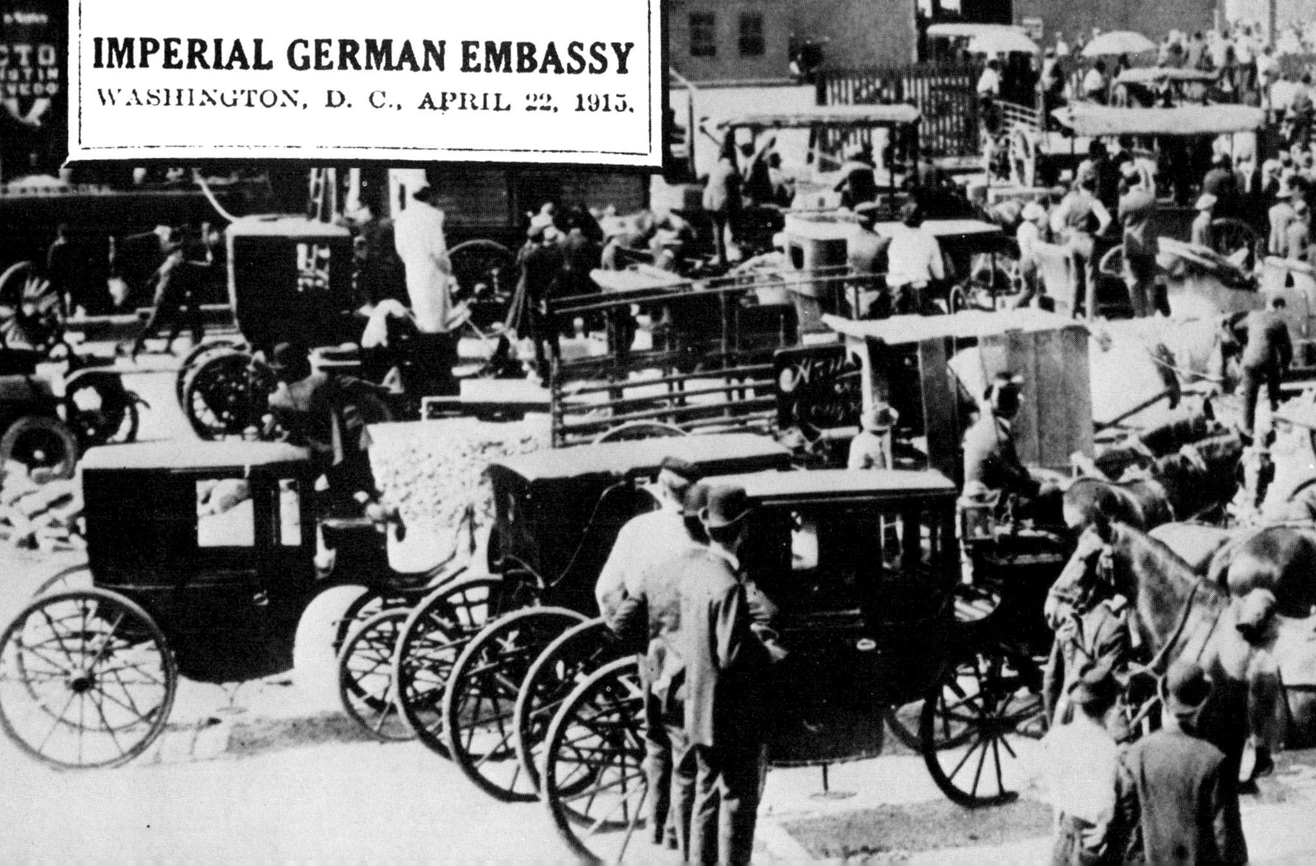

LUSITANIA
LIVERPOOL

stricted by orders that forbade them to sink passenger steamers without giving warning and saving the passengers and crew.

The bitter dispute in Britain over the conduct of the naval war, and the row between Churchill and Fisher over the Dardenelles, reached its climax early in May as the Anzac army was pinned down on the Gallipoli beaches.

At the War Council meeting of 14 May Fisher saw the continual demands on his ships as 'a progressive frustration of my main scheme and strategy,' and the next day resigned in protest.

The Leader of the Opposition and former Conservative Prime Minister, Arthur Balfour, seized upon the Dardanelles row and the scandal of the shortage of shells at the Western Front to force a vote of 'no confidence' on the Government. Asquith realized that he would have to compromise and agreed to form a coalition government with Balfour replacing Churchill as the First Lord of the Admiralty.

The Navy was relieved to see Churchill's departure; the professional officers had always felt that he had interfered too much. However this was countered by the alarm with which they viewed Fisher's departure. The pace of the Admiralty under the new regime slipped into second gear. Balfour and the First Sea Lord, Admiral Jackson, did not generate the same drive and dynamism with which the Fisher-Churchill partnership had thrust the Navy through the first critical period of the War. Balfour was a studiedly calm intellectual, a philosopher who 'had the finest brain in politics'. Jackson, whose health was deteriorating, was a technically brilliant officer whose scientific attainments (he was one of the few naval officers ever to be made a Fellow of the Royal Society) had played an important part in the development of the torpedo and wireless branches of the Service.

The slow pace of the new regime disturbed Jellicoe who was already desperately short of destroyers for fleet duties. He foresaw an increasing demand on his forces for escort duties and anti-submarine patrolling. Aggressive 'hunting' of U-boats was at the time believed to be the best method of dealing with the submarine offensive. But the tactics were rather like fishing for a single minnow in a large pond. U-boat sinkings were few considering the enormous effort of long, fruitless hunts across the North Sea and the western approaches. Only nineteen U-boats were sunk in the whole year.

Submarines were only one problem that Jellicoe had to face whilst the Grand Fleet waited for action. Another enemy was boredom. Somehow 60,000 officers and men in over a hundred warships had to be kept fighting fit and psychologically prepared for battle. Days, sometimes weeks, of semi-idleness were enforced on the ships in the bleak gale-torn northern anchorages.

The Navy's morale was suffering from this 'year of wild-goose chases' when under the timid von Pohl the German Fleet hardly ever left the safety of its harbours. A wardroom song summed up the Grand Fleet's view:

We hate this bloody war,
It gives us all the blight,
We cannot go ashore,
And yet we cannot fight.

Jellicoe, a keen sportsman with a deep concern for the welfare of his men, saw to it that a great deal of effort went into organizing sporting facilities and fleet entertainments. The only island in Scapa Flow with level ground, Flotta, was laid out with football pitches and a crude golf course where ratings and officers organized inter-ship tournaments.

The most popular ship in the whole of the Grand Fleet was the SS *Gourko*, an old supply-ship that had been fitted up as a floating entertainments centre with an auditorium and a stage that served for concert parties and the immensely successful inter-fleet boxing tournaments. It was the concert parties that proved the most enduringly popular of the entertainments; and the SS *Gourko* was always in demand to tie up alongside a battleship so that the ship's company could lay on amateur theatricals. Often lavish productions were staged like West End shows, complete with 'gaiety girls' recruited from those members of the ship's company willing to appear in drag. These concert parties gave the men an opportunity to let off steam; jokes and sketches lampooning the War, the Admiralty

Coaling HMS *Centurion* (above) from the collier alongside.

and the Germans brought the loudest reaction from the audience. In summertime, fancy-dress balls and dancing to the ship's band became popular diversions.

'Patrol' and 'coal' dominated the rhythm of life at Scapa. Fruitless patrols were made doubly depressing by the process of coaling. A battleship might load a thousand tons of coal after a long patrol in the North Sea – a task which would require hours of filthy work for officers and men. Frequently an admiral would dignify the start of coaling by appearing in a spotless white boiler suit and white gloves to ceremonially trundle the first load of coal into the bunker from a brightly polished wheelbarrow.

Coaling a ship was one part of the routine of maintaining fighting readiness. Another important element was the constant exercises and gunnery practices that Jellicoe organized for the battle fleet. But letting off salvoes at distant rocks or wooden targets towed by drifters was no substitute for shooting at targets that fired back. By the end of the year everyone longed for a taste of real action.

The British admirals might have been comforted a little had they been aware of the damaging effect inactivity was also having on the Germans. Even von Pohl's captains wrote over his head to the Chief of Naval Staff demanding offensive strikes to take advantage of the fact that the British Fleet had been weakened by the Dardanelles campaign. But all the action they saw was a series of half-hearted forays into the Bight.

In the High Seas Fleet there was none of the comradely spirit between the upper and lower deck that the British officers fostered with organized sports and entertainments. 'Deep disappointment, mingled with boredom, was rampant.'

A cut in the food rations that summer fuelled the discontent, making the men even more resentful. The food shortage was a bitter reminder of the power of the British ships they were not allowed to go out and fight. Realizing that the situation was becoming serious, a number of the senior commanders in the fleet united to press the High Command for an offensive action. Confident that he had the Kaiser's fullest authority for rejecting any action, von Pohl told the Chief of Naval Staff in no uncertain terms not to interfere.

Only the exploits of the German surface raiders like the *Moewe*, which had escaped to sink ships in spite of the British blockade, brightened the gloom that settled over the German Fleet during the closing months of 1915. The attitude of the men had sunk to a low ebb: 'A year ago we had sailed over there [England] and our cruisers had subjected three of the coastal towns to a thorough bombardment. But it was all different then; we were still idealistic,' wrote Richard Stumpf, aboard the battleship *Helgoland*, 'Our enthusiasm was such that each one of us would have been willing to lay down his life in battle. But now the very thought of a battle frightens us.'

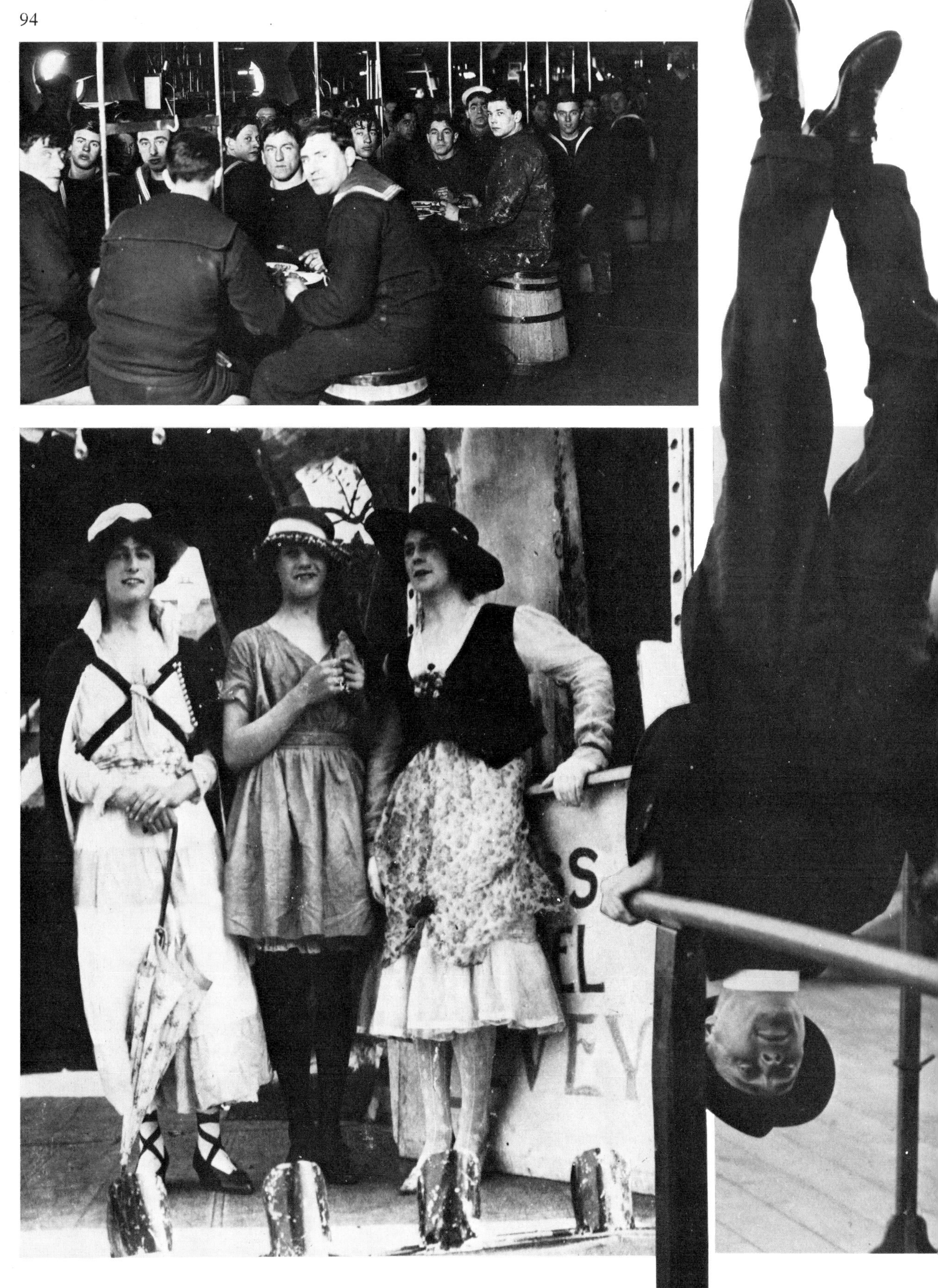

Letting off steam For the two great Fleets, boredom was the biggest enemy, shown in the miniature log of the battleship HMS *Centurion* for April 1915:

Sat. 17 – Provision ship before breakfast. Paint ship. 10.40 am out nets. 5 pm in nets. Prepare for sea and left at 9.15 pm.

Sun. 18 – Action stations 8 am till 5.30 pm (plenty of unofficial buzzes).

Mon. 19 – Gunnery for breakfast, dinner, tea, and supper.

Tues. 20 – Back to Dixie; arrived 11.45 pm.

Wed. 21 – More black diamonds 12.00, and proceeded to sea again 10.30 pm.

Living on board in crowded messes, the British (far left) paid great attention to physical exercise (centre) in the lonely anchorage at Scapa. Entertainment was provided by reviews, with 'chorus girls' supplied from the ships' companies (below left).

The Germans in austere Wilhelmshaven were less fortunate. They had little shore leave and less attention was paid to organized entertainments. This they provided for themselves (below).

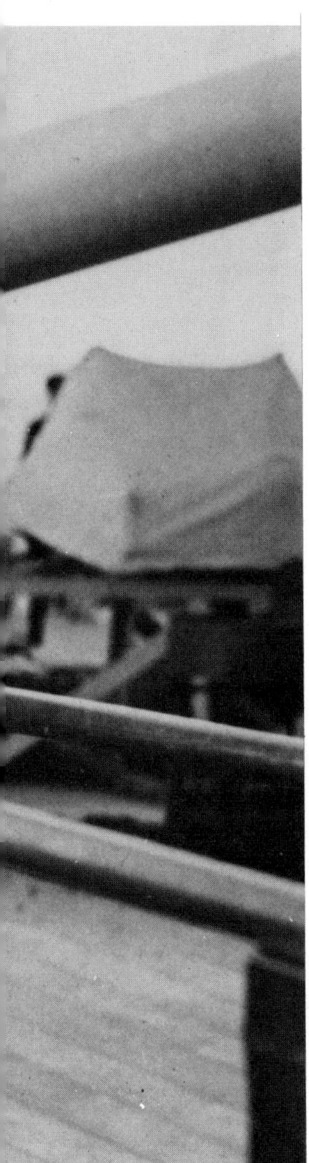

Total war After almost two years of war, the industrial might of Britain and Germany had been fully mobilized in support of the fighting services, with women recruited into munition factories. British shipyards were working round the clock to build destroyers, desperately needed to combat the submarine menace and protect the battle fleet.

BAITING THE TRAP

On 30 December 1915 General von Falkenhayn, Commander-in-Chief of the Army, summoned the Naval Staff to a series of urgent conferences at the War Ministry in Berlin. With the armies of Europe in a military deadlock, the German generals began to realize that the Navy might offer a way out of the strategic stalemate. Von Falkenhayn's purpose was to agree a strategy by which the Navy would break the blockade that was slowly beginning to paralyse the German military and industrial machine. Now that Bulgaria had entered the War as an ally, the generals felt sufficiently confident of their military position to put aside their previous reservations about an all-out submarine offensive. Convincing arguments had been put forward by economists which suggested that, on the evidence of the 1915 U-boat campaign, Britain could be broken economically in the first six months of 1916, before any anticipated U S entry into the War. Tirpitz advocated a scheme for a total 'embargo on commercial traffic to and from England', and he argued that unrestricted submarine operations were 'the last and only chance for Germany'. The generals and admirals decided to put the plan before the Kaiser and form a united front against the politicians. The date he proposed for the commencement of the new submarine war was 1 March. It would be timed to coincide with the massive army offensive against the French Meuse forts at Verdun.

'The salvation of the Navy' was how Admiral Holtzendorff, now Chief of the Naval Staff, saw the chance to resume an unrestricted U-boat campaign. It would inspire the sagging morale of the High Seas Fleet which had reached its nadir with the submission of a memorandum by a group of senior officers expressing no confidence in von Pohl's leadership. But fate stepped in; von Pohl was found to be mortally ill with a brain tumour.

The man who succeeded von Pohl as C-in-C on 24 January was Admiral Reinhard Scheer, the Commander of the 2nd Squadron of the High Seas Fleet. He possessed a determined personality, if lacking a

In January 1916 Admiral Reinhard Scheer was appointed C-in-C of the High Seas Fleet (below, no. 4) on the death of von Pohl. An established tactician, Scheer had agitated for a more offensive naval strategy. There was some surprise when Scheer was preferred to Hipper (below, no. 2), who had seen action against the British forces. Scheer immediately adopted a more aggressive policy; submarines and Imperial Navy Zeppelins were to be used in an attempt to goad the British into a false move.

certain humour and imagination, and had played a leading part in the agitation to get the fleet on to a more offensive strategy.

Scheer's appointment was enthusiastically approved by the officers and men of the fleet. They believed that their long inactivity was over. The new commander wasted no time in making it clear that he was going to restore a policy of vigorous action.

Scheer's new strategy was worked out in collaboration with his squadron commanders and, like that of his predecessors, did not aim for a headlong confrontation with the superior British Fleet. The real objective was to force Jellicoe to abandon his 'waiting' strategy by applying 'systematic and constant pressure'. It was to be effected principally through a new U-boat offensive, constant harassment with mines, and air raids by Navy Zeppelins supported by fleet sorties. Scheer believed that such attacks, if maintained, would force Jellicoe to react and divide the Grand Fleet since as a single unit it would not be able to cover the whole of the North Sea. The German destroyer flotilla

Assault from the sea The fast battlecruisers of Hipper's Scouting Force (*Seydlitz* and *Derfflinger*, right) were to be the spearhead in luring a portion of the British Fleet to destruction. Hit-and-run bombardments were planned to infuriate British public opinion and sting the Royal Navy into risky operations.

patrols and minefields in the Bight would be strengthened, in anticipation of luring the British forces into coastal waters. He also planned that the submarines should be deployed in association with the fleet as well as offensively against merchant shipping.

On 23 February, two days after the Army had launched their new offensive at Verdun, the Kaiser and his entourage inspected the fleet at Wilhelmshaven. Scheer took the opportunity to give Wilhelm a detailed briefing on his offensive plans, stressing the importance of the U-boat campaign. Noted Scheer: 'His Majesty then took the opportunity to remark that he fully approved of the order of procedure submitted to him by the Commander-in-Chief of the Fleet. This announcement was of great value to me as thereby, in the presence of all the officers, I was invested with the authority which gave me liberty of action to an extent which I myself had defined.' At last, the German Fleet Commander felt he had a free hand in its operations.

But the Emperor was clearly having second thoughts about the U-boat campaign. At a decisive audience on 6 March he capitulated to the arguments of the Chancellor and the Foreign Office. To the dismay of the generals and the admirals the U-boat offensive was 'postponed indefinitely'. For Tirpitz it was the final straw. His offer of resignation was accepted. So the man who had built Germany's *Riskflotte* only to see his Emperor refuse to risk it in action, departed from the scene. Some like the Crown Prince believed it was 'a national calamity'.

In spite of 'grave fears' that the Kaiser's postponement of the U-boat offensive knocked away a major pillar of his new strategy, Scheer realized that 'The fleet was therefore bound all the more to aim at active action against the enemy.' If the submarines were not going to be used to spur the British into action, then Scheer saw an opportunity to use the Navy Zeppelins for the same purpose. On the night of 31 January the first of a series of large air raids was launched when nine Zeppelins set off to bomb Liverpool and the Midlands. On 1 February London had been bombed. The damage caused was slight, but the furious reaction provoked in the British Press was noted with satisfaction by the Naval Staff. The irritant was having its effect.

Aware of the damaging effect of the Zeppelin raids on public morale, the British Government tried to take effective action against them. Unfortunately the Admiralty, which had been charged with the task of air defence at home, had done little about it. The task of home defence was now handed over to the Army, and the Admiralty decided to save face by striking back at the airship bases on the German coast, which was exactly what Scheer had calculated.

In the early months of 1916 Scheer's naval offensive began to take shape as German forces ventured further out into the North Sea. On 10 February a destroyer flotilla made a long sweep east of the Dogger Bank, sinking a British minesweeper and escaping before either the Grand Fleet or the Harwich forces could reach the area. The High Seas Fleet came out again on 5-6 March, this time in force, on a sweep to the south which sank two Lowestoft fishing smacks. Once again the Grand Fleet put to sea, but no contact was made. On this raid, Scheer gave a taste of his new tactics – Zeppelins had been sent ahead to bomb the Humber ports.

The Government had to act against the Zeppelin. The man on the spot at Harwich, Commodore Tyrwhitt, put forward a plan for his force to escort the seaplane carrier *Vindex* to the Horn Reefs. Here, off the island of Sylt, her five aircraft would be in range to bomb the Zeppelin sheds at Höjer.

The operation was planned for the night of 25–26

March. Beatty's battlecruiser force was to steam into German waters in close support, ready to fall back on the Grand Fleet if attacked. This was precisely the kind of attack Scheer anticipated, but he failed to appreciate that it would come so soon. On the same day of the raid the High Seas Fleet was coaling for a sweep to the north. The bombing attack at dawn on the morning of 25 March proved a complete fiasco – there were no airships in the hangars, three planes were captured, and Tyrwhitt's force, trying to escape from dangerous waters close to the coast, was hampered by gales and snowstorms that caused a collision between two of his destroyers. Hipper, Beatty and eventually the Grand Fleet were all ordered to sea but wild seas and gales frustrated any encounter.

Scheer now believed that his new policy was stirring the British into action. The Admiralty, in spite of the loss of a destroyer and three aircraft in a fruitless raid, believed that the attack 'showed that the Germans are ready to come out when their own coast is threatened.'

Jellicoe himself was of a different opinion. He confided to Beatty,

> There is a feeling at the Admiralty which I think may lead to their trying to persuade me into what is called a 'more active policy'. I notice signs of it and it shows itself in the air raids, heavily supported. I am being pressed to plan another, the idea being that it will bring the German Fleet out.

Jellicoe realized that such raids meant keeping the Grand Fleet at sea for several days close to the heavily defended and mined German coast, giving the High Seas Fleet the opportunity to come out and strike at its most opportune moment. Beatty supported his view:

> We cannot amble about the North Sea for two or three days and at the end be in a condition in which we can produce our whole force to fight to the finish the most decisive battle of the War: to think it possible is simply too foolish and tends towards losing the battle before we begin . . . my contention is that when the great day comes it will be when the enemy takes the initiative.

This opposition to rash tactics increased the tension between the Commander of the Grand Fleet and the Admiralty. In early 1916 the relationship was already under strain from a number of other causes. Principal amongst them was growing Press criticism that the Navy was not doing enough. 'Let the incomparable Navy which dominates the seas be given leave to tighten the stranglehold it has put upon Germany, and crush the life out of our perfidious foes,' cried the *Globe.* The *Morning Post* thought the Government had been 'conducting this war as if it were a General Election which could be won by fine phrases and putting their adversaries in the wrong.' Fisher reemerged to launch an attack in the House of Lords on the way the Admiralty was being run and started marshalling support for his reinstatement.

With the veteran Admiral's picture prominently displayed in shop windows and newspapers crying 'Give us back the man that won the Falkland Islands' battle', Fisher felt confident he would soon be back running the naval war again. In a London music hall the chorus sang 'Give us back our Jackie' with one side of the gallery roaring 'Yes, Yes, Yes!' and the other calling out 'No, No, No!'

Fisher, much to his dismay, was not recalled. The agitation died down, but it increased the Admiralty's impatience with Jellicoe's lack of action.

On 24 April it was Scheer's turn to escalate the naval war in the North Sea. The High Seas Fleet had set out from the Jade in an operation to bombard Lowestoft and Yarmouth. The day after, on Easter Monday, Dublin flared into rebellion against the British. After promises of German help, engineered by Sir Roger Casement, bitter fighting broke out. In this atmosphere of anxiety and distraction for the British, Scheer informed the Kaiser that it was his intention 'to *compel* the enemy to send out his ships'. There were two ways in which this could be done – 'bombardment of the coastal fortresses and airship attacks on England during the night of our approach. Both lines of action offer a possibility that the enemy will take counter measures which would present us with the chance of attacking him.'

British Intelligence warned that a new German

THE SOLILOQUY.

There is still much doubt about the German naval intentions; but to save the dynasty some development seems probable.—Daily paper.

Scene: Beside the Kiel Canal. A tumult in the distance.

Hamlet:

To sea or not to sea. That is the question.
Whether 'tis nobler in the ditch to suffer,
Or to take arms across a sea of trouble
And end things on the bottom. Spare me days!
It's suicide to send them out to fight,
But if they stay it looks like bloody murder.
There's the respect that makes calamity
Of that damned shambles—Verdun!

Risking the Fleet The Kaiser, unwilling to send out his U-boats for fear of international repercussions, sanctioned operations by the High Seas Fleet. German battle squadrons take on board ammunition for a North Sea foray (below). Allied cartoonists capture the Kaiser's deep dilemma over risking his Fleet (left).

naval operation was imminent, but it was not until the evening of the 24th that it was discovered that Yarmouth was the objective of the raid. The High Seas Fleet sailed at midday and by mid-afternoon the Grand Fleet was under orders to raise steam. Shortly after 7 pm the Grand Fleet and Beatty's battlecruisers had put to sea from Scapa Flow and Rosyth. Tyrwhitt's Harwich force (reduced to three light cruisers and eighteen destroyers because the remainder were covering bombardment operations on the Belgian coast) was already off the Norfolk ports.

Four German battlecruisers (the *Seydlitz* had struck a mine at the beginning of the operations and turned back), under the command of Rear-Admiral Boedicker in the absence of Hipper, were detached at 1.30 am, 70 miles from the English coast, and headed for Lowestoft whilst Scheer patrolled in support with the battle fleet. Tyrwhitt sighted the Germans at 3.50 am and urgently signalled to Beatty and Jellicoe, but failed to decoy the battlecruisers before they opened fire on Lowestoft. The heavy shelling destroyed the harbour batteries and 200 houses. Then at 4.20 am the battlecruisers headed for Yarmouth, opening fire some twenty minutes later. Impudently, the Germans used Nelson's column as a marker for their ranging, but the town only suffered a few minutes' bombardment before a daring attack by Tyrwhitt's force compelled Boedicker to break off the action. Both German forces could have attacked and annihilated Tyrwhitt's considerably weaker British force. But neither risked any further initiative and, content with their efforts, the Germans headed back to the Jade. Jellicoe and Beatty were still hundreds of miles away, with their long lines of battleships and battlecruisers ploughing through heavy seas.

The operation was hardly a brilliant success for either side, but the Kaiser was 'immensely satisfied' and wrote to Scheer to congratulate him. The German Admiral took this as further confirmation of his new policy but all hopes of his U-boat offensive were dashed

Under pressure of public opinion, the Admiralty forced Jellicoe to split the Grand Fleet, despatching the crack 5th Battle Squadron (right, *Valiant*, *Malaya* and *Barham*) south to join Beatty at Rosyth; Scheer's strategy was beginning to work, and his next step was to send Hipper to bombard Sunderland as a bait for Beatty's forces.

by the Kaiser's order that the trade war was to be conducted 'in strict accordance with the prize regulations'. The final decision had been taken after the American ultimatum of 20 April which followed the torpedoing of the unarmed French steamer *Sussex* on 24 March with the loss of many lives, including some American. Washington had given Berlin the stark choice between a break in diplomatic relations or 'an abandonment of its present methods of submarine warfare'.

It was now the British turn to launch an attack. Jellicoe had finally agreed to Admiralty pressure for another raid on the Zeppelin bases. At first light on 4 May seaplanes took off from their tenders close to the island of Sylt, covered by the 1st Light Cruiser Squadron and sixteen destroyers. The flimsy aircraft headed towards the coast to attack the Tondern Zeppelin sheds, but the main objective was to entice the High Seas Fleet out while the Grand Fleet waited to close the escape route to the Jade once Scheer appeared. For six hours Jellicoe steamed anxiously up and down waiting for Scheer to seize the bait. By late afternoon, with no sign of German activity, the British turned for home, unwilling to risk a night action.

But the Admiralty were not prepared to go on waiting indefinitely and planned to move some of the heavy units of the Grand Fleet further south. The Lowestoft raid had shown that the Grand Fleet could not get down from its Scapa base fast enough to trap the Germans before they retreated across the North Sea.

The Admiralty planned to reinforce Beatty's force at Rosyth with the new 15-inch-gunned super-Dreadnoughts of the 5th Battle Squadron. Jellicoe explained his serious reservations to the First Sea Lord: 'The stronger I make Beatty, the greater is the temptation for him to get involved in an independent action.' A year earlier, when Beatty's force had moved down to Rosyth after the Dogger Bank battle, Jellicoe had cautioned him about rushing ahead too freely into action, warning him that 'the Germans will sooner or later try to entrap you . . . The Germans also probably know you and your qualities very well by report and will try to take advantage of that quality of "not letting go when you have once got hold".'

Jellicoe's hand was forced by the German raid of 24 April. The First Lord of the Admiralty, Balfour, wrote to the Mayors of Lowestoft and Yarmouth assuring them that the fleet would be redistributed to prevent further attacks. The Admiralty then suggested that Jellicoe move the whole Grand Fleet south to Rosyth. This he was not prepared to do until the anti-submarine defences on the Firth of Forth had been strengthened. Instead he compromised by sending the 3rd Battle Squadron of King Edward VII pre-Dreadnoughts to Sheerness on the Thames Estuary. He at last conceded that the 5th Battle Squadron would join Beatty at Rosyth, in exchange for a battlecruiser squadron which would go to Scapa where they could undertake gunnery exercises.

The Germans were delighted to discover that the Grand Fleet was being split up. They took lightly Balfour's threats that 'another raid on the coast of Norfolk (never a safe operation) will be henceforth far more perilous to the aggressors than it has been in the past'. But such threats were liable to backfire as the *Globe* newspaper pointed out: 'The prudent cat does not indulge in vociferation when she is watching the rathole. She restrains herself until the quarry is actually under her claws.'

Scheer immediately set in motion his plans to tempt 'the cat' without delay. A week after the announcement, the Commander-in-Chief of the High Seas Fleet issued an order for the next operation which he felt 'would be certain to call out a display of English fighting forces as promised by Mr Balfour'. It was for a raid on the English coast at Sunderland and therefore much closer to the Grand Fleet base. As the plan developed in its details, Scheer prepared to launch the biggest offensive operation ever undertaken by the German Fleet.

All the available U-boats, now released from commerce warfare, were to take part together with all the ships of the High Seas Fleet and the Zeppelins. In its essence Scheer had devised a vast trap for the Grand Fleet sprung underwater, on the surface and in the air.

The jaws of the trap were the U-boats, stationed off the British bases like hungry sharks with the task of torpedoing the ships of the Grand Fleet as they

emerged. They would also act as reconnaissance outposts for the fleet. The bait in the trap would be an attack by Hipper's battlecruisers on the port of Sunderland. This was sufficiently near to Beatty's Rosyth base to tempt the admiral to attack, without waiting for Jellicoe's battle fleet to come down from Scapa Flow. The principal teeth of the trap would be Scheer himself with the rest of the German Fleet waiting to destroy Beatty's battlecruisers – or what remained of them after the U-boat attack – off Flamborough Head.

Essential to Scheer's plan were the Zeppelins which would give reconnaissance cover for the entire operation, ensuring that the Grand Fleet was not already at sea waiting for Scheer.

Unknown to the German Admiral Jellicoe was at the same time putting the finishing touches to his own scheme to snare the German Fleet. In essence the two plans were remarkably similar. The bait in the British trap was to be two light cruiser squadrons penetrating the Kattegat. The jaws of the trap would be a battle squadron patrolling the Skagerrak. The battlecruisers and the rest of the Grand Fleet would be ready to cut off any German retreat to the south. The idea was to lure Scheer so far north that the main British Fleet could block his retreat. Submarines and minefields would be laid off the Horn Reefs as a final spring to the ambush.

Jellicoe planned to launch his operation on 2 June; Scheer's operation had originally been intended for 17 May, but it was to suffer from delays. On 17 May the U-boats were on station; but Scheer had to postpone the operation, first until 23 May because of condenser problems with his dreadnoughts and delay in repairing the *Seydlitz*'s mine damage; then until 29 May because of further delay with the *Seydlitz*. Before Scheer could get to sea the weather intervened. Easterly and northerly winds made the airship reconnaissance impossible. Choosing not to risk the dangers involved in his first plan and because the U-boats could only remain on station until the 30th, Scheer abandoned the Sunderland operation and ordered an alternative plan. The object of this reserve plan was the same as the first: to lure the British Fleet forward over the U-boat trap. The bait was now a foray by the German battlecruisers into the Skagerrak to attack merchant shipping. The battle fleet would cruise off the Danish coast, its flank protected by a cruiser screen, ready to descend on Beatty's force which was expected to be sent to deal with Hipper. At the same time Scheer would be ready to retreat rapidly into the safety of the minefields of the German Bight if Jellicoe appeared on the scene.

In the days following 17 May, British Naval Intelligence knew that a major operation was afoot on the other side of the North Sea. The absence of U-boat attacks and the knowledge that at least nine were at sea set the Admiralty speculating on the next German move. Jellicoe and Beatty were warned that a big enemy operation was imminent.

The officers and men of both navies were poised for the signal that would trigger a chain of events which could finally break the deadlock.

'HOSTILE FORC

The Grand Fleet is ordered to make ready for sea. The battle fleet's communications relied mainly on signal lights and flags. Newly developed wireless telegraphy with its primitive spark transmitters and receivers was considered unreliable by Jellicoe. The equipment was prone to interference and confusion at critical moments.

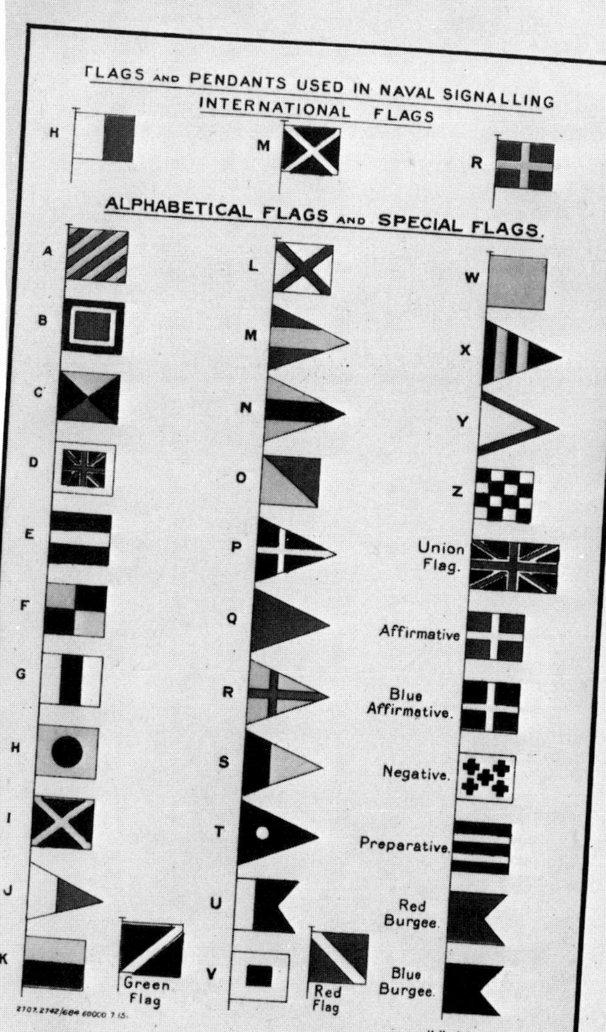

MAY PROCEED TO SEA

Tuesday 30 May found the fleet anchorage at Scapa Flow in an unusual state of excitement. It was the day set for the Grand Fleet boxing competition. Drifters and pinnaces scurried across the bright waters of the Flow, ferrying competitors and high-spirited spectators to the sportship SS *Borodino*. The boxing ring had been rigged on the main deck and draped with patriotic red, white and blue bunting.

Seven-hundred miles away at Verdun, a deadlier contest was entering its sixteenth week of attrition. General Falkenhayn's attempt to 'bleed the French Army white' had turned Verdun's battlefield into a vast 'mincing machine' that had consumed nearly three-quarters of a million French and German casualties.

In the quiet Scottish town of Dunfermline, the War seemed a long way away for the officers of the 1st and 2nd Light Cruiser Squadrons as they sipped tea in the park and listened to the band. Their ships lay peacefully at anchor in the nearby River Forth upstream from the battlecruiser anchorage.

At the great naval base at Wilhelmshaven it was a different scene as the High Seas Fleet prepared to sail. Decks were being hosed down after final coaling, loose gear stowed and life jackets issued. It all seemed a great fuss to the crews for 'just another trip'.

The same day in Whitehall's Admiralty building, the British Fleet's nerve centre, cryptographers in the top secret 'Room 40' were sifting through a stream of German signals. Something big was about to happen across the North Sea and Room 40 was hard at work trying to piece Scheer's plan together from the signals. Set up at the beginning of the war under the brilliant Director of Naval Intelligence, Captain (later Admiral) Hall – nicknamed 'Blinker' by his devoted staff – the existence of the organization was known only to a handful of top-ranking naval officers.

A network of direction-finding wireless stations strung out along the east coast constantly monitored enemy wireless messages for Room 40, and although the Germans had realized by May 1916 that their enemies might be listening in, they had no idea just how good they had become at code-cracking. The Admiralty were very jealous of their 'secret weapon'. Entry to Room 40 was forbidden except to a very few and its decoded interceptions were referred to as 'Japanese Telegrams'. A series of 'Japanese Telegrams' alerted the Grand Fleet. The first, sent from Room 40 to Naval Operations Division early in the forenoon of 30 May, contained a preliminary warning signal sent by Scheer, 'Hostile forces may proceed to sea', which was incorrectly deciphered as 'German forces may proceed to sea'. Another followed ordering the High Seas Fleet to assemble in the outer Jade by 7 pm that evening. By noon the Admiralty decided to put Jellicoe on preliminary alert. Meanwhile Tyrwhitt's Harwich force was ordered back to harbour to await developments.

Orders to sail Jellicoe's flagship HMS *Iron Duke* (seen below with the 2nd Battle Squadron) could raise steam and lead the Grand Fleet to sea in four hours. When the Admiralty ordered out the Fleet at 5 pm on 30 May, the crews were relaxing with their boxing championships and concert parties (insert). HMS *Centurion*'s 'Hearts and Flowers' was 'dramatically interrupted, when a messenger from the ship arrived to inform Lt-Comdr Godsal that the Fleet were under short notice for sea, and the performance must cease immediately and the whole party return on board'.

At 3.40 pm Scheer's coded wireless signal '31 Gg 2490' was picked up. Room 40 realized that this must be the executive order to set the operation in motion. They failed to decipher it completely, but it was clear that the '31' referred to the following day. (In fact it was 'Execute Top Secret Instruction 2490' – Scheer's alternative Skagerrak plan.) On receiving this information, Operations Division cabled Jellicoe, 'Germans intended some operations commencing tomorrow' and he was ordered to sea: 'You should concentrate to eastward of Long Forties ready for eventualities.' From Scapa and the other Scottish bases at Cromarty and the Firth of Forth, the squadrons of the Grand Fleet prepared to put to sea.

Alerted by the early messages, Jellicoe's flagship, *Iron Duke*, was already a bustle of activity by mid-afternoon. The boxing championships had been rushed to a premature final and the spectators aboard the SS *Borodino* knew that something was up when she suddenly raised steam and got under way herself to speed the sailors back to the battleships. The buzz went round, 'the German Fleet is out at last'. Most of the old hands dismissed it. This was just going to be another false alarm.

At 7.05 pm the signal flags 'Raise steam for 19 knots' were broken out from the *Iron Duke*. Within minutes clouds of black smoke began to pour from the funnels of the fleet battleships as deep in the bowels of every Dreadnought the first relays of stokers began to feed their furnaces with tons of coal. Except for the few oil

burners, the Grand Fleet was totally dependent on the muscle-power of thousands of these stokers, sweating in the heat and grime of the boiler-rooms. Unable to hear or know what was going on above the roar of the furnaces and the ventilating fans, they slogged away continuously, manhandling coal and raking the furnaces in temperatures often above 100 degrees Fahrenheit.

To those watching from the lonely Orkney crofts, the plumes of smoke drifting across the evening sky was a sure sign that the fleet would soon be putting to sea, abandoning the lonely anchorage once more to its seagulls and cormorants. On the south-west coast of the mainland at Cromarty, the eight battleships of Vice-Admiral Sir Martyn Jerram's 2nd Battle Squadron were preparing to weigh anchor, ready to sail for the rendezvous with Jellicoe's units.

At Rosyth, within sight of the great iron bridge over the Forth, the men of Beatty's 'hunters of the deep', the battlecruiser fleet, had been recalled after an off-duty afternoon ashore. Sub-Lieutenant Bickmore had been entertaining his mother and sister and, after a pleasant time playing tennis and having tea, they were waiting on the quay for the *Warspite*'s boat to ferry them back. Suddenly they saw the flag on the battleship's halyards, 'Raise steam for full speed. Clear for action on leaving harbour.' Bickmore's heart started to race with excitement, but as he recalled, 'I couldn't tell my mother and sister anything was up. We sailed at 10 o'clock that night.'

Boy Seaman E. L. Edds on the bridge of the light cruiser *Inconstant* remembers, 'At that time I had no idea of what it was all about but it was wonderful to me to see this massive might of armour proceeding ahead at line under the Forth Bridge.'

At 9.30 pm the first in the long line of warships at Scapa nosed down the Flow, which glittered red under a majestic northern sunset. In ninety minutes 148 British warships left the protection of the Scottish anchorages and headed out into the darkness of the North Sea.

It was a frustrating time for Scheer's U-boat patrol lines; during the moonless night the long lines of the Grand Fleet moved unseen through the darkness. Only the *U32* sighted the ships at first light and managed to fire two torpedoes, missing the light-cruiser *Galatea*. The U-boat trap, on which Scheer had pinned so much hope, had failed him.

Relays of stokers fed the boilers in the Grand Fleet battle squadrons (left). Some ships had as many as forty boilers, and the amount of coal they consumed was a determining factor in Jellicoe's strategy to trap the High Seas Fleet. The C-in-C could not expect to stay at sea longer than four or five days. On the bridge of the battleship HMS *Royal Oak* (below right), the officer of the watch and the look-outs at their station.

The three principal divisions of the British Fleet slipped safely out to sea, steaming in night-cruising formation, closely screened by their protecting cruisers and destroyer flotillas. The 2nd Battle Squadron was to join them at noon the following day, some 200 miles west off the tip of Norway. Further south, Beatty's battlecruiser fleet and the 5th Battle Squadron left Rosyth to head out to a position 100 miles north of the Horn Reefs light vessel at 2 pm the next afternoon, when Jellicoe planned to be some 65 miles to the north. The two forces of the Grand Fleet would then close for a rendezvous. By that time the two sections of the fleet would have swept a considerable portion of the North Sea. The Admiralty had decided that Tyrwhitt's Harwich force should wait in harbour under short notice to steam. But three submarines were sent to patrol off the Vyl light vessel in accordance with Jellicoe's original plan.

Thanks to the efficiency of the men of Room 40, all British forces were at sea and steaming to their allotted rendezvous points off the Skagerrak well before Scheer signalled the first of his ships to sea. At 1 am on the morning of 31 May, Hipper's scouting groups received their orders to weigh anchor and head out through the Schilling Roads to show themselves off the Skagerrak the following afternoon. The remaining hours before dawn saw a procession of 101 darkened German warships making their way to sea along the passage that had been specially swept through the middle of the Amrum Bank minefields. At first light, unknown to one another, the two great fleets were at sea and heading to the same small patch of sea off the Skagerrak.

Jellicoe's battle fleet of 24 Dreadnoughts was steaming from the west at some 18 knots across the North Sea in six divisions abreast, each division made up of four Dreadnoughts. Deployed in advance were the three battlecruisers of the 3rd Battlecruiser Squadron; on each of the wings were the 13 ships of three cruiser squadrons. The whole force was screened by 51 destroyers of three flotillas. This mighty naval unit was spread out across many square miles of sea and to manoeuvre it as a coherent force required considerable skills of seamanship.

The numerical odds were overwhelmingly in favour of the British Fleet. Jellicoe was superior in battleships and battlecruisers by 37:27 and excluding the German pre-Dreadnoughts the ratio was 37:21 in modern capital ships. He had a massive superiority in destroyers and cruisers of 113:72. The Dreadnought battle fleets had approximately equal speeds; but the presence of the squadron of 18-knot 'Deutschlands' reduced the High Seas Fleet speed by several knots. But it was in gunpower that Jellicoe had the decisive advantage. The British Battle Fleet totalled 272 heavy guns against the 200 German – and they were of bigger calibre. The Royal Navy's philosophy was 'to hit hard first and keep on hitting' realizing the battle would be won or lost by gunpower. Each ship and every squadron had been drilled and drilled again in the business of handling the huge weapons arrayed in the turrets of their ships.

When it came to the final confrontation both commanders knew that much would depend upon their ships' ability to withstand the huge weight of projectiles that would fall on them. The German Fleet had been built according to Tirpitz's dictum, 'the supreme quality of a ship is that she should remain afloat, and by preserving a vertical position continue to put up a fight.' Thickness of armour and effectiveness of shells were factors that could readily be as-

sessed but the training and, above all, the morale of the men were crucial factors where Britain had an immeasurable advantage. Nothing could overcome the confidence bred from a centuries-old tradition of being unbeatable at sea. Both commanders understood that the strategic *raison d'être* of the long Dreadnought battle lines was their power to devastate the enemy, but bringing about a tactical situation that would achieve this was not a simple matter. In Nelson's time, with ranges of only a few hundred yards, once the naval fleets clashed it had been almost impossible to miss at the point-blank ranges. But the rifled gun and explosive shell, together with steam propulsion and armour plate had changed all that. Battles were fought at ranges of eight miles or more at speeds of twenty knots. 'Naval gunnery', according to one officer, 'was like taking a rifle and shooting at running rabbits from the back seat of a car moving at 30 miles per hour. The wonder is we ever hit anything – but we did.'

Hits were achieved because a sophisticated director and firing system had been devised by both navies. It was controlled from a position high in the ship's superstructure, clear of spray and funnel smoke, where optical rangefinders were used to establish a target's distance, bearing and speed. This information was then fed into a mechanical computer to calculate the relative movement of the two ships during the shell's trajectory. The resultant angle of bearing and elevation was then transmitted to the turrets whose crews trained the turrets round to the given bearing and elevated the guns to the correct angle for firing. The whole process was under the control of the gunnery officer who was aloft in the armoured fighting top, spotting the fall of shot. This complicated inter-relationship of human judgement and mechanical effort depended for its accuracy on practice and skill.

In this gunnery confrontation Jellicoe knew that his overall superiority was to some extent reduced by his weakness in certain respects compared with the Germans. As a result of Admiralty shortsightedness the importance of advanced gunnery directors to control the armament of the Dreadnoughts had been ignored until the final years preceding the outbreak of war. As a result the Royal Navy's gunnery record had been less than brilliant. Although a technically advanced director system was developed by Admiral Sir Percy Scott, the Navy's leading gunnery specialist, it was not until Churchill took over at the Admiralty that it was fitted on the battleships. Even by the time of Jutland, two of the British Dreadnoughts (*Erin* and *Agincourt*) still lacked directors for controlling their main armament. The need for the director systems to control the battleships' secondary armament had only been realized after the outbreak of war and few director sets could be spared from the main armament programme. The British cruisers and destroyers carried no director systems at all.

The German Fleet's director system was more widely fitted, though technically less sophisticated than Scott's system but the German optical rangefinders far outclassed the British. The Germans attached great importance to rapid and accurate range-

Night departures Shortly after midnight on 30 May navigation officers (below) of the High Seas Fleet set course for the North Sea. By first light HMS *Agincourt* and other units of Admiral Burney's 1st Battle Squadron from Cromarty (bottom) were heading for their midday rendezvous with the Grand Fleet. Both sides had prepared a trap for the other.

finding and their 'ladder' system of firing also meant that in the early stages of an action their salvoes were quickly on target. The 'ladder' system involved firing three salvoes in quick succession in range steps a few hundred yards above or below the central step of the 'ladder', shooting on the rangefinder's precise range. The chances were that the target would lie somewhere on the spread of the ladder, the correct one could be observed from the splashes and the guns could go straight into rapid firing. Such a system was only practical with highly accurate rangefinders. The British had adopted the much slower 'bracket' system. The first salvo was fired at the estimated range and the fall of shot observed. The gun elevation was then corrected by a fixed amount, and the next salvo fired and observed. This process continued until two successive salvoes had fallen on either side of the target. When this happened the correction was halved each time until the splashes straddled the target. Only then could the guns be put into rapid fire.

The Germans had good reason not to feel overawed at the apparent British superiority in the number of guns. Their own weapons although lighter were better constructed, which balanced up the bigger British calibres. The British guns also tended to droop and lose accuracy when they grew hot.

Two other factors were to affect the battle, and both were unknown to Jellicoe.

When it came to penetrating thick armour at long ranges, British shells were inferior to the German (the over-sensitive fuses and the lyddite explosive tended

'Strategy and tactics count for nothing if we cannot hit; the only object of a man of war is to hit . . . we point the gun . . . at a certain spot; that spot is not the spot that you want to hit, the gun must be pointed high, so as to counteract the effect of gravity. The wear of the gun, the temperature of the air, the strength and direction of the wind, must all be taken into consideration. . . . When firing at a range of 5 miles . . . the shot takes 12 secs to get to its destination; during that time the ship it is being sent to, if steaming at the rate of twenty knots, will have changed her position 120 yards.' – *Admiral Sir Percy Scott.*

to ignite prematurely on oblique impact, whereas the German fuses and trotyl explosives allowed their shells to penetrate armour before exploding). But more important was the fact that the British ships' magazines were extremely vulnerable to cordite flash. Fortunately for the Royal Navy the Germans were ignorant of this, although they themselves had taken steps to overcome similar faults in their own magazine systems after the near disaster of the *Seydlitz* at Dogger Bank.

In planning the British battle tactics Admiral Jellicoe had been influenced by two overriding factors. The first was the strategic importance of the Grand Fleet. This dominated his whole thinking. The second was his conviction, as a gunnery officer, that the outcome of any Dreadnought battle was going to be determined solely by superior gunpower.

Jellicoe knew that all depended on his ability to control the huge concentration of ships in a tactically advantageous battle order. By nature a cool, almost cold man, renowned for his quiet reflective character, the neat and methodical Jellicoe had been nicknamed 'Silent Jack' by the Service. He was also polite and calm and controlled, but although he had a capacity for administration it was, according to some critics, marred by excessive attention to detail. Admiral Roger Keyes said of him that 'his precise brain made such a cold analysis of each problem that he tended to reach

On target The hitting power of the fleets was contained in the big guns. The complexities of gunnery control are explained in a contemporary diagram and the equipment can be seen on board HMS *Canada*. The guns could also be fired independently by using the periscopes clearly seen in the roof of each turret.

INTERIOR VIEW OF BARBETTE

(shewing how worked, and Method of Ammunition supply to Guns inside).

1 Sighting Hood.
2 Armoured Barbette.
3 Working Levers for Gun Mechanism.
4 Pair Quick-firing Guns.
5 Hydraulic Charge Rammers.
6 Pair 12 inch Guns.
7 Breech of Gun.
8 Emergency Hand-power for working Barbette.
9 Machinery for working Barbette.
10 Continuation of Armour from Barbette to below waterline.
11 Waterline.
12 Shaft, up which Shells are hoisted by lift to guns.
13 Powder Magazine.
14 Ditto.
15 Carrier, which conveys Powder up to Gun.
16 Shell on hoist for conveyance up to Gun.
17 Pivot on which Barbette revolves.
18 Shell Magazine.

Diagram showing Electric Control Gear for Sighting and Firing of Guns.

A. Fire Control and Range Finding Station.
B. Conning Tower (where Captain directs the fighting).
C. Barbettes and Guns.

———— Electric Control for range & sighting of Guns.
.... " " " " firing of Guns.

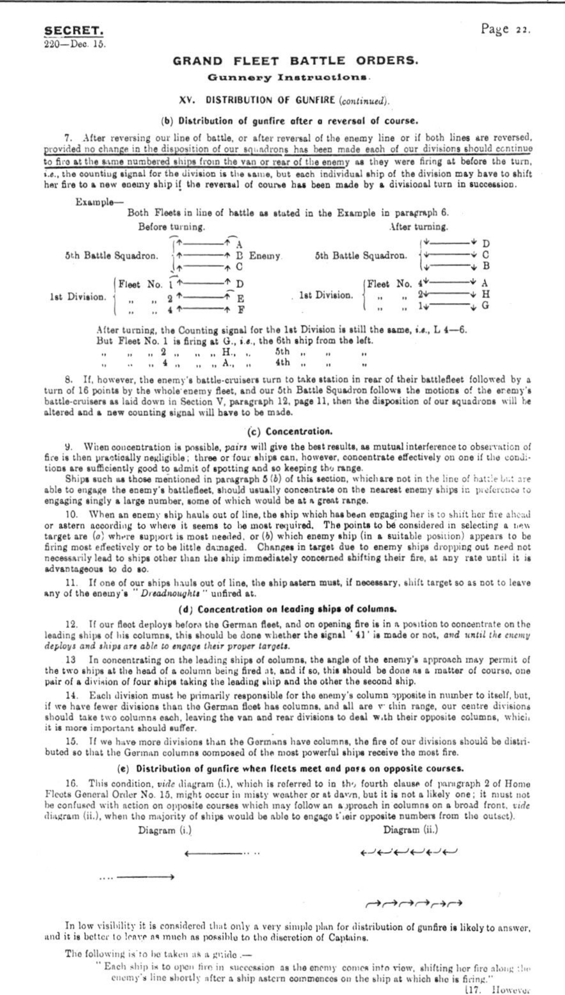

SECRET. Page 22.
220—Dec. 15.

GRAND FLEET BATTLE ORDERS.

Gunnery Instructions.

XV. DISTRIBUTION OF GUNFIRE (*continued*).

(b) Distribution of gunfire after a reversal of course.

7. After reversing our line of battle, or after reversal of the enemy line or if both lines are reversed, provided no change in the disposition of our squadrons has been made each of our divisions should continue to fire at the same numbered ships from the van or rear of the enemy as they were firing at before the turn, *i.e.*, the counting signal for the division is the same, but each individual ship of the division may have to shift her fire to a new enemy ship if the reversal of course has been made by a divisional turn in succession.

Example—
Both Fleets in line of battle as stated in the Example in paragraph 6.

Before turning.			After turning.		
5th Battle Squadron.	↑———↑	A	5th Battle Squadron.	↓———↓	D
	↑———↑	B Enemy.		↓———↓	C
	↑———↑	C		↓———↓	B
1st Division. Fleet No. 1	↑———↑	D	1st Division. Fleet No. 4	↓———↓	A
" " 2	↑———↑	E	" " 2	↓———↓	H
" " 4	↑———↑	F	" " 1	↓———↓	G

After turning, the Counting signal for the 1st Division is still the same, *i.e.*, L 4—6.
But Fleet No. 1 is firing at G., *i.e.*, the 6th ship from the left.
" " " 2 " " " H., " 5th " " "
" " " 4 " " " A., " 4th " " "

8. If, however, the enemy's battle-cruisers turn to take station in rear of their battlefleet followed by a turn of 16 points by the whole enemy fleet, and our 5th Battle Squadron follows the motions of the enemy's battle-cruisers as laid down in Section V, paragraph 12, page 11, then the disposition of our squadrons will be altered and a new counting signal will have to be made.

(c) Concentration.

9. When concentration is possible, *pairs* will give the best results, as mutual interference to observation of fire is then practically negligible; three or four ships can, however, concentrate effectively on one if the conditions are sufficiently good to admit of spotting and so keeping the range.

Ships such as those mentioned in paragraph 5 (*b*) of this section, which are not in the line of battle but are able to engage the enemy's battlefleet, should usually concentrate on the nearest enemy ships in preference to engaging singly a large number, some of which would be at a great range.

10. When an enemy ship hauls out of line, the ship which has been engaging her is to shift her fire ahead or astern according to where it seems to be most required. The points to be considered in selecting a new target are (*a*) where support is most needed, or (*b*) which enemy ship (in a suitable position) appears to be firing most effectively or to be little damaged. Changes in target due to enemy ships dropping out need not necessarily lead to ships other than the ship immediately concerned shifting their fire, at any rate until it is advantageous to do so.

11. If one of our ships hauls out of line, the ship astern must, if necessary, shift target so as not to leave any of the enemy's "*Dreadnoughts*" unfired at.

(d) Concentration on leading ships of columns.

12. If our fleet deploys before the German fleet, and on opening fire is in a position to concentrate on the leading ships of his columns, this should be done whether the signal '41' is made or not, *and until the enemy deploys and ships are able to engage their proper targets.*

13 In concentrating on the leading ships of columns, the angle of the enemy's approach may permit of the two ships at the head of a column being fired at, and if so, this should be done as a matter of course, one pair of a division of four ships taking the leading ship and the other the second ship.

14. Each division must be primarily responsible for the enemy's column opposite in number to itself, but, if we have fewer divisions than the German fleet has columns, and all are within range, our centre divisions should take two columns each, leaving the van and rear divisions to deal with their opposite columns, which it is more important should suffer.

15. If we have more divisions than the Germans have columns, the fire of our divisions should be distributed so that the German columns composed of the most powerful ships receive the most fire.

(e) Distribution of gunfire when fleets meet and pass on opposite courses.

16. This condition, *vide* diagram (i.), which is referred to in the fourth clause of paragraph 2 of Home Fleets General Order No. 15, might occur in misty weather or at dawn, but it is not a likely one; it must not be confused with action on opposite courses which may follow an approach in columns on a broad front, *vide* diagram (ii.), when the majority of ships would be able to engage their opposite numbers from the outset).

Diagram (i.) Diagram (ii.)

In low visibility it is considered that only a very simple plan for distribution of gunfire is likely to answer, and it is better to leave as much as possible to the discretion of Captains.

The following is to be taken as a guide.—

"Each ship is to open fire in succession as the enemy comes into view, shifting her fire along the enemy's line shortly after a ship astern commences on the ship at which she is firing."

[17. However

The text book battle Admiral Sir John Jellicoe had prepared seventy pages of *Grand Fleet Battle Orders* to meet every conceivable contingency in a major fleet action. In Jellicoe's view any fleet action would be decided by massed gunpower. 'In all cases the ruling principle is that the Dreadnought fleet as a whole keeps together, attempted attacks by a division or squadron on a portion of the enemy line being avoided . . . so long as the fleets are engaged on approximately similar courses, the squadrons should form one line of battle.'

the more cautious solution'. He was a very different character to his junior, the battlecruiser commander, Admiral Beatty, who was renowned for his dash, élan, and flair for publicity.

During the long hours of vigil in the Scapa Flow Jellicoe had sat alone for hours contemplating the large, tactical table in his quarters aboard the flagship on which every German and British ship was represented. Carpenters had cut holes in the middle so that he could view the different combinations and formations from new angles. As a result of his deliberations Jellicoe had produced a complete tactical bible for the Grand Fleet, a blueprint covering every way in which the battle would be fought.

His views were enshrined in the seventy closely printed pages of the *Grand Fleet Battle Orders* which incorporated all the results of hundreds of hours of close study by the Tactical Board, and Jellicoe's practical experience.

The effect of such detailed battle orders was that they

tended to inculcate a cautious approach to tactics, reinforcing the tendency to strong, centralized command and a stifling of individual initiative. Above all Jellicoe wanted to avoid 'the danger involved in leaving too much to chance in a fleet action, *because our fleet was the one and only factor that was vital to the existence of the Empire*, as indeed to the Allied cause.'

A major weakness of the Battle Orders was that they depended on carefully analysed plans of how Jellicoe believed his opponent would fight. It took to the other extreme the situation which had existed until Jellicoe assumed command in 1914, when no planning had been done at all, apart from a few pages of notes. Incredibly, the Admiralty had created a colossal naval weapon with little thought of how it would be operated in battle. The mere existence of the fleet had been considered enough. The 'Nelson touch' was optimistically relied upon for the rest. Tactical decisions were left to the admirals on the basis of the broad strategic and tactical guidelines contained in *The Regular Fighting Instructions*. But this overlooked the vital fact that the senior officers in the Navy were without formal training in tactics. As one contemporary officer put it, 'tactical thought consisted of a few catchwords and a lot of tradition'. No group of experts existed, even at the Admiralty, for studying new tactics or analysing fleet exercises. These in any case were conducted as a series of formal manoeuvres which were more appropriate to the ballroom than to the high seas. With no properly organized study of tactical development, innovation had been left up to the initiative of a handful of officers of whom, fortunately for the British, Jellicoe was one.

The technological revolution at sea had not yet – in the Royal Navy at least – revolutionized thinking about the way in which a battle should be fought.

Everything had been staked on the 'big gun' philosophy, and it was considered that the best way of achieving a decisive result was for the whole battle fleet to be deployed in line ahead. The central article of faith that a naval battle must inevitably be a line-ahead gunnery duel was fundamental to Jellicoe's tactical philosophy. Certainly it had the advantage of concentrating the maximum weight of broadside on the enemy and the potential advantage that whichever fleet succeeded in cutting across the bows of its opponent would gain the upper hand. By 'crossing the "T"' in this way the complete gunpower of the traversing fleet could be concentrated on the hapless enemy, which would then find its guns masked by its own ships. The choice for a trapped fleet was a turn through 90 degrees so that it ended up steaming parallel again (this involved ships turning in succession past a point on which the opposing fleet was able to concentrate its fire) or another riskier alternative, to turn every ship at exactly the same time on its own tracks, so that the fleet would be sailing away from the enemy. Even in peacetime this sort of manoeuvre required parade-ground precision and timing, plus an extremely efficient system of communications. With radio still in its infancy, all depended on flags and signalling lights. Under the smoke and shellfire of battle the British regarded this move as far too dangerous. In a short time their line could become disrupted and then a better-organized enemy could destroy weaker, ill co-ordinated squadrons piecemeal.

Underlying all tactical plans was a large measure of uncertainty since there had never been an occasion when two big lines of equally matched Dreadnoughts had fought each other to annihilation. The Germans, however, had paid great attention to tactics, and in prewar exercises in the Baltic they had practised their own signalling and manoeuvres (including the *Gefechtskehrtwendung* in which each ship would turn on its wake, starting from the rear vessel in the line) with Prussian attention to detail and discipline.

The very rigidity of the British single-line battle formation brought criticism from some of Jellicoe's officers for inflexibility and the necessity of centralized control. But Jellicoe believed that once battleships started to leave the line in an engagement, the situation could become chaotic as the line would start to collapse, with a real danger of ships masking each others' fire. If the Dreadnoughts had to fight an equally disciplined enemy of almost equal strength, Jellicoe had come to the conclusion that there was no alternative to the single line of battle. Such a battle line's principal drawback was that manoeuvring it was a slow process

Germany's naval might The High Seas Fleet steams steadily north on the morning of 31 May.

because the signals had to be relayed out from the flagship in the centre to the ships at either end. With 24 Dreadnoughts, each following the wake of the other at a minimum safe distance, this would result in a line of battle nearly seven miles long. Just deploying the single battle line from the six column cruising formation took up to twenty minutes. Any manoeuvre would involve the same problems of co-ordination and delay as those experienced by an arthritic Brontosaurus.

There was no doubt that Jellicoe appreciated the problem of manoeuvring and keeping his Dreadnought battle fleet together, particularly as in his Fleet it had almost become too unwieldy to control. Like the Brontosaurus, its size was beginning to sap its strength.

The alternative to the single line of battle was, for Jellicoe, to split up the fleet into separate divisions. But this produced even greater problems of control in a battle which would be proceeding at high speed over a large area of sea. But the real tactical danger that Jellicoe foresaw in dividing his fleet was that it would give the Germans more opportunity to concentrate their fire on weaker squadrons. Such tactics, Jellicoe rationalized, could only put the fleet at greater risk, and this is made clear by his Battle Orders, which stressed the importance of the battle line keeping together. But the long, formidable line of battle was particularly vulnerable to torpedo attack, and for this reason Jellicoe made it quite plain that it was not to approach too close to the enemy. Moreover the chances of achieving a torpedo hit against a line of battleships six miles long were greatly increased, so it would be the job of the destroyer flotillas and cruisers to thwart torpedoboat and submarine attacks. His subsidiary forces, therefore, were primarily for defensive purposes and were charged 'with the duty of preventing interference with our battle fleet'. In effect their task in the battle was to hold the ring whilst the Dreadnoughts fought it out in a massive gunnery duel.

But the British C-in-C's objective could only be made good if the enemy battle fleet stood and fought. Not even Jellicoe believed in his most optimistic assessment that Scheer would risk putting himself at such a disadvantage. How to cope with the almost certain probability that the German battle fleet would turn away presented Jellicoe with his most difficult tactical decision. His Battle Orders revealed his fear of mines and torpedoes being used against him if he pursued a retreating enemy:

> Exercises at sea and exercises on the Tactical Board show that one of the most difficult movements to counter on the part of the enemy is a 'turn away' of his line of battle, either in succession or otherwise. The effect of such a turn (which may be for the purpose of drawing our fleet over mines or submarines) is obviously to place us in a position of decided disadvantage as regards attack by torpedoes fired either from submarines or from destroyers. If the turn is not followed, the enemy runs out of gun range. If it is followed, we have to accept a disadvantageous position for a length of time dependent on our excess of speed over the enemy's battle line. This excess may be expected to be $1\frac{1}{2}$ to 2 knots, due to the presence of the German 2nd Squadron.
>
> It may be expected that I shall not follow a decided turn of this nature shortly after deployment, as I should anticipate that it is made for the purpose of taking us over submarines.

In effect, Jellicoe had taken the momentous decision that he would not pursue a fleeing enemy. His concern not to risk his battleships in a torpedo attack also convinced him that a 'turn away' was a preferable manoeuvre to 'turning towards' the oncoming torpedoes. Turning a ship so that either the bows or the stern 'combed' the oncoming torpedoes reduced the risk of a hit. But 'turning away' was safer, since the torpedo would be moving relatively slowly compared to the ship.

Scheer's intentions were equally clear. He was not seeking a confrontation battle and he would do everything in his power to avoid one. Great emphasis had been laid on tactics and tactical education in the High Seas Fleet and commanders were accorded more individual initiative. In one area it had a supreme advantage over the British in that night tactics had been developed as an integral part of fleet exercises. Special night signalling, searchlights and star-shells ensured that they could undertake a night battle, whereas the Grand Fleet had none of these and was determined to avoid action in darkness.

As the two titanic battle fleets steamed across the North Sea to the collision point, the battleships, cruisers and destroyers were cleared for action, every man in the British Fleet knowing what was expected of him - victory. Yet Jellicoe's master plan was one which discounted victory in its traditional Nelsonian meaning of annihilation. As Churchill succinctly summed it up:

> The standpoint of the Commander-in-Chief of the British Grand Fleet was unique. His responsibilities were on a different scale from all others. It might fall to him as to no other man - sovereign, statesman, admiral or general - to issue orders which in the space of *two or three hours* might decide who won the War. The destruction of the British Battle Fleet was final. Jellicoe was the only man who could lose the War in an afternoon.

THE BATTLE

2.20 ENEMY IN SIGHT.

A bright sun dispelled the early morning mist as the rocky fortifications of Heligoland slid past on the starboard quarter of the lines of German battleships. Ahead and already lost to sight on the hazy horizon was Admiral Hipper's battlecruiser scouting group.

On the bridge of his flagship, the *Friedrich der Grosse*, Admiral Scheer of the High Seas Fleet was in a buoyant mood. At 5.30 am he had received the first reports from U-boats patrolling off the British bases:

> The reports gave no enlightenment as to the enemy's purpose. But the varied forces of the separate divisions of the fleet did not seem to suggest either combined action or an advance on the German Bight or any connection with our enterprise, but showed a possibility that our hope of a meeting with separate enemy divisions was likely to be fulfilled.

As a final precaution Scheer had planned that five Zeppelins would set off on reconnaissance patrols covering the whole area. But the airships were not able to get airborne until late morning, by which time a deep haze and low clouds made reconnaissance impractical.

All morning there was an air of optimism and expectation in the German Fleet. Crews gathered on

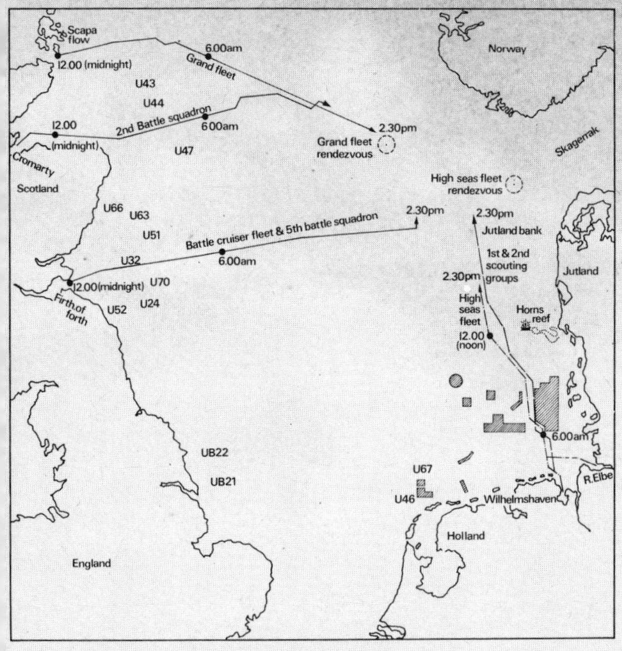

(Left) The courses of the British and German Fleets as they raced across the North Sea on the morning of 31 May 1916 to the inevitable collision off the Danish coast of Jutland. The dispositions of the U-boats which failed to attack the Grand Fleet as it left its bases are also shown, together with the minefields in the German Bight (the shaded areas).
The High Seas Fleet as it steams in line ahead, seen from the quarter deck of a battleship in the middle of Scheer's line (below).

deck beneath the guns to be briefed by optimistic commanders. On the Dreadnought, *Helgoland*, Seaman Richard Stumpf eagerly absorbed the bombastic address of Captain von Kameke:

'A really lively movement of ships has been reported up there between England and Norway. We want to take a little look at that and if it is true then we will "tickle them up a little bit". But for the English who are still in harbour we have a particular surprise; at the exits from the Forth at Rosyth, at Cromarty and Scapa Flow seven German U-boats are lying in wait . . . Our bait, the light German cruisers, will draw the stupid fools out with their wireless messages.' He said this in such a droll Berliner dialect that everyone laughed out loud. 'It will be mere child's play and it won't be bad for us at all.'

Thirty miles ahead, leading the 'bait', Admiral Franz von Hipper on the bridge of the battlecruiser *Lützow* was buoyant, confidently predicting to his staff officer, Commander Raeder, that they 'would be at it hammer and tongs by the afternoon'.

Far to the north there was no sense of urgency on the British Ships, as the Grand Fleet proceeded in stately order southeast. An officer on the light cruiser *Falmouth* scouting ahead of Beatty's forces recalled:

Many of us thought it was only one of the customary sweeps that was being carried out and that after dinner we should get the equally customary signal, 'Return to base'. It was a glorious afternoon – one of the pleasant extremes of which the North Sea is capable – everybody was enjoying a bask in the sun whilst keeping handy to their action stations.

At 11.15 am, earlier than expected, Sir Martyn Jerram's 2nd Battle Squadron from Cromarty had joined Jellicoe's ships and now the combined British

Battle Fleet steamed abreast in six columns, 24 battleships zigzagging towards the Skagerrak at 15 knots.

So far it was proving an uneventful trip, broken only by minor excitement when the destroyer screen inspected a fleet of Dutch trawlers. At 12.40 pm the 2nd Cruiser Squadron had just signalled the flagship that the destroyers had found nothing suspicious when Jellicoe received a misleading wireless message from the Admiralty Operations Room: 'No definite news of enemy. It was thought fleet had sailed but directional signal places flagship in Jade at 11.10 am. Apparently they have been unable to carry out air reconnaissance which has delayed them.'

This report profoundly influenced the course of events. It encouraged Jellicoe to continue his leisurely pace down the North Sea towards his rendezvous with Beatty, and at 2 pm he was already 16 miles, one hour's steaming time, behind schedule. Jellicoe concluded that if the Germans had not yet left the Jade, then he would have to stay at sea for as long as possible in case they put in an appearance. As he wrote later:

> The signal I made to the battlefleet at 1.55 pm enquiring the rate at which the battleships could supply oil to destroyers at sea, shows that I was expecting to remain at sea awaiting events owing to the Admiralty message indicating that the High Seas Fleet was still in harbour.

The fact that Jellicoe maintained his economical cruising speed meant that it was going to be late afternoon before he joined up with Beatty.

NO DEFINITE NEWS OF ENEMY.

Admiralty to C-in-C Grand Fleet

Jellicoe and the battle fleet (below) steamed at 15 knots to their rendezvous with Beatty on the morning of the 31st; Admiralty intelligence indicated that Scheer was still in harbour.

The fateful signal, which may have spared the Germans an annihilating defeat, was totally erroneous. The High Seas Fleet had been at sea several hours when Captain Jackson, the Director of Operations at the Admiralty, had entered Room 40. He 'displayed a supreme contempt' for the work of the civilian academics and cryptographers in the intelligence centre and in an abrupt manner he demanded to know where the directional wireless placed the DK call sign, which was employed by the German flagship. On being told 'in the Jade' he immediately left, made his own interpretation of the situation and sent the signal to Jellicoe.

If Jackson had explained why he required the information he would have been told by the Room 40 experts that the German C-in-C's flagship had adopted the usual practice of transferring his DK call sign ashore when he sailed on an operation to conceal his departure as long as possible. At that time Room 40 were in the process of deciphering another of Scheer's signals which positively indicated that he was at sea.

The erroneous signal was to have even more serious consequences than the loss of an hour of daylight for fighting the battle. Jellicoe's confidence in Admiralty intelligence reports was irreparably shaken.

There were two other signs of the casual British attitude towards a possible clash with Scheer. First the seaplane carrier, *Campania*, which had been late in leaving Scapa Flow because she had failed to read the departure signals, was sent back to base. She was so far behind that Jellicoe believed her aircraft would serve no useful purpose by the time she joined the fleet late in the afternoon. But in sending the *Campania* home Jellicoe was depriving himself of aerial reconnaissance which could have brought him early warning of enemy tactical dispositions. Of more strategic importance was the Admiralty's decision to hold back Tyrwhitt's Harwich force of cruisers and destroyers to guard against a raid on the Thames. The British C-in-C regarded these battle-hardened units as an integral part of the Grand Fleet, and their experience would have been a valuable asset in any night action. For the fiery Tyrwhitt the prospect of missing a fleet action was too much, and he took his flotillas to sea, only to be ordered back again after an hour's steaming.

In his belief that the German ships were still in port, Jellicoe saw no reason to change his tactical dispositions. Seventy miles or more separated the two British forces. Jellicoe wanted to keep his main force to the north should there be any German plan to break the blockade by attacking the northern patrol between Norway and the Orkneys. It meant however that the reconnaissance forces attached to Beatty and Jellicoe would be out of visual contact.

Scheer's simple ruse of transferring his call sign to the shore station had worked brilliantly. Both Jellicoe and Beatty believed that they had the North Sea to themselves and saw no reason to concentrate their respective forces. But Scheer was equally ignorant of the situation, while Hipper's squadron was ploughing north also unaware of what was heading straight for him directly off his port quarter. By 2 pm on an increasingly hazy afternoon, barely fifty miles separated Hipper's scouting groups from Beatty's battlecruisers.

As they approached the Skagerrak according to

THERE ARE A GOOD MANY STEAM AND SAILING TRAWLERS, DUTCH, IN SIGHT.

NOTHING SUSPICIOUS HAS YET BEEN REPORTED BY DESTROYERS.

This signal received by Jellicoe shortly after midday confirmed the general feeling in the Grand Fleet that the sunny afternoon would be 'another routine sweep'. Away to the south in HMS *Princess Royal* with Beatty's battlecruisers, when hands were piped to lunch Stoker Wood did not neglect his patent pills – or to inform the manufacturer after the dramatic events of the afternoon (left).

plan, the crews of Hipper's ships prepared for action. The Gunnery Officer of the *Derfflinger*, Georg von Hase, wrote:

> Nearly everyone was agreed that this time there would be an action, but no one spoke of anything more important than an action involving the lighter fighting forces or the older armoured cruisers. At midday the drums beat through the ship. A long roll. The signal to clean guns. Every man except the officers had to go to his action station.

The next two hours were spent going over every detail of machinery in the *Derfflinger*'s four 12-inch turrets, each named in alphabetical order ('Anna', 'Bertha', 'Caesar' and 'Dora'). Then, as von Hase recorded, 'I started some gun drill and turret exercises, my officers and men were not too pleased with this but I knew only too well how great my responsibility was. I could only answer for the perfect working of the whole apparatus if each part of it were moving once more under battle conditions.'

Sixty miles to the east of the *Derfflinger*, aboard the battlecruiser *Queen Mary*, much the same routine was going on. The gun crews were anxious to maintain their ship's reputation as the best shot in Beatty's elite force. The gunner's mate in the rearmost turret was E. Francis:

> I went over 'X' Turret from top to bottom and I really felt quite pleased with everything; it was complete right down to the spare lengths of flexible wiring, urinal bucket, biscuits and corned beef, drinking water and plenty of first aid dressings. I went to the commander and made my report. He thanked me and repeated again that he thought they were out. I said 'I sincerely hope they are, Sir, as it is uphill work keeping the men to the idea of meeting them again. If we can only manage to get a few salvoes into our old opponents the German battle-cruisers it will put new life into the crowd.'

At 2 pm Beatty believed that he had still some sixteen miles to run to the position at which he would turn north towards Jellicoe. In actual fact he was only ten miles away since zigzagging and tides had introduced an error of six miles into his estimated position. Anticipating the turn north, Beatty flashed by signal light to the four super-Dreadnoughts, *Barham*, *War-spite*, *Malaya* and *Valiant*, stationed five miles off *Lion*'s port bow: 'When we turn northward look out for the advanced cruisers of the Grand Fleet.' This disposition and order unfortunately ensured that the most powerful ships in Beatty's fleet would be farthest away, with their lookouts concentrating in a direction opposite that at which crucial developments were about to take place.

When the *Lion* ran up the signal for the 'turn to the north', only fifty miles now separated Beatty's flagship from Hipper's *Lützow*. The impending change of course could have meant that the two fleets might not have made contact for another hour, if at all. But at 2.15 pm on the afternoon of 31 May 1916, the course of history turned on the behaviour of a small Danish tramp steamer which chanced to be slowly passing south between the two battlecruiser fleets. Emitting clouds of steam from her overheated boilers, the SS *N.J. Fjord* attracted the attention of the light cruisers which fanned out on each side of their Fleets.

The first ship to investigate the smoke rising from the *N.J. Fjord* was the German light cruiser *Elbing*, the outermost ship of Hipper's port wing. A few minutes later *Galatea* on Beatty's starboard screen approached from the other direction. The *Galatea* had only spotted the smoke because she had been late in receiving the signal to turn north. It was several minutes before Commodore Alexander-Sinclair, the commander of the 1st Light Cruiser Squadron, made out the masts and funnels of what he took to be German cruisers. Immediately, *Galatea* signalled *Lion*: 'Two-funnelled ships have stopped steamer bearing ESE eight miles, am closing.'

Alexander-Sinclair, racing towards the *N.J. Fjord* and the unknown ships, flashed the current British recognition signal to confirm whether the ships were hostile before opening fire. They were in fact the torpedo-boats *B109* and *B110* sent by the *Elbing* to investigate the steamer, and as they sped away they signalled

URGENT. ENEMY SHIPS REPORTED IN MY 2.20 ARE

TWO DESTROYERS. AM CHASING. GALATEA.

Leading the 1st Light Cruiser Squadron, HMS *Galatea* (below) became the first ship to open fire in the Battle of Jutland. Fire was returned by the light cruiser SMS *Elbing* (right); she soon scored the first hit of the battle – but the shell which struck *Galatea* below the bridge failed to explode!

Elbing for *Lützow*: 'Several enemy vessels in square 164Y1V.'

At first a horrified Hipper misinterpreted the signal as a report that twenty-four to twenty-six enemy battleships had been spotted.

On board the British light cruiser, *Galatea*, now joined by the *Phaeton*, the flags, 'Enemy in sight' were fluttering proudly from the mast as the ships gave chase and fired the first shots of the battle.

Having at first mistaken the high bow waves of the British light cruisers for battlecruisers, the *Elbing* turned to cover the torpedoboats. A running gun battle between the rival light cruisers now developed. At a range of 15,000 yards *Elbing* scored the first hit of the battle of Jutland, one of her shells smashing through *Galatea*'s bridge – but it failed to explode.

The commanding admirals on both sides now anxiously awaited more reports to establish the strength of the forces opposing them. The ether was alive with wireless messages urgently commanding the ships of both fleets to raise steam for full speed. To try to find out what was going on and to counter the growing number of British light cruisers converging on the *Elbing*, Hipper ordered four light cruisers of the 2nd Scouting Group to support and investigate. At 2.35 pm *Galatea* electrified Beatty's fleet, which was still out of sight of the Germans, with her signal, 'Urgent: have sighted large amount of smoke as though from a fleet bearing ENE.'

Beatty immediately turned about to a south-westerly course to cut them off. Minutes later *Galatea* radioed, 'Urgent. My 2.35 smoke seems to be seven vessels besides destroyers and cruisers. They have turned north.'

It was now not immediately clear to the British what was happening. The confusion was maintained when Commodore Alexander-Sinclair on the *Galatea* abandoned his most important duty of reconnaissance in order to chase the German light cruisers in an attempt to lure them across to Beatty. This was to be the first of many mistakes made by the British scouting forces which fatally deprived Beatty and Jellicoe of accurate intelligence at critical moments of the battle.

The error was compounded when the 2nd Light

Cruiser Squadron, Beatty's other scouting force, which otherwise would have spotted the German battle-cruisers, rushed in to join the running skirmish started by the *Galatea*.

Vital minutes ticked away as Beatty aboard the *Lion* waited impatiently for information. On the strength of the *Galatea*'s first signals, he had characteristically headed his battlecruisers round to the South East to head off an enemy 'fleet'. But he did not know where it was or how strong it would be. To establish these vital facts the *Engadine* was ordered to send up a reconnaissance flight.

Meanwhile an appalling signals confusion almost succeeded in cutting Beatty's fleet into two separate parts. When Beatty had signalled his force to alter course to SSE and turned the *Lion* about to cut off the yet unsighted enemy fleet, the battlecruiser captains instinctively understood the way in which their Vice-Admiral 'manoeuvred his fleet like a huntsman with a pack of hounds', but the Commander of the 5th Battle Squadron, Rear-Admiral Evan-Thomas, was accustomed to the more meticulous signals procedures laid down by Jellicoe for the Grand Fleet. These insisted that all course and speed changes were to be repeated to outlying units by searchlight, which *Lion* had omitted to do, so that with the *Barham*'s lookouts searching the horizon ahead for signs of the Grand Fleet, Evan-Thomas missed the *Lion*'s signal.

His four battleships, already 4½ miles ahead of the *Lion*'s port bow before the turn, suddenly found that the battlecruisers were heading away from them in the opposite direction. In the absence of any signals that might have been expected from the *Tiger* as the sternmost and therefore the 'repeater' ship, Evan-Thomas assumed the 'Vice-Admiral wished the 5th Battle Squadron further to the northward to prevent the enemy escaping in that direction.' It took nearly eight minutes for Evan-Thomas's natural tactical instinct to overcome his reluctance to act without orders, and to decide that he must reverse course. The two forces were rushing apart at nearly forty knots before he swung around, and the gap between them had opened to over ten miles. Now his four battleships worked up to their maximum speed of 25 knots to try and close the gap with Beatty 'by cutting corners' – but it would be twenty minutes before the 15-inch guns of the Royal Navy's most powerful battleships opened fire.

Beatty's and Hipper's battlecruisers were forging,

(Opposite) Disposition of the battlecruisers shortly after Lieutenant F. J. Rutland (right) took off in his seaplane (below – being hoisted out of HMS *Engadine*'s hangar). The British and German light cruisers, after clashing an hour before over the *N. J. Fjord*, were fighting a running battle to the north as Beatty and Hipper had still not sighted each other. The 5th Battle Squadron, led by the *Barham*, having missed the earlier signal to turn, was 'cutting corners' to catch up HMS *Lion*.

as yet still unseen, towards each other, when *Engadine*'s Short Floatplane, piloted by Flight-Lieutenant F. J. Rutland with Assistant Paymaster G. S. Trewin as the observer, took off. They had a difficult time trying to see what was going on below them:

> Clouds were at 100 to 1,200 feet, with patches at 900 feet. This necessitated flying very low.
>
> On sighting the enemy it was very hard to tell what they were and so I had to close within a mile and a half at a height of 1,000 feet. They opened fire on me with anti-aircraft and other guns, my height enabling them to use their anti-torpedo armament. When sighted they were steering a northerly course. I flew through several columns of smoke caused by bursting shrapnel. When the observer had counted and got the disposition of the enemy and was making his W/T [wireless telegraphy] report, the enemy turned 16 points [i.e. 180°: each point equals $11\frac{1}{4}°$; 32 points equals 360°]. I drew his attention to this and he forthwith transmitted it. The enemy ceased firing at me. I kept on a bearing on the bows, about three miles distant from the enemy, and as the weather cleared a little I observed the dispositions of our fleet, and judged by the course of our battle-cruisers that out W/T had got through.

The remarkable first-ever aerial reconnaissance of a naval battle was cut short when the carburettor broke, forcing the floatplane down after barely half an hour aloft. The resourceful Rutland (later known as 'Rutland of Jutland') succeeded in repairing the defect with a rubber tube, but the order came to hoist the seaplane back aboard the *Engadine*.

Rutland had not actually sighted the German battlecruisers, but he had seen the scattered German light cruisers being recalled by Hipper as part of his preliminary concentration for battle.

SEND UP SEAPLANES TO SCOUT NNE .

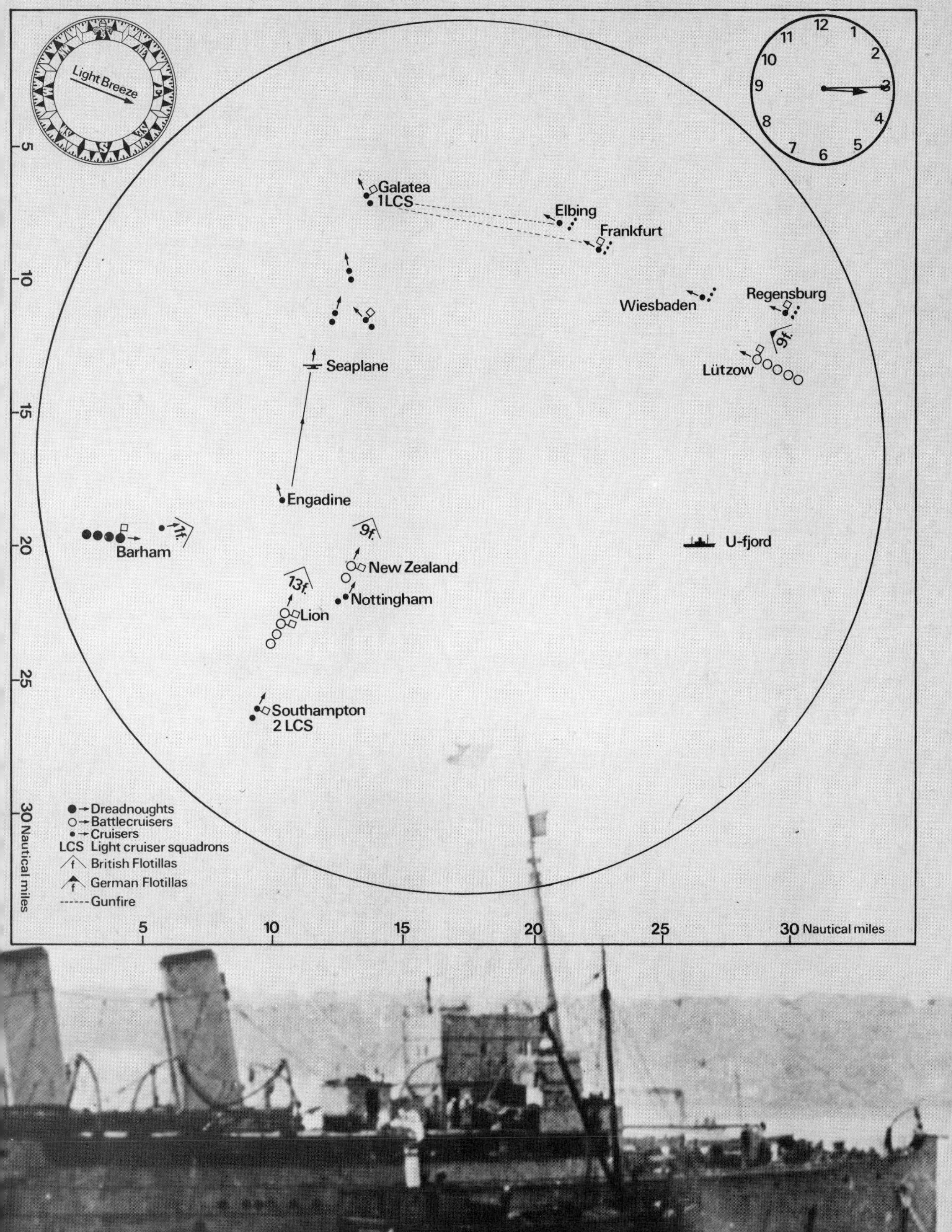

Light Breeze
12
1
2
3
4
5
6
7
8
9
10
11
Galatea
1LCS
Elbing
Frankfurt
Wiesbaden
Regensburg
9f.
Lützow
Seaplane
Engadine
Barham
1f.
9f.
New Zealand
13f.
Nottingham
Lion
U-fjord
Southampton
2 LCS
5
10
15
20
25
30 Nautical miles
Dreadnoughts
Battlecruisers
Cruisers
LCS Light cruiser squadrons
British Flotillas
German Flotillas
Gunfire
5
10
15
20
25
30 Nautical miles

PREPARE TO ATTACK THE VAN OF THE ENEMY.

HMS *Lion* leading HMS *Princess Royal* and HMS *Queen Mary* (below) photographed from HMS *Tiger* shortly before they raced into action.

CRUISERS THREE, DESTROYERS FIVE,

ENEMY BEARING AND DISTANCE FROM ME

E. 10 MILES. ENEMY COURSE NW.

Message from Seaplane.

Shortly after 3 pm the German lookouts, high in the spotting-tops of their ships, sighted the British battlecruisers. Minutes later they made out the distant shapes of the 5th Battle Squadron. It was 3.15 when the *New Zealand*, leading the *Indefatigable* in the 2nd Battlecruiser Squadron, sighted Hipper's group off her starboard bow. Soon after this, when Beatty himself aboard the *Lion* had his quarry in sight, he immed-

iately headed across to cut them off. He had everything to gain tactically by waiting for the 5th Battle Squadron to come up. But Beatty's understandable determination to get into action at his maximum speed of 28 knots resulted in Evan-Thomas's four battleships, which were then only six miles away, being left behind again.

As the six battlecruisers (*Lion*, *Princess Royal*, *Queen Mary* and *Tiger* in one column and *New Zealand* and *Indefatigable* in another) surged towards the Germans with their decks cleared for action, Hipper knew exactly what to do. Knowing that Scheer was at sea over the horizon to the south with the might of the High Seas Fleet, he swung his forces towards the long line of German battleships. He calculated that Beatty would immediately follow him without thinking of a trap.

Across the narrowing gap of thirteen miles, the gun crews stood ready, closed up for action. The great shells were rammed into the breeches as turrets turned menacingly towards the enemy. Damage parties stood by, the sick-bays were fully manned, and every telescope and rangefinder focused on the enemy.

The long-awaited battle was about to begin.

3.30 ALTER COURSE LEADING SHIPS IN SUCCESSION TO E. SPEED 25

Beatty to Battlecruiser Fleet.

'I expected to be excited, but was not a bit,' wrote a 19-year-old sub-lieutenant on the destroyer *Pelican* as his ship raced along towards the enemy.

> It's hard to express what we did feel like, but you know the sort of feeling one has when one goes in to bat at cricket and rather a lot depends upon your doing well and you're waiting for the first ball. . . . A sort of tense feeling waiting for the unknown to happen, and not quite knowing what to expect: one does not feel the slightest bit frightened, and the idea that there's a chance of you and your ship being scuppered does not really enter one's head – there are too many other things to think about.

Every man in every ship, from stoker to admiral, knew that they were closing for a titanic clash that had been planned and prayed for since war began. It was also the climax of a struggle for sea supremacy that had begun more than twenty years before in the halcyon days at the end of Victoria's reign. Every one of the 60,000 officers and men of the Grand Fleet and the 45,000 of the High Seas Fleet realized that the course of history was about to turn upon their action.

In the High Seas Fleet the 'action stations' was sounded with the 'Off into battleship' call. 'Whoever has heard this great call with drums and horn will never be able to forget the magic moment,' wrote Captain Scheike, for whom the moment was one of Wagnerian drama: 'In a few minutes the final preparations and the rush by the crew to their posts were over. In the calm that followed, it seemed to me as if the ghosts of the great dead heroes, whose names were shining brightly on the steel flanks of our ships, were assembling above the clouds to look down and judge the worth of our new generation.' For others like the medical orderlies in the German Dreadnought *König*, thoughts were on organizing for human survival: 'Masks were collected together with cotton wool to block ears, bandages and stretchers were distributed to the individual battle areas and everyone was given a small first-aid kit.'

In both fleets during those final minutes the routine was the same. In the British battlecruiser *Princess Royal*,

> 'Action stations', followed by the bugle 'double' were sounded off, and all communications, instruments, etc., etc. were quickly tested. The various parties were mustered at their stations; gas masks, goggles and life-saving belts were produced, and all the other final preparations for action made. Splinter mats, fire hoses, boxes of sand, stretchers, medical instruments and drugs, leak-stopping gear, shoring-up

GETHER THE REST

OTS.

Manoeuvring the battlecruisers at high speed by flag signals presented great problems. Beatty was accustomed to turning his ships like a 'huntsman' wheeling his pack (bottom, the *Lion* leading the *Princess Royal* in turn to starboard). This caused problems in the early stages of the action when the 5th Battle Squadron failed to observe the flag signals obscured (as here) by funnel smoke. The guns of the battlecruisers (below) probed the horizon for the enemy.

ASSUME COMPLETE READINESS FOR ACTION EVERY RESPECT.

spars, spare electrical gear, spare hydraulic gear, engineers' spare gear – all these and the other various accessories were got ready in a few minutes, as nearly everything was kept permanently ready for action when at sea.

When the alarm went on board the super-Dreadnought, *Warspite*, Sub-Lieutenant Bickmore, who had had nothing to eat all day, was in the gunroom:

> I sat down to my tea and I had a bit of bread and butter with some jam and I had just started on my first cup of tea, when outside the bugles blew 'action stations'. I went on eating my tea thinking, 'What on earth's all this; do they want us back for another practice?' Then I suddenly realized that they hadn't sounded the last 'G' which always followed when it was for practice. It was the real thing. So I grabbed everything I could get hold of and I dashed back to my turret. I got into the turret and Bertie Packer got in just before me. He clapped on his earphones and said, 'They're out, the *Galatea*'s spotted them'.

In the *Derfflinger*'s spacious wardroom the Gunnery Officer, von Hase, was taking a break for 'an excellent cup of coffee on the comfortable leather settee. I could have done with a considerably longer period in this position, but the alarm bells rang through the ship, both drums beat for action, and the boatswain of the watch piped and shouted "Clear for action".' A dozen miles across the narrowing gap of water still separating the rival battlecruisers, Captain John Green on the upper bridge of the *New Zealand* had just strapped on over his neat uniform a curious black and white rush skirt that a Maori chief had given to the ship in 1914 as a talisman. Down below in a turret Prince George of Battenberg, the eldest son of the former First Sea Lord, was already regretting that he had been refused permission to fetch his favourite cine-camera from his cabin. Through his narrow observation slit he could have shot some of the most spectacular film footage of the century. High above him in the armoured observation position on the *New Zealand*'s mast, another officer recalled how he 'had great difficulty in convincing myself that the Huns were in sight at last, it was so like a battle exercise the way in which we and the Germans turned up on more or less parallel courses and waited for the range to close sufficiently before letting fly at each other. It all seemed very cold-blooded and mechanical, no chance here of seeing red, merely a case of cool, scientific calculation and deliberate gunfire. Everyone seemed cool enough, too, in the control position, all sitting quietly at their instruments waiting for the fight to commence.'

The British battlecruisers were being followed in the periscope lenses of the *Derfflinger*'s gunnery officer:

> Magnified fifteen times I could now recognize them as six of the most modern enemy battlecruisers; six battlecruisers to our five so we went into battle with nearly equal forces. It was a stimulating majestic spectacle as the dark, grey giants approached like fate itself. The six ships, which had at first been proceeding in two columns, formed line ahead. Like a herd of prehistoric monsters they closed on one another with slow movements, spectre-like, irresistible.

At the head of the German line, in the *Lützow*'s armoured control position, Hipper personally directed every detail of the opening attack, in accordance with his maxim 'If a mistake creeps in at such a time it is all but impossible to make it good.' With the inevitable cigar at the corner of his mouth, and telescope glued to his eye, he studied the *Lion* with hawk-like intensity:

> We were lying opposite each other in two lines with a south-easterly course, the English to starboard. In front of their line were three Queen Marys, then a ship of the Tiger class (it had apparently 13.5-inch guns) then two Indefatigables. We were lying on their port in the following order – *Lützow*, *Derfflinger*, *Seydlitz*, *Moltke* and *Von der Tann*.

Commander Prentzel, Hipper's Gunnery Officer, was assessing the most appropriate moment to open fire when Hipper turned round from his telescope and sharply announced, 'I've seen everything, gentlemen,

3.48 OPEN FIRE AND ENGAGE ENEMY

Both fleets opened fire at the same time, at an approximate range of 15,000 yards. Beatty failed to take advantage of the longer range of his 13.5-inch guns because of range-finding errors and poor visibility. The German ships initial broadsides (below) were more accurate. Their better equipment and broader beam provided a more stable gun platform, and the British were silhouetted against a bright horizon.

and will give the order when the signal is to be given.' *Lützow* ran up the flag signal, 'Take targets from the port'. Hipper and his officers wondered why the British had not yet opened fire. Surely they were well in reach of the longer range of Beatty's 13.5-inch guns?

On the bridge of the *Lion* Beatty was keenly waiting for his spotters to call out when he was in range. Lieutenant Chalmers was on the bridge during those anxious minutes:

> The visibility as it happened, was extremely patchy. It was one of those typical North Sea summer days with a thin white mist varying in intensity and having too much humidity for the sun to break up . . . Unfortunately, the western horizon was clear, so to the enemy the British ships were sharply silhouetted against a blue sky, and so also would be the splashes of German shells falling around them. Due to these conditions, the British rangefinders gave readings far in excess of the actual range, which caused Beatty to hold his fire longer than was necessary. From *Lion*'s bridge the dim outline of the German ships could be seen but no details could be picked out.

'All was ready to open fire, the tension increased every second,' wrote von Hase of those last final minutes as he held the *Derfflinger*'s gunnery director locked on the *Princess Royal*,

> but I could not yet give the first order to fire. I had to wait for the signal from the flagship: 'Open fire'. Our enemy, too, were holding their fire and coming continually closer.
>
> '15,000!' As my last order rang out there was a dull roar. I looked ahead. The *Lützow* is firing her

4.01 INDEFATIGABLE BLEW UP.

The weak armour and lack of anti-flash protection in the British battlecruisers soon succumbed to accurate German salvoes. HMS *Lion* (right) receiving a hit on Q turret – in the flash explosion that followed, Beatty's flagship was only saved by Major F. W. Harvey's (inset) dying efforts to flood the magazines. HMS *Indefatigable* (left) was less fortunate; minutes later she was destroyed by a direct hit.

> first salvo and immediately the signal 'Open fire' is hoisted. In the same second I shout 'Salvoes fire,' and like thunder our first salvo crashes out. The ships astern follow suit at once and we see all round the enemy jets of fire and folding clouds of smoke – the battle has begun.

On the receiving end of Hipper's first salvoes, Chalmers noted, 'At 3.48 pm the gun flashes of their first salvoes rippled down their line, stabbing the haze, and a few seconds later the reassuring roar of the *Lion*'s first salvo rent the air. The shells from both sides fell well over the target.' At the same instant *Lion* ran up the flags 'Open fire and engage the enemy'. Beatty's battlecruisers fired uncertainly at first. Just how poor it was in the opening stages was revealed by the light cruiser, *Regensburg*, a mile on the disengaged side of Hipper, which passed through mountainous shell splashes and was in greater danger than the German battlecruisers. One British ship, the *Tiger*, actually held her guns on the *Regensburg* for 10 minutes.

Beatty had planned to open fire at his maximum range of 18,000 yards taking advantage of his 13.5-inch guns, which outranged the German guns by some thousand yards. But the British rangefinders had not kept pace with the development of their guns and were under-reading by as much as 2,000 yards. Not only did the German line open fire first with the advantage of light on their side, but the British gunners were handicapped by the light grey of Hipper's ships merging into the grey horizon and coastal haze. The British gunnery was also considerably hampered by funnel smoke blowing across the range in front of them, whereas the light north-easterly wind cleared it away behind the German ships.

Beatty's ships handicapped themselves still further by mismanaging their firing distribution. Hipper had one less battlecruiser but the *Derfflinger* found herself unengaged for nearly ten minutes. Von Hase could hardly believe it:

> By some mistake we were being left out. I laughed grimly and now began to engage our enemy with complete calm, as at gun practice, and with continually increasing accuracy. All thought of death or sinking vanished. The true sporting joy of battle awoke in me and all my thoughts concentrated on the one desire: to hit, to hit rapidly and true, to go on hitting and to damage the proud enemy in any possible way or place.

At last the *Queen Mary*'s gunnery officer, who had concentrated on the *Seydlitz*, realized his mistake and turned his guns on to the *Derfflinger*; the ship, true to her fine shooting reputation, scored the first British hits to cause major damage to the enemy. At 3.55 pm two shells pierced the *Seydlitz*'s forward turret, putting it out of action and starting a cordite fire that could have spread to the magazine had it not been for the new anti-flash doors and the prompt flooding of the magazine.

On the bridge of the *Lion*, Lieutenant Chalmers found the *Lützow*'s gunfire unpleasantly accurate:

> The first German salvoes fell well over us, but within four minutes we were hit twice. On the bridge we were blissfully ignorant of the fact that two large shells had exploded in the ship: the rush of wind and other noises caused by the high speed at which we were travelling, together with the roar of our own guns as they fired four at a time, completely drowned the noise of the bursting shell.
>
> There was no doubt, however, that we were under heavy fire, because all round us huge columns of water, higher than the funnels, were being thrown up as the enemy shells plunged into the sea. Some of these gigantic splashes curled over and deluged us with water. Occasionally, above the noise of battle,

LION BEING FREQUENTLY HIT BY ENEMY.
TURRET WRECKED AT 4 PM.

(Opposite) The battlecruiser action soon settled down into a running battle as the British and German ships fired at each other at near maximum ranges. Admiral Franz Hipper (left) was skilfully luring Beatty south on to the guns of the High Seas Fleet. Shortly after the destruction of HMS *Indefatigable* Hipper came under heavy attack from the rear as HMS *Barham* and the 5th Battle Squadron entered the fray.

we heard the ominous hum of a shell fragment and caught a glimpse of polished steel as it flashed past the bridge.

Now, at a critical moment in the battle Beatty's flagship narrowly missed destruction. One of *Lützow*'s shells pierced the midships 'Q' turret's 9-inch armour and burst inside, killing the crew and setting fire to the cordite charges in the reloading cage. With supreme presence of mind the ship was saved by Major Francis Harvey of the Royal Marines, the turret commander. He was fatally wounded and had lost both legs but managed to order that the magazine doors be closed and flooded (he was awarded a posthumous VC – the first of the battle). 'By the time the flash reached the handling room, the crew of the magazines had just closed the doors, some of them were found dead afterwards with their hands on the door clips.' The destructive power of the cordite flash was appalling:

> Everyone in the path of the flash was killed, including a surgeon lieutenant and his stretcher party who were stationed just above the escape hatch. The clothes and bodies of the dead men were not burned, and in cases where the hands had been raised to protect the eyes, the parts of the face actually screened by the hands were not even discoloured.

On the bridge, the first Beatty heard of this incident was the appearance of a dazed and bloodstained sergeant of the marines who reported: '"Q" turret has gone sir. All the crew are killed and we have flooded the magazines.'

Beatty's own judgement was that 'the firing of the enemy was very rapid and effective', and shortly after the *Lion* was hit, disaster struck the British battlecruiser line. The 18,750-ton *Indefatigable* was hit, as the *New Zealand*'s torpedo officer reported:

> She had been hit aft, apparently by the mainmast, and a good deal of smoke was coming from her superstructure aft, but there were no flames visible. We thought it was only her boom boats burning. We were altering course to port at the time, but her steering gear was damaged as she did not follow round in our wake, but held on until she was about 500 yards on our starboard quarter, in full view from the conning tower. Then she was hit by two shells, one on the fo'c'sle and one on the foreturret. Both shells appeared to explode on impact. Then there was an interval of about 30 seconds, during which there was absolutely no sign of fire or flame or smoke, except the little actually formed by the burst of the two shells, which was not considerable. Then the ship completely blew up, commencing apparently from for'ard. The main explosion started with sheets of flame, followed immediately afterwards by a dense, dark smoke, which obscured the ship from view. All sorts of stuff was blown into the air, a 50-ft steam picket boat, for example, was blown up about 200 feet, apparently intact although upside down.

One thousand and fifteen officers and men disappeared in the shattering explosion. Two seamen were picked up later by a German torpedoboat from water strewn with wreckage and littered with the 'bodies of thousands of dead fish floating tummy upwards'.

Then like a vision in the midst of the destruction the two battlecruiser fleets, racing southwards, overtook a sailing vessel – to the astonishment of both sides: 'A large barque with full sail set was lying becalmed between the two fleets about this time, and the feelings of her crew may be imagined as salvo after salvo fell in their direction.'

The destruction of the *Indefatigable* was greeted on the *Von der Tann* with elation; but when the news was first reported to Hipper he was sceptical that a great British battlecruiser could just blow up and disappear. It was only after he had counted the five remaining enemy battlecruisers through his own telescope that he grunted his approval to his staff and lit a fresh cigar. The odds between the battlecruisers were now even.

The battle had reached such an intensity that many of the British ships were unaware that the *Indefatigable* had gone. In the *New Zealand*, 'An assistant paymaster,

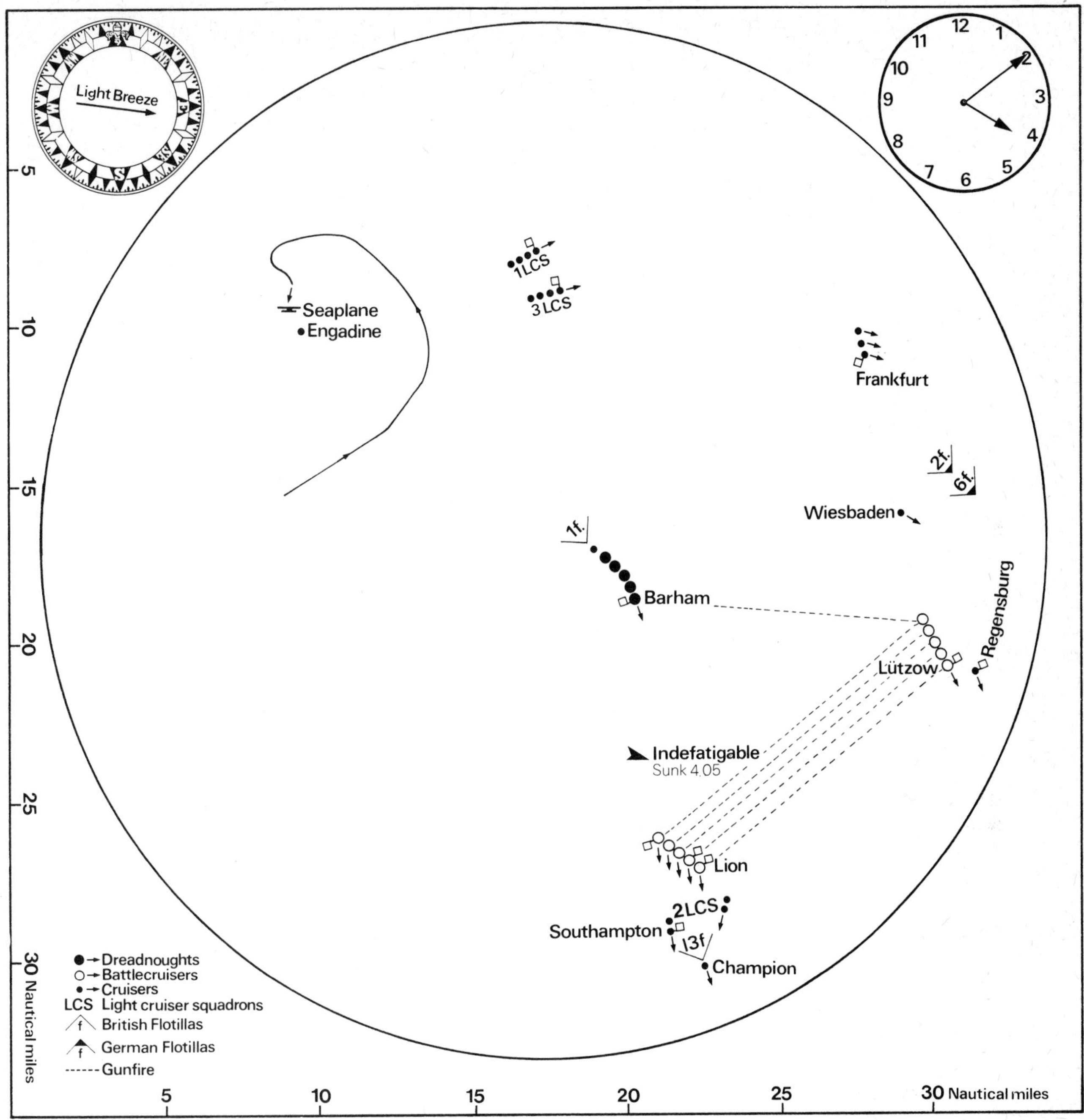

who was keeping a record of the action immediately behind me, said, "*Indefatigable* – hit"; he was going to say "sunk" but thought it might rattle the control party. The captain then passed the order to engage the rear ship of the enemy's line, which we did, straddling her at once. Hits were at this time observed on both the fourth and fifth ships.'

To relieve the pressure on his battlecruisers against the devastatingly accurate German gunnery, which had now hit *Lion* again and set fire to *Princess Royal*, Beatty decided that the moment had come to launch his destroyers against the enemy line. But before he could transmit the signal 'Attack the enemy with torpedoes' to the 13th Destroyer Flotilla, a shell from the *Lützow* shot away the *Lion*'s main wireless. All Beatty's signals now had to be laboriously passed to the *Princess Royal* by lights before being wirelessed to his other ships. The battle had become so intense that he decided to use his superior speed to open up the range by turning away slightly, to give the British ships a chance to put out their fires. It was several minutes before the range opened and the shooting ceased.

4.30 THERE SEEMS TO BE SOMETHING WRONG WITH OUR BLOODY SHIPS TODAY

Vice Admiral Beatty.

As the first firing clash withered away, Jellicoe, still forty miles to the north, was trying to piece together what was happening to the battlecruiser fleet from the incoherent wireless signals. Sensing that Beatty might need early assistance, at 4.05 pm he detached the 3rd Battlecruiser Squadron with the order 'Proceed immediately to support BCF'.

But powerful help was nearer at hand for Beatty. Some twenty minutes after the battlecruisers had opened fire, Evan-Thomas's 5th Battle Squadron was racing towards the sound of gunfire with his four powerful battleships. As the *Indefatigable* blew up, the big battleships, with *Barham* in the van, broke through the smoke and haze, scattering the German light cruisers which had now fallen astern of Hipper's fleet speeding south. Hipper soon discovered that he was out of gun range due to Beatty's small turn away, but now, at 4.10 pm, 15-inch shells crashing around the *Von der Tann* at the end of his line revealed that the battleships had found his range. Hipper knew he now had to link up with Scheer at all possible speed and this conviction was soon reinforced by the accurate shooting of the *Barham*. Even at the extreme range of 19,000 yards hits were being scored.

Increasing speed to 23 knots Hipper started to zig-zag, but the rear of his line was exposed to heavy fire. One of the *Barham*'s first salvoes hit the *Von der Tann*'s stern and damaged the steering engine. Damage control parties worked feverishly in the oily smoke and darkness to repair the steering engine,

otherwise the *Von der Tann* would have been delivered into the hands of the oncoming battleships as in the case of the *Blücher* during the Dogger Bank action. After a short interval the steering gear functioned again. It was found possible to shore up the bulkhead forward of the after engine and only 600 tons of water were finally left in the ship, producing a list of two degrees and increasing the draught aft to 33 feet.

As the *Valiant*, *Warspite* and *Malaya* came into range the next German battlecruiser in line, the *Moltke*, began to be hard-pressed and, after many straddling salvoes, she was also hit. A 15-inch shell penetrated a coal-bunker, tore open one of the ammunition hoists to the 6-inch guns and pierced the casemate deck close to one of the guns, putting it out of action, whilst flames entered the handling room and injured the ammunition-room hands.

Seeing that Hipper was under heavy fire from the 5th Battle Squadron, Beatty decided to close the range again and send in his destroyers for a torpedo attack.

After waiting impatiently for months to come to grips with the High Seas Fleet, 45-year-old David Beatty, celebrated for his love of action, found himself engaging the German battlecruisers with odds in his favour. As his battlecruisers were knocked out and his superiority diminished he coolly ordered the battlecruiser fleet to 'engage the enemy more closely'. (Below) HMS *Queen Mary*, third in Beatty's line (right) is hit amidships seconds before a fatal salvo struck her for'ard.

At 4.17 pm the battle flared up into a three-sided gunnery duel.

> The German shooting at this time was very good [reported an officer in the *Tiger*'s conning tower] and we were repeatedly straddled, but funnily enough we were not being hit very often. I remember watching the shells coming towards us. They appeared just like big bluebottles flying straight towards you, each time going to hit you in the eye; then they would fall and the shell would either burst or else ricochet off the water and lollop away above and beyond you, turning over and over in the air.

In the *Derfflinger*, von Hase saw the British shells as,

> elongated black spots. Gradually they grew bigger and then – crash! they were here. They exploded on striking the water or the ship with a terrific roar. After a bit I could tell fairly accurately from watching the shells whether they would fall short, or over, or whether they would do us the honour of a visit. The shots that hit the water raised colossal splashes. Some of the columns of water were of a poisonous yellow-green tinge from the base to about half their height. These would be lyddite shells. The columns

The 26,500-ton battlecruiser explodes after being hit by the *Derfflinger*, whose log described her throes (below). 'First of all a vivid red flame shot up from her forepart. Then came an explosion which was followed by a much heavier explosion amidships. Black debris of the ship flew into the air; immediately afterwards the whole ship blew up with a terrific explosion. A gigantic cloud of smoke arose, the masts collapsed inwards; the smoke cloud hid everything and rose higher and higher. Finally nothing but a thick black cloud of smoke remained where the ship had been.'

stood up for quite five to ten seconds before they completely collapsed again.

The *Lion*'s damage-control parties were still struggling to bring her fires under control. As she was still obscured by smoke, the *Derfflinger*, mistaking the *Princess Royal* for the enemy flagship which was being engaged by *Lützow*, moved her guns to the next astern which was the *Queen Mary*. She was already under fire from the *Seydlitz*'s three remaining turrets. A bitter gunnery duel now developed between these three ships. The *Queen Mary*'s guns-crews were still keeping up their reputation. According to von Hase: 'I could see the shells coming and I had to admit that the enemy was shooting superbly. As a rule all eight shots fell together. But they were almost always over or short – only twice did the *Derfflinger* come under this infernal hail, and each time only one shell hit her . . .'

Disaster now struck the *Queen Mary*, as Gunner's Mate E. Francis in 'X' turret recalled:

Immediately after that came what I term the big smash, and I was dangling in the air on a bowline which saved me from being thrown on to the floor . . . No. 2 and No. 3 of the left gun slipped down under the gun, and the gun appeared to me to have fallen through its trunnions and smashed up these two numbers. Everything in the ship went as quiet as a church, the floor of the turret was bulged up, and the guns absolutely useless. I must mention here that there was no sign of excitement. One man turned to me and said, 'What do you think has happened?' . . . I put my head up through the hole in the roof of the turret and I nearly fell back through again. The after 4-inch battery was smashed right out of all recognition, and then I noticed the ship had an awful list to port. I dropped back inside the turret and told Lieutenant Ewart the state of affairs. He said, 'Francis, we can do no more than give them a chance; clear the turret.' 'Clear turret,' I called out . . .

I went through the cabinet and out through the top with the lieutenant of the turret following me: I believe he went back because he thought there was someone left inside . . . I was halfway down the ladder at the back of the turret when Lieutenant Ewart went back; the ship had an awful list to port by this time, so much so that men getting off the ladder went sliding down to port . . . When I got to the ship's side there seemed to be quite a fair crowd and they did not appear to be very anxious to take to the water. I called out to them, 'Come on you chaps, who's coming for a swim?' Someone answered, 'She will float for a long time yet,' but something, I don't pretend to understand what it was seemed to be urging me to get away, so I clambered over the slimy bilge-keel and fell off into the water, followed, I should think, by five other men. I struck away from the ship as hard as I could, and must have covered nearly 50 yards when there was a big smash and, looking round, the air seemed to be full of fragments and flying pieces.

4.20 QUEEN MARY BLEW UP.

Log of HMS Lion.

Following only a few hundred yards astern, the *Tiger* and the *New Zealand* had to take prompt evasive action. An officer on the bridge of the *New Zealand* reported:

> The *Tiger* was steaming at 24 knots only 500 yards astern of *Queen Mary* and hauled sharply out of line to port and disappeared into this dense mass of smoke. We hauled to starboard and *Tiger* and ourselves passed on each side of the *Queen Mary*. We passed her about 50 yards on our port beam, by which time the smoke had blown fairly clear, revealing the stern from the after funnel aft afloat and the propellers still revolving, but the for'ard part had already gone under. There was no sign of fire or cordite flame, and men were crawling out of the top of the after turret and up the after hatchway. When we were abreast and only 150 yards away from her, this after portion rolled over and as it did so, blew up. The most noticeable thing was the masses and masses of papers which were blown into the air as this after portion exploded. Great masses of iron were thrown up into the air, and things were falling into the sea around us.

Only twenty survivors out of a ship's company of 1,266 were later rescued by destroyers.

Standing beside Beatty during this awful spectacle of destruction was his Flag Captain, Ernle Chatfield. 'We both turned round in time to see the unpleasant spectacle . . . Beatty turned to me and said, "There seems to be something wrong with our bloody ships today."'

Whether the destruction was caused by inadequate armour or poor flash protection in the magazines will never be established, but Beatty's famous *sangfroid* passed into naval legend.

His immediate reaction, in his characteristic style and in keeping with the Nelson tradition, was to order his remaining battlecruisers to 'Engage the enemy more closely'. This was not mere bravado. Beatty had lost

The British destroyer flotillas pressed forward to attack (racing past HMS *Lion* below). As they came between Beatty and the German line their funnel smoke obscured Hipper's ships, but they were being severely punished by the 5th Battle Squadron, including the *Moltke*. 'A 15-inch shell penetrated a coal bunker, tore open one of the ammunition hoists to the 6-inch guns and pierced the casemate deck close to one of the guns, putting it out of action with all its crew.'

two ships but he calculated that the position of the German battlecruisers must now be desperate. With *Barham*, *Valiant*, *Warspite* and *Malaya* firing from the rear, it seemed that Hipper must be trapped between the two forces in a pincer movement. Beatty had no idea that Scheer's full battle fleet was steaming straight at him and was at that moment just over the horizon.

Hipper realized that he was running close to destruction: the 32 15-inch guns of the four battleships had shown what their gunnery could do at extreme range, and they were closing on him fast. A hail of shells was slowly incapacitating his ships. Although he had spectacularly sunk two enemy battlecruisers his own were being severely damaged. The last of his line, *Von der Tann*, only had two guns still in action from the punishment that was being meted out by the *Barham*; the *Seydlitz* three. Had it not been for the fact that many of the British hits exploded on impact the German battlecruisers would have been beyond Scheer's help. Hipper wrote after the action: 'It was nothing but the poor quality of the British bursting charges that saved us from disaster.'

The shooting of the Germans was becoming increasingly erratic under the heavy enemy fire when Hipper saw the British destroyers coming out to attack. Beatty had wirelessed the Captain of the 13th Destroyer Flotilla twenty minutes earlier that 'opportunity appears favourable for attacking', and urged both the 1st Flotilla and the 13th by flags to 'Proceed at your utmost speed'. This was to have unfortunate consequences. His destroyer flotillas were not all in position to launch an immediate attack. The rush into action had left the 9th and 10th Flotillas far back from their position in the van of the fleet. During the gunnery action, the smoke made by the 9th and 10th Flotillas steaming through the lines interfered with the battlecruisers' gunnery – so much so that the *Lion* had signalled to all destroyers at 4.11 pm 'Clear range'. Five minutes later the effort had paid off and the light cruiser *Champion* had assembled sufficient forces ahead of the *Lion* to launch into the attack eight destroyers from her 13th Flotilla and four from the 10th Flotilla.

But the German light forces were already heading out for a counter-attack. Commodore Heinrich in the light cruiser *Regensburg* acted on his own initiative to relieve the pressure on Hipper's battlecruisers by leading out to attack the 5th Battle Squadron with his twenty-five torpedo-boats of the 9th Flotilla. Both British and German destroyers tangled in a wild mêlée between the two fleets.

The German torpedo-boats heading out to launch their torpedoes at the four battleships met a fiery response: 'We started on at them with 15-inch shrapnel', remembered Sub-Lieutenant Bickmore who was in one of the *Warspite*'s main turrets, 'and

4.26 KEEP CLEAR OF SMOKE.

Beatty via Princess Royal *to destroyers.*

4.30 ENEMY DESTROYERS ATTACKING.

Southampton *to Beatty.*

The high speed and manoeuvrability of the light craft (left) made them extremely dangerous to capital ships. Commander Barrie Bingham (right) raced at 35 knots to within 5,000 yards of the *Lützow* before firing two torpedoes as Hipper turned away.

they turned back at once. 15-inch shrapnel takes a bit of stopping, since with shells 6-feet high and 15 inches in diameter the shrapnel balls inside are as big as your fist and there are dozens of them. It was rather like using a shotgun at rabbits.'

The British attack was led with extraordinary dash by Commander 'Barrie' Bingham in *Nestor*: 'We ran full speed at 35 knots . . . we observed the enemy's fifteen destroyers coming out with the object of making a similar torpedo attack on our battlecruisers.' Accompanying *Nestor* was the *Nomad*, captained by Lieutenant-Commander Whitfield:

> I ordered fire to be opened on the third destroyer of the line. It would seem that the enemy considerably underestimated the speed of our division, as the *Nomad* was soon being badly hit, while *Nestor* and *Nicator* seemed to suffer less. A shell close by the bridge brought down the wireless gear, and at the same time dislocated the searchlight. Firing at the enemy's destroyers was carried out with precision, resulting in the turning of the enemy's destroyers and rendering at least two out of action. During this encounter and before being close enough to fire our torpedoes with good effect, a shell entered the engine-room tearing up the deck for about 8 feet and, bursting in the engine-room, shattered the starboard bulkhead valve destroying all the steam-pipes in the vicinity . . . Steam poured into the engine-room and the main engines and auxilliary engines came to a standstill.

Bingham in the *Nestor* pressed on with the *Nicator* and, 5,000 yards from the *Lützow*, fired two torpedoes; both missed when Hipper turned his ships away.

After the first attack Bingham gallantly went in for a second try just as the German torpedo-boats were returning: 'Thus I found myself with the solitary *Nicator* hot in the track of the fleeing destroyers, and now rapidly approaching the head of the German battlecruiser line, who were not slow in giving us an extremely warm welcome from their secondary armament. At a distance of 3,000 to 4,000 yards the *Nestor* fired her third torpedo.' Unfortunately the bold attempt failed and Bingham's ship was halted by a shell from the *Regensburg*, and she came to a stop only two miles away from where the *Nomad* lay crippled.

But the attack under Bingham's leadership (for which he received a VC) had sunk two German torpedo-boats, *V27* and *V29*. The fierce skirmish between the battlecruisers had blunted both destroyer attacks; of the twenty torpedoes fired by the British destroyers, two from the *Petard* had struck home: one hit the sinking *V27* and the other caused damage to the *Seydlitz*. The German torpedo-boats, with their weaker armament, had been unable to press home their attack with the same determination as the British: of the eighteen torpedoes they fired, none reached a target. But the ten that were fired at the 5th Battle Squadron by Captain Goehle's 9th flotilla had forced the 5th Battle Squadron to break off their devastating firing.

When the British battleships turned away to avoid the German torpedoes, it gave Hipper's ships a much needed respite. He also took the opportunity to make a larger turn away to dodge the *Nestor* and *Nicator*'s attack. The destroyer flotillas were ordered back and at 4.36 pm firing petered out.

Then suddenly, just as Beatty was preparing to inflict a punishing defeat on Hipper, a momentous signal arrived from the *Southampton*, which was scouting ahead: 'Urgent. Priority. Have sighted enemy battle fleet bearing approximately SE. Course of enemy N.' Now the battle was totally transformed. Beatty realized that Hipper had led him straight into a trap.

4.38 URGENT. PRIORITY. HAVE SIGHTED EN

BEARING APPROX SE. COURSE OF ENEMY N

Directly ahead of Beatty's four battlecruisers and four battleships the entire German High Seas Fleet was coming up in an apparently endless procession from the south. There were 22 capital ships, with 6 light c uisers and 31 destroyers. For the first time the Royal Navy witnessed the full deployment of the rival High Seas Fleet. On board the cruiser *Southampton* officers and men were almost spellbound. At first those in the cruiser's control top, with the exception of the gunnery lieutenant, were convinced that the new arrivals were the British Grand Fleet, regardless of the fact that the ships were approaching from the wrong direction. Optimism and anticipation rose in the German Fleet as Hipper's wireless messages informed Scheer that at any moment the British battlecruisers were expected to appear with the scouting groups leading them into the trap. Seaman Stumpf was in the *Helgoland*, the eleventh battleship in Scheer's line:

> How beautiful it was to see our 21 primeval elephants charging forward quickly to the roar of the guns! Everything within me stormed and tossed in happy excitement. My mind already visualized the trained guns and exploding shells all around. I was burning with impatience and it seemed to me that everything was happening much too slowly. Quickly, quickly, staunch ship, up ahead our brave cruisers are already fighting and bleeding. If you don't hurry they will sacrifice themselves.

Scheer's original intention had been to head his battle line across to the north-west to make certain of trapping the British ships between his own and Hipper's fire, but the intervention of the 5th Battle Squadron spoilt his plan:

> While the Main Fleet was still altering course, a message came from Scouting Division II that an English unit of warships, five ships (not four!) had joined in the fight. The situation was now becoming critical for Scouting Group I, confronted by six battlecruisers and five battleships. Naturally, therefore, everything possible had to be done to get in touch with them, and a change was made back to a northerly course. The weather was extremely clear, the sky cloudless, a light breeze from the NW and a calm sea. At 4.40 pm the fighting lines were sighted.

On board the *Lion*, Chalmers witnessed the drama: 'This was the supreme moment of Beatty's career . . . almost immediately a forest of masts and funnels

Southampton *to Beatty.*

Hipper had succeeded in luring the British Battlecruisers into the jaws of a trap. It was 'the supreme moment' of Beatty's career, demanding all his skill and judgement. Once he spotted the masts of Scheer's battlefleet curving into the distance (below), Beatty ordered his ships to turn north towards Jellicoe, in order to lead the Germans on to the Grand Fleet.

appeared on the southern horizon, where the visibility happened to be clear. Without hesitation, Beatty at 4.48 pm swung his battlecruisers round in succession, 180 degrees to starboard to a northerly course, and settled down at full speed to close the Commander-in-Chief by the quickest route.'

Beatty passed a message to the *Princess Royal*, by signal light, for immediate transmission to Jellicoe: 'Urgent. Priority. Have sighted enemy's battle fleet, bearing SE. My position Lat. 56° 36′ N, Long. 6° 04′ E.' This news transformed the situation for Jellicoe, who increased speed and signalled the fleet: 'Enemy battle fleet is coming north' and wirelessed to the Admiralty the long awaited wireless message from the flagship: 'Urgent. Fleet action is imminent.' The news swept the Grand Fleet plunging south towards Beatty, and electrified the Admiralty departments and bases far removed from the fighting lines. Tugs started to raise steam to go to the aid of crippled ships, hospitals prepared to receive casualties and even the normally imperturbable First Lord of the Admiralty, Arthur Balfour, was 'obviously in a great state of excitement'. The 'second Trafalgar' seemed imminent.

Beatty's battlecruisers were now the bait with which he had to deliver the High Seas Fleet into the jaws of the Grand Fleet. The British ships wheeled to the north to follow the *Lion.* But some three miles ahead of the flagship, Commodore Goodenough chose, like Nelson, not to see the signal, being determined to fulfil his reconnaissance. According to one of his officers, Lieutenant Stephen King-Hall:

> We disobeyed the signal, or rather delayed obeying it, for two reasons. Firstly, we wished to get close enough to the High Seas Fleet to examine them and report accurately on their composition and disposition; secondly, we had hopes of delivering a torpedo attack on the long crescent-shaped line of heavy ships which was stretched round on our starboard bow. It was a strain steaming at 25 knots straight for this formidable line of battleships, with our friends going fast away from us in the opposite direction . . . Seconds became minutes, and they still did not open fire, though every second I expected to see a sheet of flame ripple down their sides and a hail of shell fall around us.

Having closed to within 13,000 yards, Goodenough wirelessed a complete report before leading his squadron west to clear the German guns. 'Urgent. Priority. Course of enemy's battle fleet N, single line ahead. Composition of van Kaiser class. Bearing centre

'Look sir, this is the day of a light cruiser's lifetime. The whole of the High Seas Fleet is before you, Commodore Goodenough recalled being told as he surveyed the High Seas Fleet from the *Southampton*'s bridge. It was: sixteen battleships with destroyers around them on each bow. That was reported. We hung on for a few minutes to make sure before confirming the message. My Commander, efficient and cool said: "If you're going to make that signal, you'd better make it now, sir. You may never make another."'

URGENT. PRIORITY. COURSE OF ENEMY N.

SINGLE LINE AHEAD . . .

Southampton *to C-in-C.*

HMS *Southampton* (below) leading the 1st Light Cruiser Squadron within 13,000 yards of the German battlefleet. Commodore Goodenough (left) ignored Beatty's signal for a turn North in a bid to provide detailed reconnaissance.

E. Destroyers on both wings and ahead. Enemy's battlecruisers joining battle fleet from northward. My position Lat. 56° 29′ N, Long. 6° 14′ E.' Only then did the whole German battle line erupt into fire on the four light cruisers.

Secure in his armoured control position on the *Friedrich der Grosse*, the German C-in-C watched Goodenough's cruisers speeding away at 25 knots as the German guns began to do 'a sort of target practice in slow time' with the squadron.

'We crouched down behind the tenth-of-an-inch plating and ate bully-beef,' wrote Stephen King-Hall, 'but it didn't go down very easily. It seemed rather a waste of time to eat beef, for surely in the next ten minutes one of those 11-inch shells would get us; they couldn't go on falling just short and just over indefinitely and, well, if one did hit us – light cruisers were not designed to digest 11-inch explosives in their stomachs'. But his captain succeeded in skilfully dodging the salvoes to bring their light cruisers unscathed through the barrage, after forty-five minutes of hectic manoeuvering.

Fate was harsher to the two crippled British destroyers which suddenly found they had become the targets for the whole of the advancing German battle fleet. *Nestor* was lying just astern of *Nomad* and Commander Bingham, after refusing to put the destroyer *Petard* at risk by accepting a tow, faced an appalling ordeal with his crew.

'We were heavily shelled, and the enemy's shooting was very good. We did not reply; the other ships did, with I think no possible effect. Heavy shells were falling all round the four ships and to me it seemed unlikely that we should get away at all. One salvo fell around us about abreast the after-funnel, three to starboard, and so close that the ships shook as if we had rammed something. I do not think the three starboard ones fell 20 feet away at the outside. I had the time of flight taken and it was about 40 seconds towards the end of shelling. Splinters were painfully audible and often visible, and the noise of the bursting shells very impressive.'

4.47 PICK UP MEN IN WATER ROUND US.

Beatty to destroyers.

The German battle fleet concentrated its fire on Goodenough's light cruisers (below). HMS *Birmingham* like HMS *Southampton*, *Nottingham* and *Dublin* raced after Beatty at high speed, dodging the salvoes from Scheer's battleships. But the crippled British destroyers HMS *Nomad* and *Nestor* could not escape and were used as target practice for the German gunners.

The High Seas Fleet opened fire on *Nomad* and she sank after a few minutes. From the time that we realized that our destruction was imminent, all preparations were made with a view to saving as many lives as possible, and all confidential matter was thrown overboard and seen to sink. The motorboat and whaler were lowered to the water's edge and the wounded were later placed in the motorboat. The Carley floats were hoisted out and placed alongside, the dingy being damaged by shellfire was useless. The cables were got ready on the fo'c'sle in the unlikely event of a tow being forthcoming; this was done on the suggestion of Lieutenant M. J. Bethell with a view to keeping the minds of the men occupied. The High Seas Fleet then drew up and we were very soon straddled, not before however we had fired our fourth and remaining torpedo. The *Nestor* now occupied the unrivalled attention of the High Seas Fleet and was hit in many places, principally aft, and rapidly commenced sinking by the stern. Immediately I saw that she was doomed I gave my last order, 'Abandon ship'. This was carried out in perfect order and discipline. The boats and Carley floats worked their way clear of the ship which all the time was being subjected to a tornado of fire. A few minutes later she reared up in a perpendicular position and sank by the stern. Three cheers were given for the *Nestor* and *God Save the King* was sung.

Commander Bingham was saved with 'the greater part of his crew', and spent the rest of the battle cooped up below decks on the German destroyer, *S16*.

Beatty was now in headlong flight and Hipper, confident that the 5th Battle Squadron must soon be forced to follow Beatty or risk destruction by the High Seas Fleet, decided to pursue the British battlecruisers.

In spite of signalling difficulties when the *Lützow*'s wireless aerial was hit, Hipper brought his ships round to snare Beatty. But as his ships made the turn in succession, the 5th Battle Squadron opened fire again and scored more hits. Evan-Thomas's action covered

4.50 PASSED 5TH BATTLE SQUADRON STEERING ON OPPOSITE COURSE.

HMS Lion*'s log.*

(Opposite) The dispositions at 4.48 immediately after Beatty turned, following his sighting of the High Seas Fleet. It was now his turn to act as a decoy and he set off north towards the Grand Fleet with Scheer in pursuit. But his signal was once again missed by Rear Admiral Evan Thomas (inset) and the *Barham* (below) continued towards Scheer's guns. HMS *Southampton* was now heading north dodging German shells.

Beatty's skilful manoeuvre, which had extricated the battlecruisers from the trap. Goodenough's warning had given Beatty enough time to turn before Hipper could cut across to box him in, but Beatty's escape was largely due to the 5th Battle Squadron which had unwittingly continued to steam south straight for the enemy battle fleet. Now a series of signalling errors almost led to the destruction of Evan-Thomas's battleships.

When Beatty sighted the masts and funnels of Scheer's ships at 4.40 pm and commenced his turn, Evan-Thomas's ships was still some eight miles astern and had neither seen the German battle fleet nor received Southampton's signals. Beatty's flag-lieutenant used flags to make the signal to turn, 'Alter course 16 points to starboard', and once again did not repeat the message by searchlight. For the second time that afternoon Evan-Thomas saw the battlecruisers turning without him. But as he was in hot pursuit of a fleeing Hipper and could not see Scheer's fleet, he pressed on. It was not until seven minutes later when *Barham* drew abreast of the *Lion*, which was then heading in the opposite direction, that Beatty repeated his signal by flags.

Vital minutes were again lost since Evan-Thomas waited for the signal to be hauled down, in accordance with standard naval practice, before commencing his turn. The 5th Battle Squadron then finally began to turn in succession, and the following battleships continued ahead to round the same point one by one. The High Seas Fleet, closing at a combined speed of 40 knots, concentrated all its guns on the point of turn.

Evan-Thomas's ships suffered heavily; as the *Barham* turned, the High Seas Fleet had already come abreast of her and she was hit almost immediately. Her wireless was put out of action and there were heavy casualties. Scheer ordered his battle line to close the range, turning his fleet by divisions. The *Valiant* and the *Warspite* were fortunate and turned without being hit at all, but when the last ship, the *Malaya*, arrived at the turning point it was a 'very hot corner', and she was hit repeatedly.

'The fighting which now ensued developed into a stern chase,' wrote Scheer, who was at this time confident that the concentrated fire of his whole fleet must knock out one of the battleships. The Germans were oblivious of the fact that Beatty was heading straight for Jellicoe's Grand Fleet; Scheer did not stop to

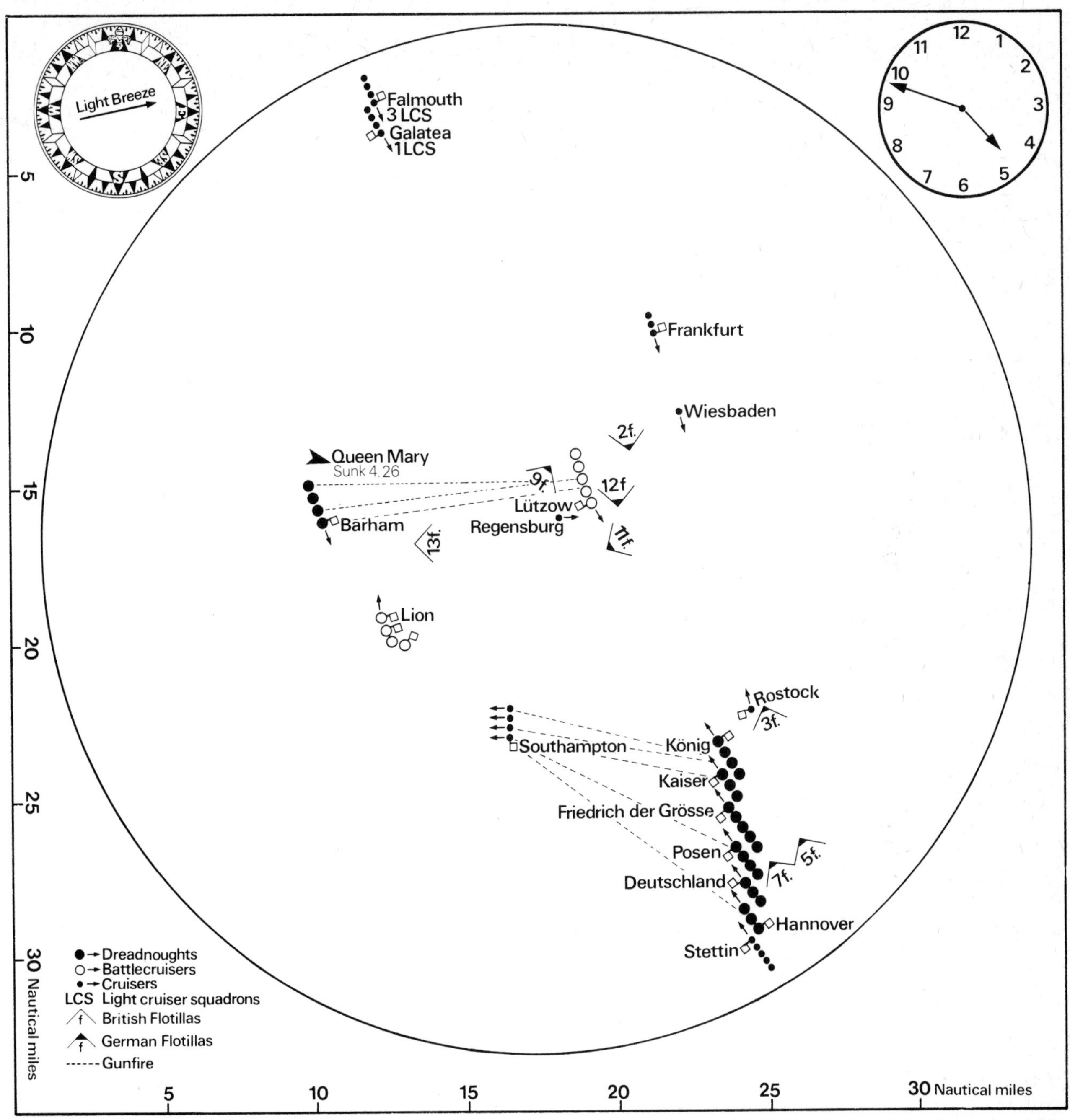

consider why Beatty was apparently fleeing north, not west towards England, as might have been expected.

As all the British ships were heading north at full speed, two isolated destroyers of the 13th Flotilla were dashing south at 30 knots. The *Onslow* and the *Moresby* had been standing guard over the seaplane-carrier, *Engadine*, whilst she hoisted her seaplane aboard, but as soon as this had been completed and she was under way again. Lieutenant Tovey (later to become Admiral and Commander-in-Chief of the Home Fleet during the Second World War) of the *Onslow* asked permission to be released and 'proceeded to close with the nearest squadron, the 5th Battle Squadron, at 30 knots'. Anxious to get into the action, he led his two ships across to the engaged bow of Beatty's flagship and soon found that he was,

> rapidly opening from *Lion* and closing enemy's battlecruisers about 5 points (56.25 degrees) on their engaged bow, distance 18,000 yards. I was unable to see any enemy's light cruisers or destroyers ahead of their battlecruisers and it seemed a favourable

5.21 CAN YOU SEE ENEMY CRUISER RIGHT ASTERN?
REPLY: YES I THINK THEY ARE FIRING
AT US BUT ARE 1,000 YARDS SHORT.

3rd Light Cruiser Squadron.

opportunity to deliver an attack with torpedoes, and with this idea proceeded to close the enemy more. Shortly afterward four enemy light cruisers appeared ahead of their battlecruisers and closed *Onslow* and opened heavy and accurate fire on both *Onslow* and *Moresby*. Realizing that I should be unable to get within torpedo range, at 4.50 pm I returned NW in the direction of *Lion*.

The two destroyers by themselves could not stop Hipper, and Tovey's gallant attempt was foiled; he extricated his destroyers and headed back for Beatty's flagship.

Thundering after its quarry the High Seas Fleet saw the British ships clearly against the yellow western horizon, except when the low sun broke through the thin hazy clouds to dazzle the German gunners.

The leading division in the German line was led by Rear-Admiral Paul Behncke in the *König*, and his ships soon engaged the *Malaya* and *Warspite* at the rear of the 5th Battle Squadron. Ahead of the *König*, *Barham* and *Valiant* continued to fire at Hipper's ships and in spite of the poor visibility scored further hits on *Lützow* and *Derfflinger* as well as keeping up the battering of the *Seydlitz*. The High Seas Fleet were concentrating an awesome fire on to the *Malaya* and *Warspite*, whose tough armour was proving capable of standing up to the punishment.

According to the official German account, every ship within range was joining in:

As the head of the enemy's line moved further from the German guns, the concentration of fire on the last ship of the squadron, the *Malaya*, increased. At 5.27 pm the *Lützow* was still firing at the *Barham*, the *Derfflinger* at the *Valiant*, and the *Seydlitz* at the *Warspite*, but the *Von der Tann* had commenced firing at the *Malaya* at 5 pm. The *Kronprinz* joined in at 5.08 pm, the *Kaiser* at 5.10 and the *Moltke* at 5.27 so that from 5.05 until 5.30 the *Malaya* was, according to observations made on board her, constantly covered by straddling salvoes. These usually

During the run north, for nearly an hour, the stout armour and construction of the super-Dreadnoughts like HMS *Malaya* (below) stood up to the German shells.

'As I was training my turret round to the starboard side, now the engaged side, I saw that our battlecruisers were already 7,000 or 8,000 yards ahead of us. I then realized that just the four of us of the 5th Battle Squadron would have to entertain the High Seas Fleet – four against perhaps twenty.'

fell at the rate of six a minute but at one time nine to the minute were observed in uninterrupted succession all round the hard-pressed ship.

On board the *Malaya* one officer recalled:

I expected at any moment that if any one of those shells should hit us in the right place our speed would be sadly reduced, and then we should fall behind and probably be sunk . . . On going back into the turret I found everyone very cheery and full of go. They had no thought that we should come off worse than the enemy, but only wanted to know how many German ships were left afloat requiring to be finished off. They were full of confidence that every shell was doing its bit, and many and varied were the benedictions they sent with each round.

The superior speed of the British battleships was the deciding factor in this phase of the action, and slowly the range began to open up, much to the chagrin of the pursuing Germans:

Very clear silhouettes could be seen of the battleships against the orange skyline. It was possible to almost make out the guns on the turrets with the naked eye . . . They were like the feelers of black monstrous beetles as they moved up and down. One hit was observed after another. . . . But the English are faster than the 'cowardly Germans' and they gradually creep out of the ranges of our guns so that at 5.30 pm the battle had stopped.

5.20 PURSUE THE ENEMY BATTLECRUI

Scheer to Hipper.

Throughout the one-and-a-half-hour run north Beatty was confident that nothing could prevent him leading Scheer into the Grand Fleet and certain destruction. He had lost two of his battlecruisers, but the remaining four were battle-worthy. Despite two turrets being put out of action and extraneous damage, they could still steam at full speed. 'Morale was high,' according to Chalmers; 'the knowledge of the loss of the *Indefatigable* and *Queen Mary* was shared only by a few observers who kept it to themselves. This was fortunate, for if the vulnerability of the ships and men had been generally known, the effect on the men might have been disquieting.'

But one important factor was beyond Beatty's control – there were only a few hours of daylight left, and visibility was rapidly deteriorating. The gunnery officer of the *Lion* found that

> the bad light and the mist, together with the smoke of our guns firing and the smoke of the enemy shells bursting, make long-range action impossible; the action consists of a series of comparatively short bursts of firing with longer intervals during which the enemy are not in sight. From the turn at 4.40 pm until the end of the day's action, the firing of our four battlecruisers only consists of five separated and short engagements. From time to time the course is altered to close the enemy and search the mist and smoke-laden atmosphere for a possible target, but almost as soon as it is sighted and opened fire upon, the target alters course away and disappears behind a smoke-screen.

The sun was now over the western horizon behind the British, and the light and poor visibility were even more trying for the Germans. From the *Derfflinger*, 'the ranges are scarcely ever less than 18,000 metres'.

The British battlecruisers were taking advantage of the mist patches, and the *Lion*'s gunnery report showed how fire was kept at Scheer's battleships whenever they were spotted: 'At 5.08 pm the enemy were lost to sight, but were sighted again at 5.12, and then again at 5.33 though insufficiently clearly to enable fire to be opened on them. The next engagement is of longer duration, and lasts from 5.38 until 6.01 at ranges varying between 13,000 and 15,000 yards.'

Scheer now began to realize that the British were using their superior speed to escape. Hipper's battlecruisers were steaming at over 20 knots and the High Seas Fleet a knot or two slower. The pre-Dreadnoughts of the 2nd Squadron were already falling well behind. 'The hope that one of the ships pursued would be so damaged as to fall prey to our Main Fleet was not fulfilled', wrote Scheer, 'although our firing was effective, and at 5.30 pm it was seen that a ship of the Queen Elizabeth type (*Malaya*), after she had been hit repeatedly, drew slowly out of the fighting line with a heavy list to leeward.'

Poor visibility started to hamper Scheer; 'the previously clear weather had become less clear; the wind had changed from NW to SW. Powder fumes and smoke from the funnels hung over the sea and cut off all view from the north and east. Only now and then could we see our reconnaissance forces.'

Maintaining top speed by the German ships was hampered by difficulties being experienced in the boiler-rooms 'owing to the stony nature of the coal fires which had not been cleaned since 1 pm and had become very dirty'. General fatigue was also becoming serious, 'the ships' companies had had no food since noon, and stokers and trimmers particularly began to show signs of exhaustion.'

In response to Scheer's urgent signal at 5.20 pm for 'General chase', Hipper turned his ships to the north-west to try and engage the British battlecruisers again. In doing this he unwittingly assisted Beatty, who some four minutes later hoisted the signal, 'Prepare to renew action', and turned eastwards. Judging that the Grand Fleet would shortly be appearing over the northern horizon, Beatty wanted to prevent Hipper spotting them and warning Scheer.

The Germans still did not suspect the real purpose of Beatty's move; according to von Hase:

> At the time we did not grasp the object of the manoeuvres . . . Admiral Beatty, by completely outflanking us in spite of our highest speed, accomplished an excellent tactical manoeuvre, and his

The superior speed of the British enabled them to draw out of range of the guns of the German battle fleet. Scheer ordered Hipper to make use of the faster speed of the German battlecruisers to prevent Beatty's escape. But the stokers in the German boiler rooms (below) were suffering from fatigue and the furnaces badly needed raking out.

ships carried out an admirable feat of technique. He accomplished the famous 'crossing the "T"', compelled us to alter course, and finally brought us into position where we were completely enveloped by the English Battle Fleet.

Hipper's battlecruisers soon found themselves under fire from two directions: the *Lion* and the other three battlecruisers fired from ahead; the *Valiant* and *Barham* joined in from Hipper's port quarter. Almost immediately Hipper's flagship, *Lützow*, was hit, and so was the *Derfflinger*. A shell landed in the bows of the *Seydlitz*, and hundreds of tons of water poured into the ship so that she started to sink by the bows. Only the strenuous efforts of her damage-control parties managed to shore up the bulkheads and save the vessel, but fires broke out on deck following repeated hits. Beatty was now able to take full advantage of the light and to keep the Germans under fire whilst taking care to keep out of range himself. 'It was highly depressing, nerve-wracking and exasperating', according to von Hase; 'our only means of defence was to leave the line for a short time when we saw that the enemy had our range.'

Hipper was becoming increasingly worried. Chewing on his cigar, his anxiety was evident to his staff as he cursed the delay which the pre-Dreadnoughts had imposed on Scheer bringing his battle fleet up in support. With his radio shot away and his ships being hit and helpless to hit back, Hipper realized that his

5.25 PREPARE TO RENEW ACTION.

Beatty to Battlecruisers.

(Opposite) The disposition of forces after an hour's run to the north. Beatty, knowing that Jellicoe would shortly appear from the northwest, sought to conceal the Grand Fleet from Hipper and to prevent a warning reaching Scheer's battlefleet (below) whose ships were spread out over ten miles after their vain chase of the *Barham* and the 5th Battle Squadron. Visibility was deteriorating and out of the mist on Hipper's unengaged flank emerged the light cruiser HMS *Chester*. The 3rd Battlecruiser Squadron led by HMS *Invincible* was moving into the attack.

damaged battlecruisers were now at serious risk. He decided to abandon Scheer's order for a hot pursuit. He eased away first to the north-east, then to the north to open up the range. 'Mark my words, Harder,' Hipper told his flag-captain, 'there's something nasty brewing. It would be better not to get in too deep.'

Hipper's foreboding was soon justified, but from a totally unanticipated direction. Shortly before six o'clock his 2nd Scouting Group of six light cruisers, which was probing the mist to the north, suddenly ran into the British light cruiser *Chester*, which was scouting on the starboard wing of the 3rd Battlecruiser Squadron.

The *Invincible*, *Inflexible* and *Indomitable*, under the command of Rear-Admiral Hood, had been sent ahead by Jellicoe to aid Beatty. Through Beatty's navigational errors they had missed him and steamed on to find themselves nearly ten miles east of the German battlecruisers. But Hood's forces now made a fortunate surprise appearance on Hipper's disengaged flank, and the *Chester* opened fire on the startled Germans.

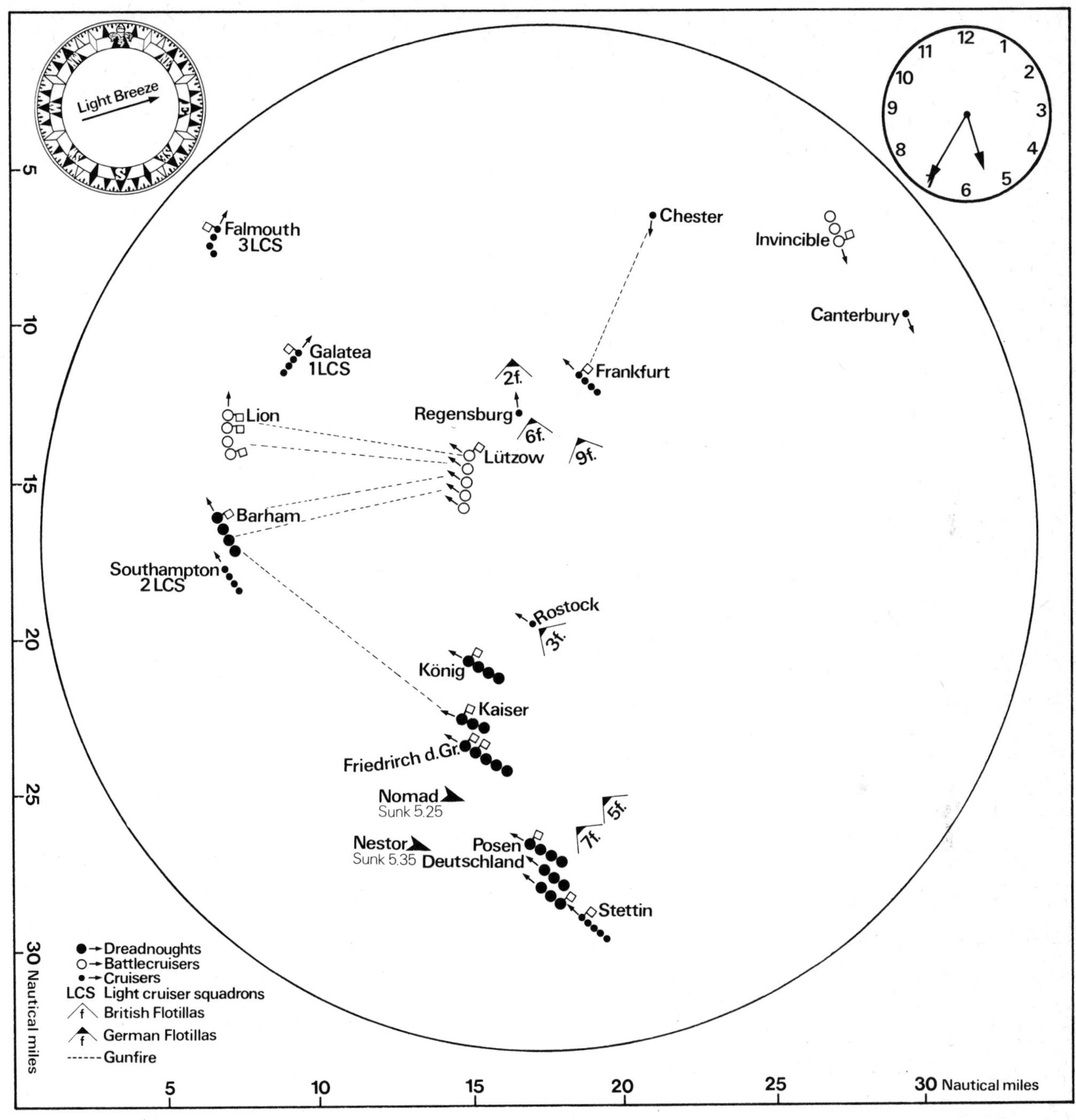

Rear-Admiral Friedrich Bödicker's four ships, *Frankfurt*, *Wiesbaden*, *Elbing* and *Pillau*, outnumbered the *Chester*, where 'things became pretty brisk aboard, the whole of the enemy light cruiser squadron concentrating on us, and several salvoes hit us.' Heavy casualties amongst the gun crews resulted from the eighteen shells that hit the ship. Amongst them was the sixteen-year-old Boy First Class, Jack Cornwell who, though wounded, refused to desert his post at the forward 5.5-inch gun (his heroism later became nationally acclaimed with the award of a posthumous VC). The *Chester*'s engine-room had a lucky escape from a hit which penetrated the port side and went out of the starboard side. 'The engine-room mascot, a black kitten, was taken to its action station below when action sounded off and apparently it did its duty nobly.' Luck held long enough for the *Chester* to head for the three massive shapes of the British battle-cruisers as she was pursued through the mist by the German ships. Now it was Bödicker's turn to be surprised as the *Invincible*, leading the *Inflexible* and *Indomitable*, loomed out of the smoke:

5.34 INVINCIBLE OPENED FIRE .

Log of HMS Indomitable.

A few minutes later we sighted gun flashes, and the next minute the *Chester*, surrounded by shell splashes, came out of the mist on our port bow heading across the bows of the squadron from port to starboard, and was followed a minute later by three German light cruisers. As soon as the latter saw us they turned starboard to pass on opposite courses. At 5.34 pm we opened fire on them but only had five minutes firing before they disappeared. *Invincible* and ourselves managed to hit one which blew up, and the *Indomitable* apparently damaged another.

Stoker Zenne was the sole survivor and witness to the saga of the *Wiesbaden*, which began when his ship was hit by the *Inflexible*:

A tremendous blow was felt and the light went out. As soon as it was switched on again from the accumulators, it was found that a shell had penetrated in Compartment 6, putting both engines out of action. There was a great danger from the escaping steam. All the after part of the ship was full of it, and the heat could be felt even at the fans. The fan turbines slowed down, and then suddenly stopped altogether.

The *Pillau* also received a hit which knocked out four of her boilers, but her engine-room staff managed to maintain enough steam for her to escape in company with the *Frankfurt* under a smoke screen. But there was no escape for the *Wiesbaden*: 'Once again the order was passed down, this time by word of mouth like a cry of despair through the ship: "Full speed ahead both engines", but the reply came back: "Engines disabled, struck by heavy shell, engine-room abandoned." The ship was a helpless target, disabled by the hated British at the very first shot.'

The *Wiesbaden*'s difficulties were only beginning as she lay motionless before the British guns. 'Hit after hit followed', wrote Zenne, 'and each time a tremor ran through the ship, but she remained afloat. The guns' crews who had suffered heavy casualties, and whose places had been filled by some of the stokers off duty, gallantly poured salvo after salvo from their nearly hot guns.'

Whilst the *Wiesbaden* was being helplessly battered

When German light cruisers scouting ahead of Hipper suddenly ran into HMS *Chester* (right) the lone British light cruiser was damaged and Boy Seaman Jack Cornwell (inset) was awarded the Victoria Cross for remaining at his post beside the wrecked for'ard turret. Hipper's forces had encountered Admiral Hood's 3rd Battlecruiser Squadron. HMS *Invincible* accompanied by HMS *Indomitable* and *Inflexible* (below) raced into action crippling the light cruiser SMS *Wiesbaden*.

by Hood's battlecruisers, Bödicker and the five remaining cruisers of his 2nd Scouting Group reported the presence of heavy British forces to Hipper. Only able to catch a brief glimpse of them through the mist, Hipper assumed they were battleships and drew the immediate conclusion that they were at the head of the Grand Fleet. Accordingly, just before six o'clock he ordered the leader of his torpedo-boat flotillas, Commodore Heinrich in the light cruiser *Regensburg*, to switch his 31 torpedoboats to attack the enemy forces on the east rather than Beatty on the west. Flying the pennant 'Z', the order for attack, the destroyers sped away past the smoking *Wiesbaden* to attack Hood's battlecruisers. At 5,000 yards *Invincible* ordered her four screening destroyers out to counter the attack. The British destroyers, led by Commander Loftus Jones in the *Shark*, accompanied by *Acasta*, *Ophelia* and *Christopher*, turned towards the enemy with thick smoke pouring from their funnels and bow-waves streaming over their narrow fo'c'sles. Their attack foiled the German onslaught, so that only twelve torpedoes were actually fired at Hood's battlecruisers, all of which were skilfully avoided. But the *Shark* and the *Acasta* were badly mauled. After ploughing on through the British lines out of control, the *Acasta* was finally taken in tow and saved; but the *Shark* lay stopped and sinking. Able Seaman C.C. Hope later gave his account from a hospital bed:

> We had been in action 10 minutes when the fore part of the ship was struck and the steering gear put out of action . . . We suffered very heavy casualties, the foremost and after guns being put out of action and their crews killed. We were then engaging enemy destroyers with the midship guns, but all the guns' crews were killed or badly wounded except A.B. Howell and myself. Captain Jones controlled the gun and set the sights, and Midshipman Smith trained the gun. A.B. Howell was then badly wounded and Captain Jones had his leg shot away.

'. . . almost immediately we saw the flash of gunfire ripple along the side of the leading light cruiser, and at the same moment we sighted a destroyer with her mast stepped aft – a sure sign of a Hun.'
– *Officer, HMS* Chester.

5.47 ATTACK ENEMY WITH TORPEDOES.

Beatty to destroyers.

Under pressure from the renewed action by Beatty's forces and the 3rd Battlecruiser Squadron from the north Hipper turned north-east. At the same time he sent his torpedo-boats to make a covering attack on the 3rd Battle Squadron, countered with great gallantry by four British destroyers led by Commander Loftus Jones (inset) in HMS *Shark*.

'. . . on the bridge we were all soaked through by the spray thrown up by shell, causing the sub-lieutenant to remark that "an umbrella would be handy" . . . After a while we received our first direct hit, which was right forward on the waterline, and gave us a feeling that the ship had been pushed bodily sideways. . . .' – *Lieut. Cmdr Barron, HMS* Acasta.

After a gallant struggle by her crew against fearful odds, the destroyer finally sank.

The survivors of the *Shark* were later picked up by a Danish steamer; but Captain Jones was not amongst them. A few weeks later his body was washed ashore on the coast of Sweden, and buried in the village churchyard of Fiskenbacksie. Thanks to the devotion of his wife, who collected reports from the survivors, he was awarded a posthumous VC. The surviving members of the crew received the DSM. The failure of the destroyer attack compelled Hipper immediately to fall back on Scheer. Abandoning the *Wiesbaden*, he joined Scheer and soon his battlecruisers were steaming north-east again, leading the High Seas Fleet's battle line.

So it was that Hipper was one of the first Germans to see the awesome spectacle of the Grand Fleet when at 6.22 pm 'out of the mist and across the horizon ahead appeared the enemy battle line with all its heavy guns firing.'

The High Seas Fleet had headed straight into the jaws of Jellicoe's trap. Beatty's move which forced Hipper to the east was instrumental in pulling off this brilliant coup. For the German Fleet the situation was perilous, particularly as Hipper's destroyer flotillas had spent themselves in their massed attack on the four British destroyers led by the *Shark*. Had they attacked north-west, they could have 'played the role of a wolf in a flock of sheep', and completely disrupted the critical deployment of the British battle line.

In the German view, 'the English main force won time to deploy, luckily for England', and shortly before his death Admiral Scheer confided that 'it was the thought of how providence had given them opportunities for a *complete* annihilation of the British Fleet that still robbed him of sleep.'

6.01 WHERE IS THE ENEMY'S BATTLEFLEET?

C-in-C to Beatty.

Shortly after 6 pm as the unseen destroyer battle moved to a crescendo, Admiral Jellicoe stood analysing his plot in the *Iron Duke*. 'At this stage there was still great uncertainty as to the position of the enemy's battle fleet: flashes of gunfire were visible from ahead round to the starboard beam, the noise was heavy and continuous.' Yet Jellicoe now had to make the crucial decision of how to deploy his twenty-four battleships. Seldom can one man have had to stake so much on so little information; the British C-in-C in the flagship had received no clear news of where Beatty's force was precisely, nor what they were doing. He was at a loss to understand the failure of so many of his captains to send sighting reports. The enemy had been engaged for nearly two hours and yet from the time of the *Southampton*'s first signal of the sighting of the German Battle Fleet at 4.38 pm, only eight accurate reports and a handful of indefinite sightings, interrupted by long periods of silence, had provided the Grand Fleet with any evidence of what was happening.

Of the eight reports, no less than six were from Commodore Goodenough in the *Southampton*, whose exemplary performance the other scouting captains failed to emulate. It was a reflection on the poor performance of British reconnaissance and communications, which contributed so much to the lost opportunities of Jutland, that Beatty's report, wirelessed as 'Enemy battle fleet bearing SE' had first been garbled in transmission and deciphered as '26–30 battleships, probably hostile, bearing SE', and it was never clarified by another message which assessed Scheer's strength. Jellicoe's inability to gauge the exact degree of superiority of the Grand Fleet over the German battle squadrons was relatively unimportant compared to the approaching decision he had to make on deployment. His six columns of battleships were in cruising division, spaced some 2,000 yards apart, resembling a giant rake five miles wide.

To transform the rake into a single line of battle Jellicoe could waste no time, and he had little margin for error. If he deployed in the wrong direction the oncoming Scheer would be able to cross Jellicoe's line at right angles. He would then 'cross the "T"', bringing all the German guns to bear whilst Jellicoe's were masked, cancelling out the superior fire power of the British ships. If, on the other hand, Jellicoe delayed until he could see the German battle line, he ran the risk of being caught in the process of manoeuvring his ships under the guns of the approaching enemy. In such a situation the British battleships would find their field of fire restricted by their own squadrons, and a fast torpedo attack by the German forces would have a disastrous effect.

Waiting for the vital news of the enemy's dispositions in order to deploy the full destructive power of Britain's main strategic instrument of war, Jellicoe found himself in the appalling situation of not knowing where the enemy were! Unfortunately Beatty overlooked his responsibility to keep Jellicoe informed, so did the *Chester* which made no report; as well as Hood's battlecruisers, which were engaging Hipper when the Grand

As the battle fleet (below) raced towards the sound of gunfire and flashes on the horizon in its six columns, Admiral Jellicoe (left) had no clear idea of the enemy's whereabouts. He still lacked vital information in order to deploy the British battle line. The outcome of the battle – and the fate of the war – depended upon his decision.

Fleet was most in need of information. The Admiralty had been of little assistance, sending out reports from Scheer's intercepted radio messages that proved to be widely at variance with the few reports which the British C-in-C was actually receiving from the scouting forces.

Between 5.40 pm and 6.03 pm Jellicoe received three reports from Goodenough, the last of which threw little light on the situation: 'Urgent. Have lost sight of enemy's battle fleet. Am engaging the enemy's battle-cruisers. My position is Lat. 56° 57′ N, Long. 5° 43′ E, course NEE, speed 26 knots.' Jellicoe's other armoured cruisers which had been deployed ahead, 'the eyes of the fleet', were of little use to him. They had become so strung out that the chain of visual contact with the flagship was broken.

With great urgency, Jellicoe signalled the *Marlborough*, leading his starboard division and supposedly the one nearest the approaching enemy, 'What can you see?' At 6 o'clock *Marlborough* replied unhelpfully: 'Our battlecruisers bearing SSW, steering east. *Lion* leading ship.' Five minutes later *Marlborough* signalled again: '5th Battle Squadron bearing SW.' This information revealed an eleven-mile error in the position of Beatty's ship. According to information he had been given, Jellicoe expected that he would sight the *Lion* some twelve miles south-east of the *Iron Duke*. In fact it appeared that she was actually 5½ miles to the south, which was confirmed by the *Iron Duke*'s sighting shortly after six. Not only was the *Lion* 6½ miles closer than anticipated, but she also appeared on

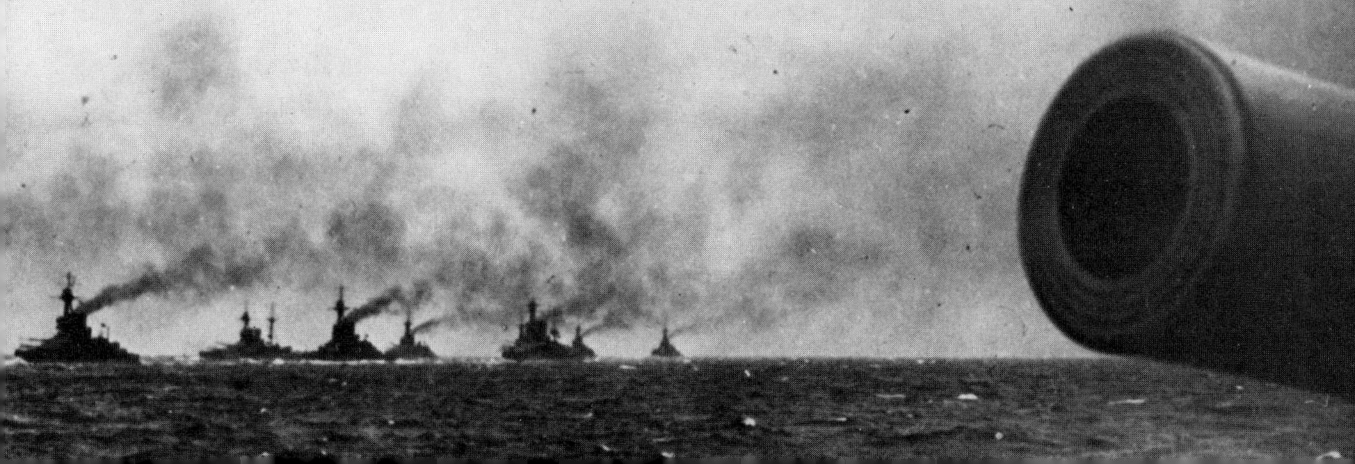

6.15 EQUAL SPEED CHARLIE LONDON.

C-in-C to Fleet.

(Opposite) The dispositions that Jellicoe, with a visibility of 6 miles, had to guess in the final moments before deployment. By forming his battle-line on the *King George V* (signalled, left, with the 'equal speed' pendant above and the C(harlie) L(ondeon) flags beneath), Jellicoe succeeded in crossing the German 'T', cutting Scheer off from his bases. But he could not appreciate that his instinct had been right because the funnel smoke from the battlecruisers (below) concealed the Germans. Ahead, Hipper's engagement drew off the German torpedo-boats in the crucial minutes of deployment.

the starboard bow rather than dead ahead as expected.

The picture now building up before Jellicoe, with the Germans still over the horizon, was that the High Seas Fleet would be upon him much sooner than he had calculated. The British battleships might have barely fifteen minutes in which to deploy into line of battle – a manoeuvre which normally took twenty minutes. Jellicoe would have no margin for error, and a mistake could be disastrous. The sound of gunfire was growing louder to those on the bridge of the *Iron Duke*, and they were still uncertain of the course and bearing of the Germans. Jellicoe's normally cool manner was momentarily ruffled when he said, 'I wish someone would tell me who is firing and what they are firing at.'

To try and find out, *Iron Duke* flashed *Lion*, 'Where is the enemy's battle fleet?' The reply from Beatty, who had last sighted Scheer an hour earlier, was vague: 'Enemy battlecruisers bearing SE.'

Iron Duke immediately signalled *Lion* again. Fortunately, between the exchange of signals *Lion* had caught a glimpse of Scheer's van far away on the horizon, and at 6.14 pm *Lion* replied, 'Have sighted enemy battle fleet bearing SSW.' This was confirmed by a following report from *Barham*, 'Enemy's battle fleet SSE.'

Precious time was running out. The High Seas Fleet would be in range within minutes. 'The point of decision,' as Jellicoe himself put it, 'was whether to form the line of battle on the starboard or on the port wing.' At that moment the Grand Fleet was still sailing directly south-east in its six lines.

> 'My first and natural impulse', wrote Jellicoe, 'was to form on the starboard wing column in order to bring the fleet into action at the earliest possible moment, but it became increasingly apparent, both from the sound of gunfire and the reports from *Lion* and *Barham*, that the High Seas Fleet was in such close proximity and on such a bearing as to create obvious disadvantages in such a movement.'

The mist would assist an attack by enemy destroyers which Jellicoe assumed to be in front of the German battleships. 'It would be suicidal to place the battle fleet in a position where it might be open to attack by destroyers in such a deployment.' Deployment to port would also put the *Marlborough*'s division (the weakest in Jellicoe's fleet) at the head of the line where the heaviest fire would be concentrated. A third drawback to deploying to port was that it might provide the enemy with a substantial overlap: 'The overlap would necessitate a large turn of the starboard wing division to port to prevent the "T" being crossed and each successive division coming into line would have to make this turn.' Every minute that passed brought the enemy fleet three-quarters of a mile closer. Nelson had nearly two hours to consider his final deployment before Trafalgar, but on the bridge of the *Iron Duke* Jellicoe made his final judgement in twenty seconds. His Flag-Captain, Dreyer, was impressed by the cool way in which Jellicoe finally reached his momentous decision: 'I was watching the steering of the ship when I heard the sharp, distinctive step of the Commander-in-Chief. He looked in silence at the magnetic compass for about 20 seconds. I watched his keen, brown, weatherbeaten face, wondering what he would do. He was as cool and unmoved as ever. Then he looked up and broke the silence with the order to Commander A. R. W. Woods, the Fleet Signal Officer: "Hoist equal speed pendant south-

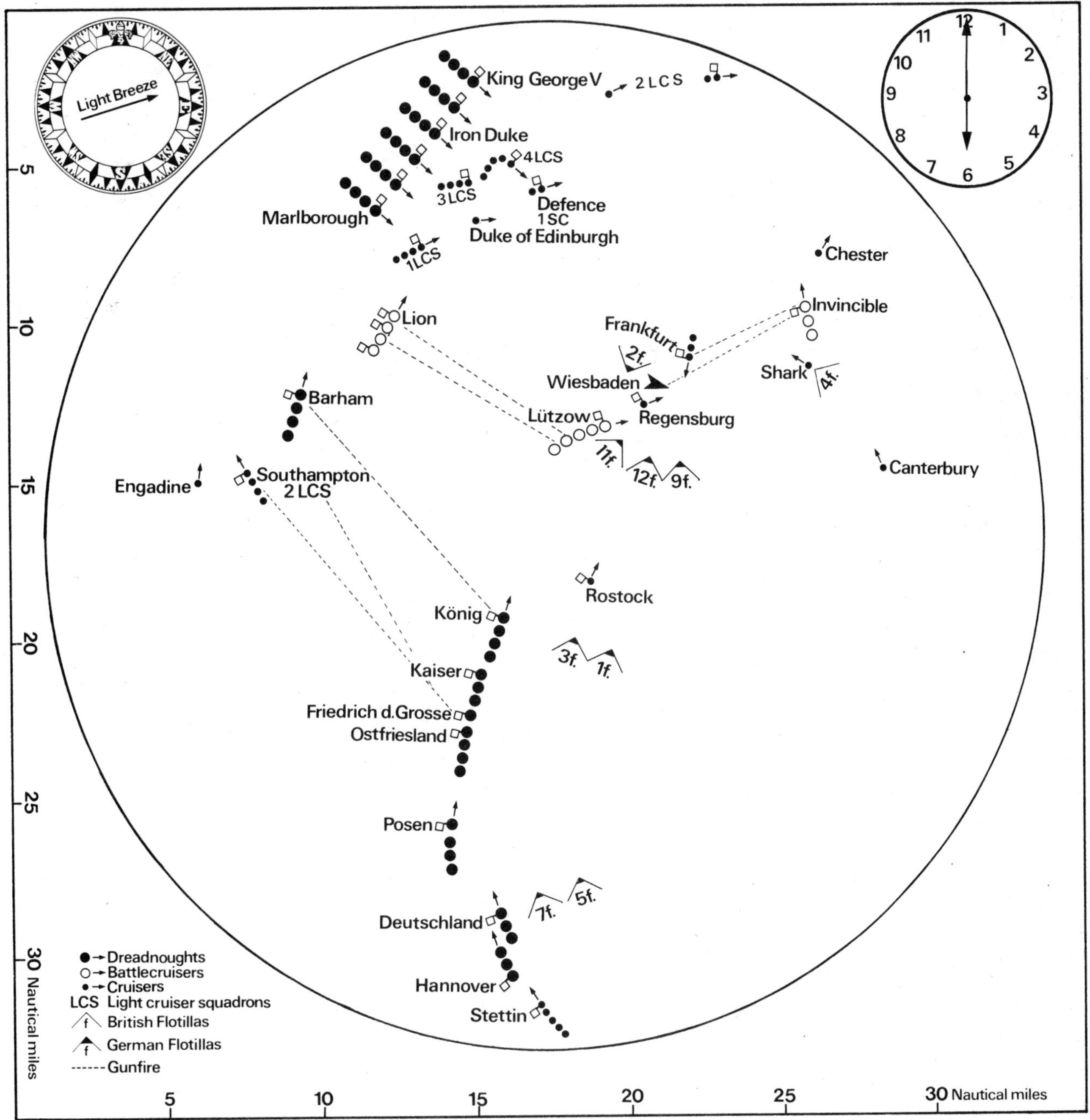

east." Woods said: "Would you make it a point to port sir, so that they will know it is on the port wing columns?" Jellicoe replied: "Very well. Hoist equal speed pendant SE-by-E."'

At 6.15 pm the pendant and flags, 'Equal speed Charles London' fluttered from the *Iron Duke* and the wireless message confirmed, 'The column nearest SE-by-E is to alter course in succession to that point of the compass, the remaining columns altering course leading ships together, the rest in succession so as to form astern of that column, maintaining the speed of the fleet.' The ponderous mechanism began to get under way as the columns of battleships, led by *King George V*, unravelled into a battle line $6\frac{3}{4}$-miles long.

Although Jellicoe did not appreciate it at first, he soon realized that he had achieved a highly important objective, the Grand Fleet had come between the enemy and his base. With only two hours remaining until darkness this now became the vital factor in determining the course of the battle.

Standing on the bridge of his flagship watching the

impressive manoeuvring of twenty-four British battleships, Jellicoe cut an unlikely figure. At Trafalgar, Nelson had stood resplendent on the quarterdeck of the *Victory* in full dress uniform; now as the Royal Navy headed for its 'second Trafalgar', the small figure on the *Iron Duke*'s bridge wore a tarnished cap, an old blue Burberry, and a twisted white scarf round his neck. One of his divisional commanders, Rear-Admiral Gaunt in the *Colossus*, was however seized with the spirit of the occasion and made by semaphore the somewhat incongruous signal: 'Remember traditions of Glorious First of June and avenge Belgium.'

Fifteen minutes passed. Finally Jellicoe saw the German battle line, but it was only a fleeting glimpse. Patches of mist combined with spreading clouds of smoke from hundreds of funnels now seriously obscured the scene. Years afterwards when he attended a demonstration at the Tactical School, Jellicoe emphasized how the poor visibility had been such a tremendous handicap by taking a duster and laying it round the models of the four leading German battleships. This, he explained, was all he ever saw of Scheer's twenty-two battleships. When he wrote to the First Lord of the Admiralty immediately after the action he explained, 'The whole situation was so difficult to grasp, as I had no real idea of what was going on and we could hardly see anything except flashes of guns, shells falling, ships blowing up, and an occasional glimpse of an enemy vessel.'

Beatty's battlecruisers did not improve the Grand Fleet's view of the enemy. They raced across the front of the fleet to take up their position at the head of the line. To avoid running them down, Jellicoe had to order his ships to reduce speed, delaying his contact with the enemy battle line. Evan-Thomas realized that the 5th Battle Squadron would never get to their appointed position at the head of the line, and after initial hesitation he led his ships to the rear without waiting for orders. As the battle unfolded with Jellicoe's battleships stretching for seven miles across the horizon, the armoured cruisers, *Defence* and *Warrior*, dashed forward between the battle lines to play a heroic, if short-lived, part in the battle. Rear-Admiral Sir Robert Arbuthnot, leading his four ships of the 1st Cruiser Squadron as an advanced screen for the Grand Fleet, had sighted Bödicker's five light cruisers of the 2nd Scouting Group. The sight of the German ships was too much for the Admiral to resist, and without heeding the consequences he raced for the enemy light cruisers and opened fire on the *Wiesbaden*.

The *Wiesbaden* was still managing to fire her remaining guns and the German Battle Fleet directed a tornado of fire on to Arbuthnot's two cruisers. On the *Derfflinger*, von Hase, directing the guns, was seized with fury. 'I abandoned my former target, had the English cruisers' range measured, gave the range and deflection, and "crash!" – a salvo roared out at the *Wiesbaden*'s tormentor. One more salvo and I had him. A column of smoke rose high into the air. Apparently a magazine had exploded. The other cruiser turned away and hauled out at top speed whilst I peppered her with two or three more salvoes.' Lieutenant Bickmore

6.14 HAVE SIGHTED ENEMY BATTLEFLEET BEARING SSW

Beatty to C-in-C.

Moments before the battle fleets sighted each other Rear Admiral Arbuthnot (inset left) led his 1st Cruiser Squadron in a reckless attempt to finish off the *Wiesbaden*. His flagship HMS *Defence* was blown up and HMS *Warrior* (left) badly damaged. Her escape was covered by HMS *Warspite* (below) circling in front of the High Seas Fleet with her helm jammed.

on the *Warspite* was a witness to the abrupt end of Admiral Arbuthnot's intervention and was about to find himself in an equally dangerous predicament:

> Arbuthnot's ships temporarily masked our fire, and ran slap into a concentrated salvo from the German Fleet which was probably aimed at us. *Defence* blew up at once, the whole of her bottom being visible some fifty feet in the air, an extraordinary sight. The *Warrior* was also heavily hit, as was the *Black Prince*. This occurred at what was known afterwards as 'Windy Corner'. At this critical moment the *Malaya*, our next astern, closed up and looked like colliding with us. Our helm was put hard over to avoid the collision, and the steering gear, already weakened by the shell hits we had received in the stern, jammed. The ship turned to starboard and continued in large circles (coming all the time nearer the German line), during which we passed close to the stricken *Warrior* which was stopped and we thus took the German fire from her.

The *Warspite* in fact made two complete turns because, although the Captain had extricated his ship from the first circle by skilful use of the engines, the emergency steering gear was hastily connected with the rudder on, and the battleship then swung wildly around to starboard. This resulted in another circle in front of the German guns and the *Warspite* received thirteen hits from heavy enemy shells:

> For about 30 minutes we were receiving the concentrated fire of some 30 German ships at comparatively point-blank range, and the noise of the shells hitting the ship sounded like a full battery of small guns firing. The ship was heavily hit and badly damaged. I personally counted over 150 holes in the ship after the action, the funnels were like colanders. The mainmast had received a direct hit, and another had put 'B' turret out of action. 'A' turret, in which I was myself, was still in action. Both our 6-inch batteries had been hit, resulting in cordite fires with many casualties. It was in one of these batteries that our Catholic Padre won the DSC for rescuing men from the flames and dragging them out until every stitch of clothing had been burnt off him. When we finally came out of it we were on fire in seven places and down at the stern until our quarterdeck was awash, with only two large guns and two small guns still capable of firing.
>
> Having nothing else to do, and as the firing had now wandered away from us, I climbed onto the top of the turret to watch the Grand Fleet deploying and open fire. It was the most magnificent sight I've ever seen in my life. It filled the horizon from one side to the other; six miles of ships turning into line and as they did so they opened fire. It was a marvellous sight. We knew we had been licked, but it was now clear that the Germans were going to get a darn sight worse than we had.

6.17 LARGE EXPLOSION SEEN IN E

FURTHER EXPLOSION SEEN.

Log of HMS Fearless.

'The entire arc stretching from north to east was a sea of fire. The flash from the muzzles of countless guns was distinctly seen through the mist and the smoke on the horizon, though the ships were not distinguishable.' As he peered at the horizon through the North Sea mist Scheer must have felt that his battle fleet faced a grim *Götterdämmerung* in the early evening of 31 May.

Scheer's squadrons were steaming at 20 knots straight into Jellicoe's battle line. According to the textbooks it was one of the worst positions any battle fleet commander could encounter. The Grand Fleet had crossed the German 'T' and was deployed across the whole horizon.

On board the *Marlborough*, the nearest ship to the German line: 'As the battlecruisers drew ahead and their smoke cleared, the German line could be more easily seen and 4 Kaisers and 4 Helgolands could be dimly made out. *Marlborough* opened fire at 6.17 pm at a battleship of the Kaiser class – range 13,000 yards, about Green (Starboard) 110 degrees.' She was followed by the 12-inch batteries of the *Agincourt*: '6.24 pm. Opened fire on enemy battlecruiser; range 10,000 yards. Target could just be made out.' Then *Bellerophon* and *Hercules* opened fire followed one by one by the other ships until in little more than six minutes the whole British line was thundering broadsides. Every ship joined in; if the mist obscured the German battle line then the guns were turned on to the unfortunate *Wiesbaden* which now found herself in the middle of the arc of fire.

The next few minutes seemed liked an age to the men on the leading German ships as the great crescent of British battleships directed all their guns on to the High Seas Fleet. In the van, Hipper's battlecruisers were only saved from destruction by their immense strength. Behncke's 3rd Battle Squadron, leading the German battleships, received terrible punishment. On board the *Kaiser*, the fourth ship in the battle line, an officer recorded his personal impression of the ordeal:

> How small one feels with all these elements wanting to harm us. Even one salvo could finish our ship, could tear it apart and make an end of us. Later I heard that someone had said to the captain of the fleet flagship which was astern of us, and who had once been commander of the *Kaiser*, 'There goes your old ship'. But the *Kaiser* was not ready to go yet – in spite of the fact that we were right in the thick of it, surrounded by clouds of dirty smoke,

As HMS *Iron Duke* leading the 4th Battle Squadron (bottom), HMS *Royal Oak*, HMS *Superb* and HMS *Canada* turned into the battle line, the poor visibility evident in this photograph was soon added to by the enormous volume of smoke pouring from hundreds of funnels (below) and the fumes from thousands of gun discharges.

getting blasted by masses of flying steel and at the same time being drenched with water from the mountainous foundations thrown up by the near misses.

We survived this hell-fire and kept right on behind our admiral's ship, even though the smoke was biting into our eyes – and we kept on firing through it all.

On board Behncke's flagship, *König*, the hits she received were giving her medical staff no respite:

Soon the battle dressing-station was so full that treatment had to be made on the deck above. Every badly wounded man received a morphine injection immediately and we had to concentrate mainly on carrying out first aid and bandaging wounds and applying splints for broken limbs . . . then casualties were admitted suffering from gas poisoning; their symptoms were irregular breathing, pallid features and a sweet and sour odour. Several needed artificial respiration and their hearts stimulated. The small oxygen cylinders were rapidly used up. It turned out that the gases were due to shells which pierced the starboard casemates and set off a fire in the ammunition hoist. These gases then leaked through into nearby compartments and the problem was also increased by fumes that leaked through from a hit in the smoke uptake into the third boiler-room.

Yet the first clash between the British and German battle fleets when it finally occurred, late on the afternoon of Wednesday 31 May 1916, lasted for barely quarter of an hour. When the long-awaited moment of trial had

'We could hear firing plainly on the starboard bow, and a few minutes later we saw flashes running right round the starboard beam. By this time all the turrets' crews were on top of the turrets, and everybody was highly excited. Action was sounded off again, and the turret crews went down to their turrets.' – *Midshipman Hoyle of HMS* Monarch.

(Opposite) The Grand Fleet, still deploying, opens fire on the van of Scheer's 10-mile battle line. Mist patches and smoke obscured visibility, which was less than six miles, for British battleships in the middle of the line, like HMS *Superb* and HMS *Canada* (left). The *Wiesbaden* was trapped between the lines and HMS *Warspite*'s gyrations covered the escape of the *Warrior*. Hipper's battlecruisers still concentrated their fire on the 3rd Battle Squadron, destroying HMS *Invincible*.

come at last, the years of economic, industrial and technological effort represented by the two great fleets, the zeal and training of the thousands of men, the tactical schemes of the commanders and the destiny of two nations depended on the vagaries of sea-mist and the uncontrollable funnel smoke from the ships themselves. Swirling smoke and mist only cleared briefly in patches. Momentary improvement in visibility allowed the battle to erupt in a series of spontaneous engagements reaching out along both battle lines. 'Ships fired at what they could see, whilst they could see it', said Jellicoe. Had it been clear, the High Seas Fleet would have been routed within minutes. But poor visibility and concealment of the target ships by clouds of smoke and shell splashes undoubtedly saved the Germans.

To the British gunnery control officers high above the shell-torn water, the situation was 'galling and trying to the last degree'. The account by the spotting officer of the *Benbow* was typical:

> For some seconds after each salvo my vision was blanked by smoke, my glasses shaken off the object and, owing to the short range and subsequent short time of flight in which to recover (to say nothing of the fact that between the moment of firing and the fall of shot there was often a small change of helm) it was practically impossible to be certain that one was spotting on the ship fired at.

The gunnery records indicate just how blindly the British battleships were firing: '*Bellerophon*. 6.15 pm sighted some grey, misty objects. 6.25 opened fire . . . Impossible to count enemy.' '*Benbow*. 6.29 pm. Lützow class. 1,000 yards. Opened fire. Shots lost in haze.' '*Conqueror*. 6.31 pm. Opened fire on Markgraf class; rough range 12,000 yards. This ship quickly disappeared in haze.' '*Monarch*. 6.33 pm. Sighted five battleships, 95 Green, three Königs, and two Kaisers; range 12,000 yards. Opened fire on leading König, two salvoes, first right and over, second appeared to straddle quarterdeck. The ships disappeared from view, but we fired one salvo at one of the Kaisers, the result not seen.'

On the German battleships the arrival of the enemy shells sounded like 'a goods train from a distance rolling over a bridge.'

Every British battleship desperately tried to outshoot her neighbour whenever a target appeared through the mist and smoke. The pent-up enthusiasm after the long months of waiting found expression in the number of battle ensigns flying proudly from every mast. In the spotting-top of the *Neptune*, a young midshipman noticed that 'in about ten minutes the air seemed to be thick with white ensigns, large and small, silk and bunting, hoisted wherever halyards could be rove.' He was well placed to see this historic encounter.

> The two fleets were now heavily engaged, but the enemy were rapidly becoming more indistinct in the gathering haze, which was soon to end the action.
>
> . . . It is a curious sensation being under heavy fire at a long range. The time of flight seems more like 30 minutes than the 30 or so seconds that it actually is. A great rippling gush of flame breaks out from the enemy's guns some miles away, and then follows a pause, during which one can reflect that somewhere in that great 'no-man's-land' 2 or 3 tons of metal and explosive are hurtling towards one. The mountainous splashes which announce the arrival of each successive salvo rise simultaneously to an immense height. One or two salvoes fell short of us early in the action and the remainder, I suppose, must have gone over as I did not see them . . . The enemy, however, clearly received some punishment as two battlecruisers, which were rather closer than were their other ships, were engaged by us and by most ships of the rear squadron at one time or another, and we saw at least two of our salvoes hit, after which the enemy battlecruisers dropped astern, to all appearances badly damaged. The warm red glow of a 'hit' is easily distinguishable from the flash of a salvo, and is extremely pleasant to look upon.

When the British gunnery officers lost sight of the German battle line, they opened up on the unfortunate

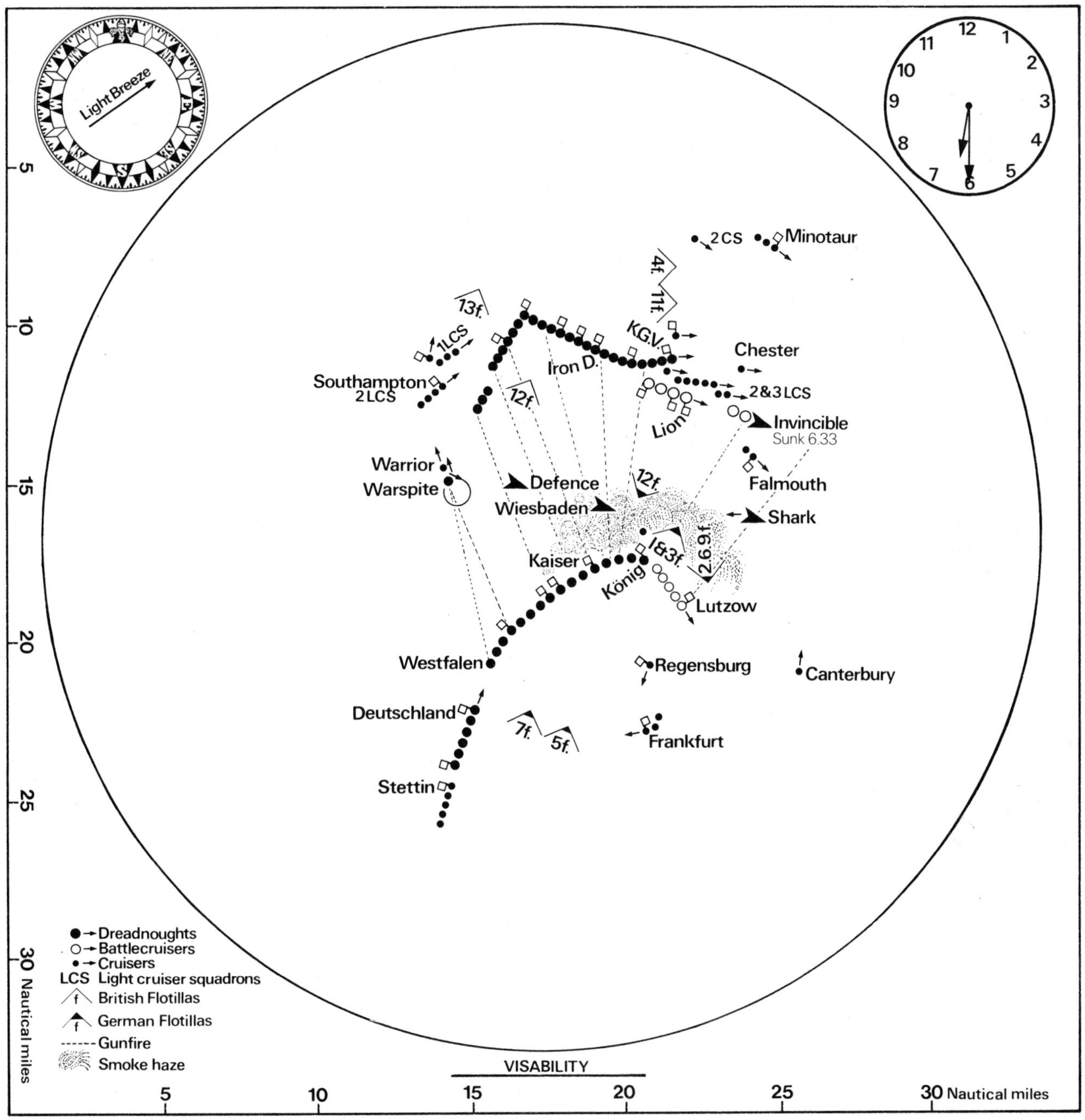

Wiesbaden which was still afloat. Not all the British ships were happy at the prospect of using the *Wiesbaden* as a target. Aboard the *Iron Duke*, 'They all had a sort of sympathetic feeling it was bad luck to go on hammering a poor sinking ship', recalled the gunnery officer who had to obtain Jellicoe's reluctant permission before ordering the fleet flagship to open fire. But somehow the *Wiesbaden* stayed afloat, a remarkable tribute to her shipbuilders, although 'ships were shelling her from all sides, weak and isolated as she was, causing fresh devastation every moment.'

The British line was now being led by Hood in the *Invincible*, with Beatty coming on behind. They concentrated on their old enemies, the German battlecruisers. A 'severe and unequal struggle' developed between Hipper's force and the British battlecruisers. At first the British had the advantage of the light, and *Lützow* was badly hit on the bow, setting her on fire and making fire-control impossible. 'A heavy turret was hurled overboard and water poured into the forward compartments, the gunnery control, and the torpedo broadside room. The ship was obviously

settling down by the head and could only steam at fifteen knots.'

The battlecruisers leading the British line were able to keep Hipper's ships under almost continuous observation and fire. On the battlecruiser *Indomitable*, 'The noise of firing now became like a roll of continuous thunder and the horizon to port was filled with whirling sheets of flame.' The *Invincible* had the leading enemy ships engaged as the range closed. Her gunnery officer, Commander Dannreuther, later reported: 'Fire was opened at the enemy at about 8,000 yards, and several hits were observed . . .' Admiral Hood hailed the control officer in the control-top from the fore bridge: 'Your firing is very good, keep at it as quickly as you can; every shot is telling!'

> At 6.31 pm the *Derfflinger* fired another salvo at this ship [according to von Hase] . . . for the third time we witnessed the dreadful spectacle that we had already seen in the case of the *Queen Mary* and the *Defence*. As with the other ships there occurred a rapid succession of heavy explosions, masts collapsed, debris was hurled into the air, a gigantic column of black smoke rose towards the sky, and from the parting sections of the ship, coal-dust spurted in all directions. Flames enveloped the ship, fresh explosions followed, and behind this murky shroud our enemy vanished from our sight. I shouted into the telephone, 'Our enemy has blown up!' and above the din of battle a great cheer thundered through the ship.

Commander Dannreuther was one of the only six survivors from a complement of 1,037 picked up from the wreck:

> The ship had been hit several times by heavy shells, but no appreciable damage had been done when at 6.34 pm a heavy shell struck 'Q' turret and, bursting inside, blew the roof off. This was observed from the control-top. Almost immediately following there was a tremendous explosion amidships indicating that 'Q' magazine had blown up.

The visibility was so bad during this stage of the battle that in the foretop of the *Indomitable*, which was bringing up the rear of the 3rd Battle Squadron, the sinking of Hood's flagship had gone unnoticed:

> Then upon the starboard bow I saw two ends of a ship standing perpendicularly above the water, the ship appearing to have broken in two halves amidships, each half resting on the bottom. My gunlayer took her for a hun, and the crew cheered wildly, but I could read the name *Invincible* on the stern and so knew better. Four or five survivors were clinging to

6.30 INVINCIBLE BLEW UP.

Log of HMS Inflexible.

The last minutes of Admiral Hood (inset) and his flagship – steaming into action (far left) and (left) enveloped in flames after being hit by the *Derfflinger*. The 18,000-ton battlecruiser – victor of the Falklands Islands battle – was split into two halves by the explosion. These came to rest vertically on the shallow North Sea floor (below). The destroyer HMS *Badger* rescues survivors as Jellicoe's battle line steams past in the background.

floating wreckage; I have never seen anything more splendid than these few cheering us as we raced by them.

The British destroyer *Badger* had also assumed that the wrecked ship was German and had an armed guard ready. One of the rescue party was struck by the fact that when they picked up the gunnery officer 'the commander was really marvellously self-possessed. I can hardly understand to this day how a man, after going through what he had, could come on board us from the raft as cheerily as if he was simply joining a new ship in the ordinary course of events. He laughed at the armed guard and assured us that he hadn't a scratch on his body, and that he had merely – as he put it – stepped into the water when the foretop came down.'

Hipper's battlecruisers had scored another spectacular victory but this could not reverse the increasingly desperate situation now facing the High Seas Fleet. Heavily outnumbered and outgunned, the situation was made worse because his battle line had become extended to over ten miles. Scheer was facing the British Fleet's overwhelming firepower, concentrated into a 6-mile arc of deadly fire.

The predicament of the German Fleet was revealed in the reports of the leading ship, the battlecruiser *Lützow*, Hipper's flagship. Already damaged from the earlier action with Beatty, Captain Harder's position was rapidly becoming untenable:

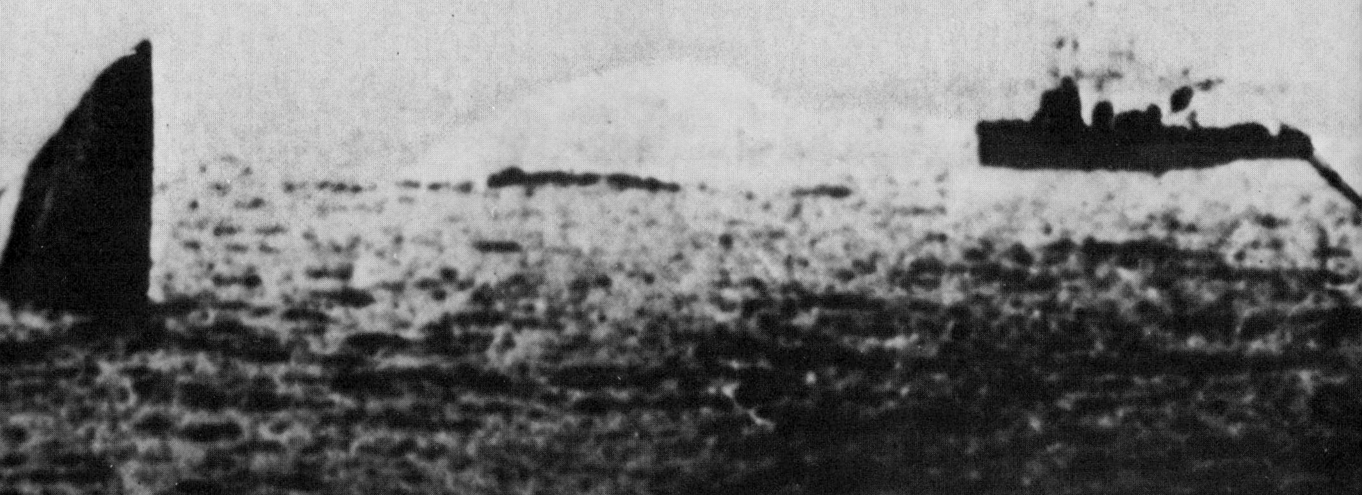

The immense firepower of Jellicoe's Dreadnoughts (below HMS *Royal Oak* firing a broadside) forced Scheer to extricate his ships by making a battle turn under cover of the smoke. In the poor visibility only a few of Jellicoe's ships spotted the move – and it was not immediately reported to the C-in-C. Within minutes, the first great clash fizzled out as the Germans disappeared.

Lützow came into heavy fire from the starboard from the enemy which could be seen only very infrequently, so that we could not return the fire very often. Our guns were interrupted because the right-hand gun of 'A' turret was hit right in front of its sight and was useless; the right side of turret 'B' was hit through the rear. This destroyed the loading machinery and the right-hand gun hoists were also put out of action. A cordite fire put the whole turret out of action for a time.

A hit between turrets 'D' and 'C' destroyed the electricity supply cables for turret 'D'; and this had then to be manually operated. The command telephone system was knocked out and although for a time the firing control instructions were given through the voice-pipe, this had to be abandoned because of the danger of gas coming through from 'B' turret. However through the use of head-sets firing control was continued.

The devastation on board was described by a crew member who had been ordered to assist in the fore dressing-station, but who on arrival found that it had been already hit. 'It was impossible to remain as the doctors had all been killed and the numerous wounded who had been taken there to await treatment were nothing more than arms and legs caused by shells penetrating the hull of the ship.'

The *Lützow* finally extricated herself from this very serious situation at 6.45 pm. Under cover of the smoke-screen she hauled out of line and changed course from south-west to west, away from the enemy fire.

6.48 THE ENEMY WAS OBSERVED TURNING AWAY TO SOUTHWARD.

Gunnery Report HMS Benbow
– 4th Battle Squadron.

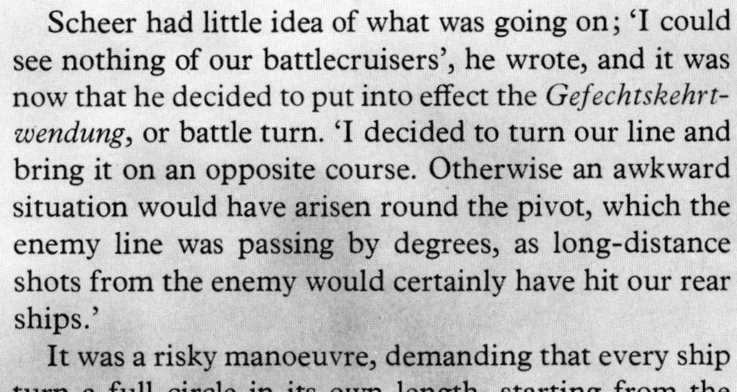

Scheer had little idea of what was going on; 'I could see nothing of our battlecruisers', he wrote, and it was now that he decided to put into effect the *Gefechtskehrtwendung*, or battle turn. 'I decided to turn our line and bring it on an opposite course. Otherwise an awkward situation would have arisen round the pivot, which the enemy line was passing by degrees, as long-distance shots from the enemy would certainly have hit our rear ships.'

It was a risky manoeuvre, demanding that every ship turn a full circle in its own length, starting from the rear ship. Although the fleet had practised it many times on manoeuvres, it now had to be performed in poor visibility and under heavy enemy fire. There was a serious risk of collision and total chaos in the battle line. Scheer resolved to take the risk, for his alternative was destruction. The signal was given and in minutes the whole line had reversed course and was steaming away from the British battle line.

> The swing round was conducted in excellent style [Scheer reported]. At our peace manoeuvres great importance was always attached to their being carried out in a curved line and every means employed to ensure the working of signals. The trouble spent was now well repaid; the battlecruisers were liberated from their cramped position and enabled to steam away south . . . The torpedoboats too, on the leeside of the fire, had room to move to the attack and advance.

Scheer now headed off to the south with his battle fleet still intact; only Hipper's force and Behncke's 3rd Battle Squadron had suffered serious damage. The other two squadrons of battleships never came within range of the British fire. The first clash of the titanic fleets was over.

6.55 CAN YOU SEE ANY ENEMY BATTL

C-in-C to Beatty.

REPLY: NO.

The gamble of the *Gefechtskehrtwendung* manoeuvre extricated the High Seas Fleet from the brink of disaster, and Scheer realized that he had gained an important initiative. If Jellicoe had anticipated and followed his turn it 'would have greatly impeded our movements'. As a leading analyst of the battle, Admiral Dewar, wrote: 'When Scheer hoisted the signal for the battle turn, the British plan collapsed like a house of cards, but it left the High Seas Fleet in a very vulnerable and unenviable position.' But Jellicoe did not immediately realize what was happening.

When the Germans disappeared from sight at 6.42 pm Jellicoe like most of his commanders assumed that this was due to 'merely the thickening of the mist'. The *Iron Duke* had only fired nine salvoes in an action that one observer recorded was like 'a game of hide-and-seek, the enemy at times being enveloped in mist and smoke, appearing out of it for only short intervals like rabbits running from one hole to another.' Nearly ten minutes passed before the British Commander-in-Chief appreciated 'that there must be some other reason'. Once again there was a paralysing breakdown of communication in the Grand Fleet. The enemy turnabout had been spotted as it occurred by many ships in the British line, including the *Falmouth* and *Canterbury* whose prime responsibility as part of the scouting light cruiser screen was to report continuously on the enemy movements. But, inexplicably, Jellicoe received no report which could enlighten him as to why the Germans had suddenly vanished. Records from the *Iron Duke*'s own gunnery transmitting-room indicate that the flagship knew that the enemy had altered course by nearly 180 degrees; but the vital information was not relayed to the bridge, nor did the other captains who saw it communicate their observations to the flagship. At 6.44 pm Jellicoe ordered a cautious turn towards the direction in which the enemy disappeared. To carry this out as rapidly as possible the fleet turned in succession, which split it into its six component squadrons again. When after nearly ten minutes the enemy had still not reappeared, Jellicoe realized that Scheer's alteration of course must have been more drastic than he had previously anticipated, and he ordered a further change of course to the south. At the same time, at 6.55 pm, he signalled Beatty who was at the head of his line, 'Can you see any enemy battleships?' To which the prompt and frustrating reply, 'No', was flashed back from the *Lion*.

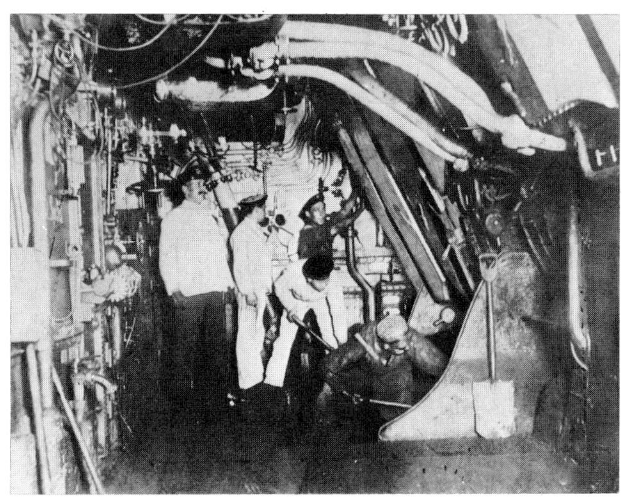

It now became clear that Scheer must have drawn farther away to the west, but Jellicoe hesitated to turn his ships after the retreating enemy in the 'resolute and immediate chase' that was the only effective counter to the *Gefechtskehrtwendung*. He knew that the Germans had practised such a manoeuvre, but the British C-in-C's analysis had convinced him that it was part of a German plan to lure him over mines and towards a torpedo and submarine attack.

Out in front of the fleet Beatty had raced ahead with the battlecruisers at 25 knots to probe the other wing of the enemy positions. But this attempt to regain contact was interrupted for nearly ten minutes whilst Beatty, for reasons which have never been satisfactorily explained, turned to starboard shortly after 6.50 pm, continued with the turn a full circle, followed round dutifully by his four battlecruisers. This circle was to take him some 5,000–8,000 yards farther away from the course of the German battleships. This added vital minutes to the delay in re-sighting the German Fleet.

During this lull in the action an incident occurred which, Jellicoe wrote, 'was an indication of the spirit prevailing in the fleet, of which it is impossible to

IPS?

Scheer's brilliantly executed '*Gefechtskehrtwendung*' which his battle fleet had rigorously practised (below) had taken Scheer away from Jellicoe at 19 knots. Vital minutes passed before the C-in-C, after signalling Beatty, realized what had happened. Scheer's escape now depended on the German stokers and engine room staff (below left).

'All around shells were bursting with deafening explosions; exhalations of poisonous gas floated about, bringing death to those who fully breathed them in and in any case violent coughing and sickness. The men's faces and hands had been stained a dark yellow by the gases from the guns and they had become completely deaf. . . . The ship from bow to stern was a smoking heap of ruins. *Stoker Zenne, SMS* Wiesbaden.

speak too highly.' The *Acasta*, crippled earlier in the action, passed by on the engaged side of the battleships, flying 'out of control' and with her engines disabled and 'The ship's company was observed to be cheering each ship as she passed.'

After a further quarter of an hour, when the enemy still did not reappear, an immediate turn to the west was obviously needed. But Jellicoe's decision not to risk close pursuit seemed justified when shortly before 7 pm the *Marlborough*, leading the last division, signalled, 'Urgent, have been struck by a mine or torpedo, but not certain which.' Jellicoe's fears about a possible trap were reinforced almost at once by a report from the *King George V* leading the wing division, 'There is a submarine ahead of you.' It was one of many false reports made during the battle. Although no submarines were within a hundred miles, the Grand Fleet was still suffering from 'submarine-itis'.

In fact the *Marlborough* had been struck by a torpedo (the only capital ship on the British side to be so hit during the battle) during a torpedo-boat attack that developed around the crippled *Wiesbaden*. The 3rd German Torpedo-boat Flotilla had originally been ordered by Scheer to attack the head of the British battle line and to make smoke to cover the turn-away, but after approaching to within 7,000 yards they had veered off under heavy fire.

Isolated torpedo-boats of the 3rd Flotilla then attempted to rescue the *Wiesbaden*'s crew under devastating fire. The attack was boldly pressed home, watched by an officer on board the *Colossus*: 'It shows how one end of a line is dependent on another for support that the enemy small craft were nearer to us although they were attacking the 1st Battle Squadron. We opened fire on them with 4-inch guns and 'A' turret, and claim to have sunk one at least, and they had already fired their torpedoes when they came down on the tail of the line like a swarm of hornets.' The attack ended when the *V48*, which had pressed in closer than the others, was sunk by heavy gunfire. The other torpedo-boats then disappeared back through the mist and abandoned the *Wiesbaden*.

The *Wiesbaden* was once again to be instrumental in affecting the course of the action when Goodenough in the *Southampton* pressed in on the last sighted position of the German line. The battered German light cruiser attracted his squadron's attention, only to reveal that he was once again facing the enemy battleships, which had suddenly reversed course again: 'Enemy's turn ESE was reported by *Southampton* at 7.04 pm. The squadron now came under heavy fire from the German Battle Fleet and it became necessary to return to the rear of our battle line. Between 6.55 and 7.05 pm water and spray was constantly coming on board the *Southampton* from enemy's salvoes which were dropping all round the ship.'

The *Southampton*'s report, hard on a signal received minutes earlier from Beatty, 'Enemy are to westward', indicated that the Germans were turning round again. The subsequent sighting of enemy torpedo-boats heading for the British lines confirmed the surprising fact that Scheer was once more steaming towards the British Fleet.

It is one of the enigmas of the battle that twenty minutes after successfully executing a desperate manoeuvre to extricate his fleet from destruction, Scheer signalled for another *Gefechtskehrtwendung*, which brought the German battle line back into the devastating fire of the British Fleet. In his written report to the Emperor, Scheer tried to justify the move:

> It was as yet too early to assume 'night cruising order'. The enemy could have compelled us to fight before dark and could have prevented us exercising our initiative, and finally he could have cut off our retreat to the German Bight. There was only one way of avoiding this: to deal the enemy a second blow by again advancing, regardless of consequences, and to bring all torpedo-boats to attack. This manoeuvre would necessarily have the effect of surprising the enemy and upsetting his plans for the rest of the day and, if the attack was powerful enough, of facilitating our extricating ourselves for the night.

Scheer's explanations after the battle clearly attempt to present his astonishing decision in the best tactical light. He later admitted in his oral report to the Kaiser that 'In peacetime . . . one would have denied that I had

7.00 ENEMY ARE TO WESTWARD

Beatty to C-in-C.

Twenty minutes after he had extricated his fleet from defeat Admiral Reinhard Scheer (below) gave the order for another 'about turn'. The explanation for this incredible decision – Scheer claimed it was inspired by Nelson's tactics – was that he believed Jellicoe to be further south, so that the High Seas Fleet could escape across the rear of the British. As his flagship SMS *Friedrich der Grosse* (bottom) in the middle of the German line came about he found that his fleet was heading straight back into the British lines.

any ability to lead a fleet!' The Official German Naval History sought to draw comparisons with Nelson's tactical decisions at Trafalgar, 'I think it will surprise and confound the enemy! They won't know what I am about.' But in the vastly different circumstances of Jutland, a close engagement with the British at that stage could only have brought destruction to the High Seas Fleet.

It is more probable that Scheer was unaware that Jellicoe's battleships were still in front of him. Their last reported position at 6.45 pm had inaccurately placed the British ships about eight miles south-eastward of its actual position. Bödicker's 2nd Scouting Group, after their recent hammering, had only made a half-hearted reconnaissance and Scheer perhaps presumed that by reversing course he might slip across behind the rear of the Grand Fleet as it searched for him to the south-west. He also claimed that his novel move would 'succour the hard-pressed *Wiesbaden*', but his real intention according to Weizacker, his Flag-Lieutenant, was 'to leg it for home'. It was reported that the Commander-in-Chief told his staff at the time, 'If I am chucked out of the Navy because of this, it's all one to me.' According to Weizacker, Scheer also remarked shortly after the battle, 'The thing just happened – as the virgin said when she got a baby.'

Whatever the real reason behind Scheer's order, it was he, rather than Jellicoe, who was surprised and found his plans upset when his leading ships once more ran headlong into the full fire of the British Grand Fleet.

For the leading divisions of British battleships, the sudden reappearance of the enemy came as a surprise. During the break in the action some ships had given their turret crews the opportunity to come up for a breather, and as shooting started again there was a rush back to magazines and handling rooms.

For Hipper's damaged battlecruisers at the forefront of the line the renewed action could not have come at a worse time. The *Lützow* was trying to limp away escorted by her destroyers, and the *Derfflinger* under Captain Hartog had assumed temporary leadership of the damaged squadron. When firing broke out again

Hipper was in the process of transferring his flag from the *Lützow* to a torpedo-boat which was drawn up alongside. An eye-witness reported that Hipper 'seemed entirely unconcerned with all the clamour and horror about him and leaped lightly from the side of the battlecruiser to the forecastle of the torpedo-boat.' 'Get away to *Seydlitz* as fast as you can so that I can take over command again', was Hipper's order. While *G39* was steering away *Lützow* 'was hit badly in the second forward turret. Several charges caught fire and tongues of flame leaped up. And now we saw the other ships of the 1st Half Flotilla and two ships of the 12th Half Flotilla belching forth smoke to form a screen between the wounded ship and the enemy.'

When *G39* had raced across to the *Seydlitz* Hipper found that a huge hole in her bows and flooding made it impracticable to employ her as a flagship, moreover her wireless had been shot away. Next in line was the *Von der Tann*, but with all her turrets out of action she was a helpless decoy for the enemy guns, so the hectic chase under heavy gunfire continued as *G39* searched for the *Moltke* whilst Hipper's staff argued that one of the Königs would be a better choice for a new flagship.

The situation was becoming desperate for the German battlecruisers. 'We had experienced all the wild splendours of a sea action. Now we were not to be spared its terrors', wrote von Hase, whose ship the *Derfflinger* was now the leading ship of the High Seas Fleet:

7.13 SCHLACHTKREUZER RAN AN DEN FEIND, VOLL EINSETZEN.

Scheer to Hipper.

Faced once again with the concentrated might of the Grand Fleet, Scheer gave orders to 'Charge the Enemy, regardless of losses'; Captain Hartog bravely headed the *Derfflinger* (left) and the three damaged battlecruisers into the British guns.

The enemy ships were again at the extreme limit of visibility. Now they opened a lively fire, and I saw that the ship I had selected as a target was firing full salvoes from four double turrets. The light round the enemy cleared for a moment and I saw distinctly that they were battleships of the heaviest class with 13.5-inch guns. Fire was now flashing from them ... The van of our fleet was shut in by the semi-circle of the enemy. We were in a regular death trap.

By 7.10 pm the whole of the British Fleet was in action with the enemy, 'a marvellously impressive spectacle as salvo after salvo rolled out along the line.'

In response to this concentrated barrage the German line was 'only able to reply feebly to the British fire which very soon became effective. Only a few shells fell round the *Hercules* and the *Agincourt* and only the *Colossus*, closest to the enemy and leading the 5th Division, was hit.' The fire was building up to a crescendo, creating a serious problem for Behncke's leading battleship division:

> Some ships of this division and also some of the 6th, had to stop engines and even go astern, owing to the whole line being checked. For some time therefore they lay almost without making any way, bunched together so forming an admirable target for the enemy's guns. The *König* had to turn to the SE to bring her guns to bear on a course parallel to the enemy, and it already looked as if serious casualties would be unavoidable during the further course of action.

With the head of the German battle line being remorselessly pushed round by the heavy fire and the virtual halting of the middle of his line, Scheer was threatened by the risk of collisions and the loss of his battle formation. Every second brought the German ships closer to catastrophe as the British fire reached farther and farther down Scheer's line. On board the *Helgoland* in Seaman Stumpf's turret, which was unable to fire the starboard midship guns because they were on the disengaged side, the tension had reached breaking point:

> We had nothing to do so we yelled and carried on without restraint. Deep in our hearts we were all afraid and tried to still our fear by making noise. Once more I put my ear to the deck to listen to the crash, crash, crash. Suddenly I got a terrific slap. All at once everything became still. It was 7.19 pm. The ship had been hit. 'Thank God!' someone called out, 'now we'll get leave to go home.' He was silenced at once. 'Shut up! Who knows how many got killed.' 'A hit in compartment 15 above the waterline. No dead,' reported the bridge at last. Everyone felt relieved. Then we began to discuss how long it would take to repair, whether we would get leave, and so on.

(Opposite) Scheer's second battle turn brought the High Seas Fleet back into the range of the Grand Fleet. Rear Admiral Paul Behncke (left) in the *König* took the brunt of the devastating fire before Scheer signalled another about turn. It was the crisis for the High Seas Fleet as the danger of collision threatened the manoeuvre.

> The shells rained down like hail on the outside armour while splinters dashed themselves to pieces against the armoured sides of the ship . . . We fired very slowly with deliberation while the Kaiser class ships in front of us shot like mad.

The damage was piling up on the other German battleships as damage control parties struggled to control flooding and suppress fires. The head of the battle line was struggling to manoeuvre and taking the worst punishment; the *König* was hit and Behncke wounded. The *Grosser Kurfürst* was damaged and so was Scheer's flagship, *Friedrich der Grosse*: 'The fire directed on our line by the enemy concentrated chiefly on the battlecruisers and the 5th Division. The ships suffered all the more as they could see little of the enemy beyond the flash of fire at each round, while they themselves apparently offered a good target to the enemy guns.' Now it was clear to Scheer that desperate measures were needed. Realizing that another *Gefechtskehrtwendung* would not by itself be sufficient this time, he decided to sacrifice his battlecruisers in a bid to cover the withdrawal of his battleships. At 7.13 pm he ordered '*Schlachtkreuzer ran an den Feind, voll einsetzen*' ('Battlecruisers at the enemy, give it everything'). It was a desperate order received with stoic resolution in the badly damaged battlecruisers. Led by the *Derfflinger*, they set off at top speed on what many of their captains believed was a 'death-ride' into the enemy guns. As they did so, Hipper's torpedoboat had just run alongside the *Moltke* and the Admiral was at that very moment attempting to transfer his flag. It was nearly two hours before he finally managed to resume command of his battered squadron. As they sped away from him, supported by the massed torpedoboats to press the attack close to the enemy lines, Hipper must have wondered whether he would see them survive the desperate charge on the iron ring of British gunpower. Scheer reported to the Kaiser that their conduct was 'especially deserving of the highest praise. Although a number of the guns were unable to fire and some of the ships were severely damaged, they nevertheless advanced recklessly towards the enemy.'

Captain Hartog's official report barely summarizes the spirit of self-sacrifice with which the German battlecruisers faced the might of the Grand Fleet: 'Order from the Fleet Commander, "Charge the enemy". We headed towards the enemy line with the utmost speed. *Derfflinger* got heavy fire from both sides. At a distance of 8,000 metres a new force had come up from the south-east.' (These were Beatty's battlecruisers which had closed up.) Von Hase's vivid testimony stands as a memorial to the courage of the four battlecruisers' crews: 'We were steaming at full speed into this inferno, offering a splendid target to the enemy while they were still hard to make out . . . Salvo after salvo fell around us, hit after hit struck our ship. They were stirring minutes. Hitherto I had continued to fire with all my turrets but at 7.13 pm a serious catastrophe occurred. A 13.5-inch shell pierced the armour of Caesar turret.' Minutes later, according to Engineer-Lieutenant Ismail, '"D" turret was penetrated from above by a shell which burst inside the top flat killing everyone there. Flames arose from both turrets and water was immediately pumped into them to prevent the fire from reaching the magazines. There were 120 men and an officer in each turret and all except one man were either killed by the British fire or drowned when the water was pumped in. Fires broke out in other parts of the ship.'

It was the same desperate story from each of the German battlecruisers, the closer they got to the British, the more they suffered. Then almost when the *Derfflinger*'s destruction seemed imminent, Scheer sent a signal that ended the charge, and the battlecruisers headed back from the devastating fire.

Although they came out of the ordeal badly damaged with the *Derfflinger* fighting fires for a further hour, and the *Seydlitz* already sinking by the bows with flames 'as high as houses' leaping from a damaged turret, the survival of the four German battlecruisers was a tribute to their construction – a vindication of Tirpitz's insistence on armour rather than hitting power. Their heroic charge had played an important part in giving Scheer the vital cover he needed to execute a third *Gefechtskehrtwendung*.

The crucial minutes required for this battle turn marked the greatest point of crisis in the battle for the

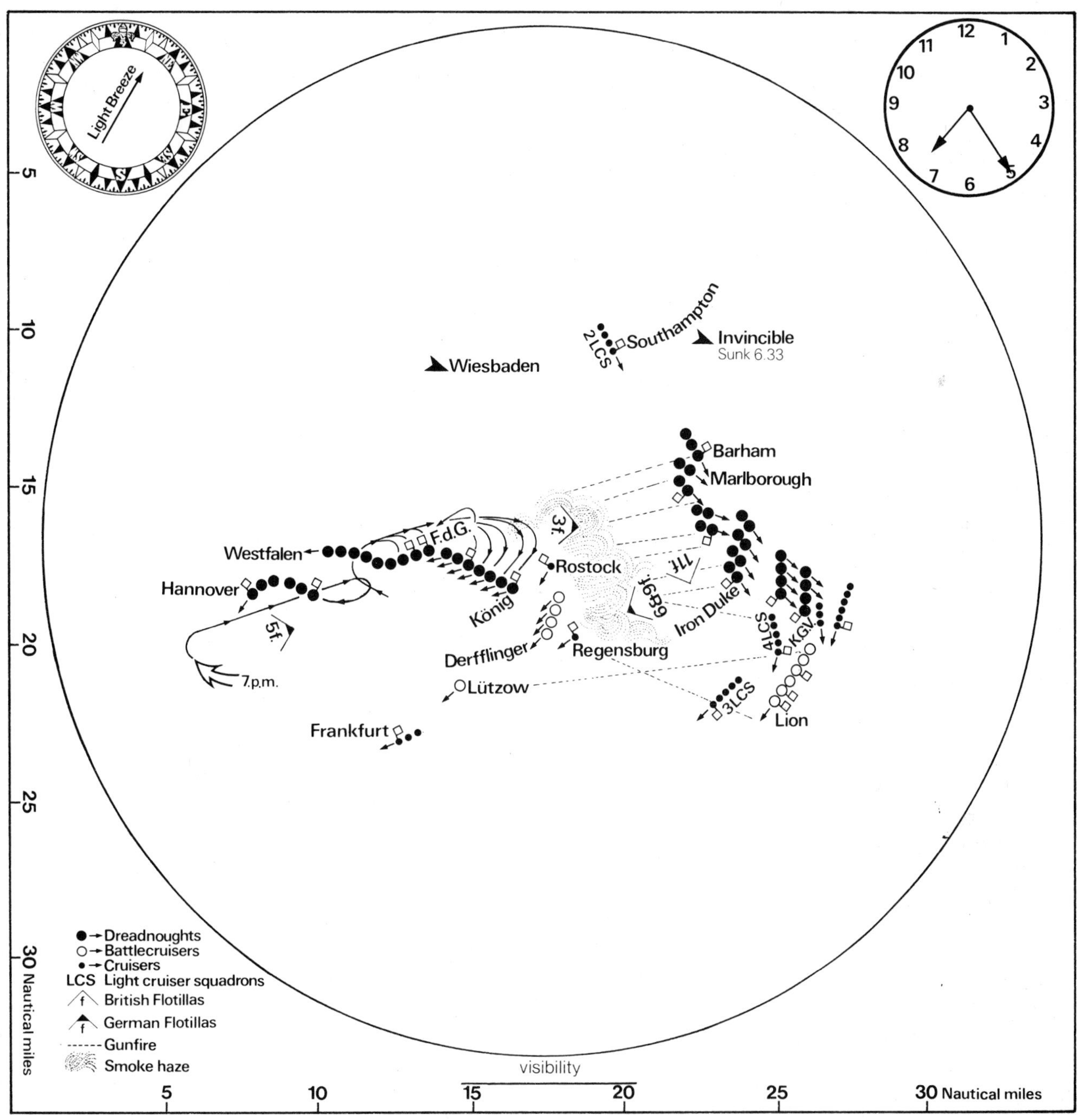

High Seas Fleet. If the 'death-ride' of the battle-cruisers and the massed destroyer attack could not hold off the enemy, then Scheer knew he faced a rout that would make Trafalgar look like a skirmish. The disorganized state of the battle line very nearly brought about disaster without the aid of British shells. According to the Official German Record, 'For several perilous minutes the ships of the 5th and 6th Divisions and the fleet flagship were consequently proceeding at slow speed very close to one another and almost in line abreast, and again it was only the seamanship and splendid tactical training of the admirals and captains that prevented collisions.' Scheer had to order his flagship *Friedrich der Grosse* out of the line to make its turn to port in order to make room for the other divisions to complete the turn without colliding. Even ten minutes later when, according to Scheer 'the line was for the third time swung round on to a westerly course', it was still under heavy fire. All semblance of an effective battle line had been lost and it was the torpedo-boat attack and smoke-screens that finally saved Scheer. The British firing gradually died away,

Scheer's third battle turn was nearly disastrous because of the ragged state of his line. A massed torpedo-boat attack and the cover given by the battlecruisers enabled him to retreat. The price was heavy. SMS *Seydlitz* (below) was on fire from stem to stern, sinking and only able to stay afloat by the supreme skill of her damage control teams. The *Lützow* had already dropped out of action in a sinking condition and early the following morning she foundered. Her crew were rescued by torpedo-boat *V45* (inset).

even though Beatty's battlecruisers were able to keep the rear of the German Fleet under fire until 7.35 pm. Once again the crews of the High Seas Fleet were hardly able to believe their good fortune in surviving the concentrated salvoes of the British battleships.

Scheer was now tactically beaten and his ships were rushing in confused retreat. The British were for a few minutes presented with their chance of achieving a complete victory but Jellicoe did not seize this opportunity to finish off the High Seas Fleet.

7.20 SUBDIVISIONS SEPARATELY ALTER COURSE IN SUCCESSION TWO POINTS AWAY FROM ENEMY PRESERVING THEIR FORMATION.

C-in-C to Battle Fleet.

7.22 PREPARE TO ATTACK THE THE ENEMY.

Jellicoe's decision not to pursue Scheer spared the Germans a humiliating rout. A ruthless British attack would at the very least have finished off the German battlecruisers. But Jellicoe's natural caution was justified by the simple fact that he did not have a clear picture of what was going on. Visibility was deteriorating rapidly and had been reduced even further by the thick blanket of smoke-screens laid by the enemy destroyers. The British C-in-C was also let down, yet again, by his reconnaissance ships. Even Goodenough's 2nd Light Cruiser Squadron this time unaccountably failed to report Scheer's change of course. As late as 7.32 pm Jellicoe still assumed that the High Seas Fleet was near at hand when he signalled to Commodore Le Mesurier, who was leading the 4th Light Cruiser Squadron, 'Do not go too near the enemy's battle fleet.' At this time the rear of the enemy battleships was some ten miles away and heading west at nearly 19 knots.

The German torpedo-boats were also highly successful in forcing the British ships to turn away at the critical moment. The decisive attacks came in three waves.

First, the 11th Half Flotilla raced out shortly before 7.15 pm and fired eleven torpedoes at extreme range at the 1st Division of British battleships, led by *King George V*. Jellicoe ordered Admiral Jerram to turn his ships 45 degrees *away* immediately, in order to comb the enemy torpedo tracks. Using the 'Preparative' signal, the rest of the fleet was ordered to turn away by half that amount in anticipation of more torpedoes. Shortly afterwards this was increased to the full 45 degrees then prescribed by the Battle Orders. The enemy attacks came at the worst possible time for the British, as their own destroyer flotillas had not yet caught up with the battleships' rapid manoeuvres and only Le Mesurier's five light cruisers were near enough to lead the counter-attack.

The second attack was made by seventeen boats of the 3rd Flotilla against the heavy concentration of battleships at the rear. This was broken up by the 12th British Flotilla after only one torpedo had been fired.

EDO VESSELS OF

When the German ships disappeared for the second time Jellicoe confronted a mass attack from German torpedo-boat flotillas (below). Jellicoe sent in the British destroyers to foil the move and the battle line turned away preparatory to dodging any torpedoes. This manoeuvre gave Scheer the time to make good his second escape.

Ten minutes later came the third wave. The thirteen boats of the 6th and 9th Flotillas made a determined attack against the fierce opposition of Le Mesurier's cruisers. When the German torpedo-boats finally broke through the barrier of mist and smoke, they met the full might of the Grand Fleet. The battleships opened up on the German destroyers and the *Conqueror* was in the thick of it:

> At 7.26 pm we opened fire on attacking German destroyers, which employed the tactics of turning away as we fired and turning back again as soon as the salvo landed, the result for us being like trying to hit snipe with buckshot. But our last salvo landed in the smoke made by one particular boat and in the midst of the splash and smoke there appeared to be debris, and when the smoke cleared away we saw an overturned destroyer where the target had been.

The destroyer *S35* had been sunk, two others badly damaged: 21 torpedoes finally reached the British divisions, and the battleships easily avoided them.

The torpedo attacks did no damage, but by turning away to avoid them the British battleships opened up the range by 3,000 yards. Scheer was given precious minutes which he badly needed to make his escape. Admiral Drax (who was aboard the *Lion*) wrote many years later, 'The Grand Fleet was, due to short visibility, about to break off the action and probably lose the best chance it ever had of achieving a decisive victory. I remember thinking then that I was witnessing a regrettable movement which I should remember to the end of my days.' The decision to comb the enemy torpedoes by turning away was to become the centre of the Jutland controversy.

Jellicoe's determination to play safe was entirely consistent with the cautious tactics on which he based the *Grand Fleet Battle Orders*. A turn away was marginally safer than a turn towards the torpedoes, and Jellicoe sought to avoid the 30 per cent hit ratio which calculations showed destroyers could achieve when they fired torpedoes at a line of battleships. It was not realized until the battle that tracks made by

7.47 URGENT. SUBMIT VAN OF BATTLESHIPS
FOLLOW BATTLECRUISERS.
WE CAN CUT THEM OFF WHOLE
OF ENEMY'S BATTLEFLEET.

Beatty to C-in-C.

By the time that Jellicoe received this signal, the British destroyer flotillas had been withdrawn (below) after breaking up the German attacks. The enemy had disappeared and Beatty was trying to probe to the south-west to locate them. Unfortunately he had not given an accurate position and the C-in-C was uncertain of the course of the High Seas Fleet.

German torpedoes were far more visible than had been expected. The decision to turn away was based on purely theoretical analysis, but in the circumstances that faced him, with the enemy torpedo-boats disappearing into the thick smoke and possible further attacks being prepared, and without the slightest idea of what the enemy battle fleet was doing, it was entirely reasonable that he should have adopted the course he did. After all he knew he had an immeasurable advantage: his fleet lay between the Germans and their base.

It was 7.35 pm before Jellicoe judged that the torpedo threat was over and ordered, 'Alter course leading ships together rest in succession to S by W', thereby assuming that this turn back would soon bring him in gunnery range again. It was a cat and mouse game with the British determined to manoeuvre the Germans into a final action. Scheer had in the meantime altered course from west to south-west once he had believed he was clear of the Grand Fleet. But the British were still between him and safety.

Scheer soon found that his new course brought him again in sight of Beatty, who at 7.40 pm reported, 'Enemy bears from me NW by W distance 10–11 miles. My position Lat. 56° 56′ N, Long. 6° 16′ E, course SW. Speed 18 knots.' Unfortunately, Beatty's reported position was wrong, it placed him just two miles away from the battle fleet when Jellicoe calculated that he must be six miles ahead because he was out of sight. But he ordered the fleet into a single line ahead and on to the south-westerly course.

The position was not finally clarified until Beatty's report, made by signal lights, which reached Jellicoe shortly before 8 o'clock, informed him that the leading enemy battleship was bearing north-west by west on a south-westerly course. Scheer was by this time some fifteen miles away so Jellicoe turned his fleet west, but his speed was held to seventeen knots because of the damaged *Marlborough*. Then the situation was thrown into confusion again when he received an urgent wireless signal from Beatty: 'Urgent. Submit van of battleships follow battlecruisers. We can then cut off the whole of enemy's battle fleet.'

Some twenty minutes had in fact elapsed before Beatty had realized that there was a danger of the battle fleet losing contact with the enemy's course and by the time his signal had reached Jellicoe, the *Lion* was over thirteen miles away and out of sight. Nevertheless Jellicoe signalled to Admiral Jerram on the *King George V*, to take the 1st Battle Squadron

ahead to join the battlecruisers. This became almost impossible because Beatty had neglected to give his last position, so Jerram headed in the direction where the battlecruisers had last been seen. In fact this took him on a divergent course away from the German battle fleet.

But Scheer had already altered course to the south and Jellicoe was therefore still on a converging course. Scheer was very concerned that every mile he sailed to the westward put him further from the safety of Germany. 'It had to be taken for granted that the enemy would endeavour to force us to the westward by attacks with strong forces during the hours of dusk and by destroyer attacks during the night, in order to give battle at daybreak.' To avoid this he hoped to 'succeed in checking the enemy's enveloping movement and reaching the Horns Reef before them'.

Beatty made contact again with the head of the German line at 8.09 pm. *Calliope* and the 4th Light Cruiser Squadron had already headed in to attack:

> We turned on to a course parallel to them after closing to about 8,500 yards to fire a torpedo. We were not fired at previous to turning, possibly because they could not make us out as friend or enemy, but they quickly proceeded to rectify the error as soon as we turned and got our range, straddling us before we got our submerged torpedo-tube flooded. Having fired our torpedo, we turned and proceeded full speed, zigzagging two points each way on an easterly course to join our own ships, which were by this time out of sight.
>
> We were in sight of the German battleships for perhaps ten minutes and under fire during this time from two Kaiser class battleships and one Helgoland, whose shooting was very accurate, and only our high speed and zigzagging saved us from annihilation . . . We were hit five times in all, three of which did serious damage to personnel.

At the rear of the German line, Admiral Napier had succeeded in bringing the 3rd Light Cruiser Squadron within range of the German 4th Scouting Group. The *Yarmouth* was soon in action:

> We were ordered to sweep to the westward to locate the head of the enemy's line and were in the process of spreading from the *Falmouth* when at 8.20 pm five enemy light cruisers were observed bearing NNW. They were followed by three battlecruisers.

PRESENT COURSE OF FLEET IS WEST.

Beatty to C-in-C.

Shortly after this sighting the battlecruisers once more attacked the head of Scheer's line supported by the 4th Light Cruiser Squadron, which included HMS *Caroline* (below).

We formed a single line and engaged the enemy light cruisers at about 7,000 yards. Their salvoes were all short, and ours may have been as bad for it was impossible to spot under the almost hopeless conditions of light. The enemy drew off and we never saw them again.

Beatty steamed towards the noises of gunfire and at 8.23 pm sighted his old opponents again and opened fire on the German battlecruisers steaming on the wing of Scheer's battle line. A shell knocked out the *Seydlitz*'s remaining turret and for von Hase on the *Derfflinger* it seemed as though the horrors of the engagement an hour earlier might be repeated:

A heavy shell struck 'Anna' turret and bent one of the rails on which the turret revolves, so that it stuck. Our last weapon was snatched from our hands. Then Stukmeister Weber, with great presence of mind, ran out of the turret and, with the help of some petty officers and gun hands cleared away the bent rails with axes and crowbars and put the turret in action again, so that it was again possible

'By 8.26 we were hard at it again at a range of 8,800 yards. By 8.42 they had had enough and drew off, so we ceased firing. Should it be my good fortune to be engaged in another action, I shall take care that only one gramophone is taken into the turret. We had one in the gunhouse and one in the working chamber and during every lull these two were playing simultaneously, each with a different record. The result was one of the real horrors of the war.'
– *Turret Officer HMS* Indomitable.

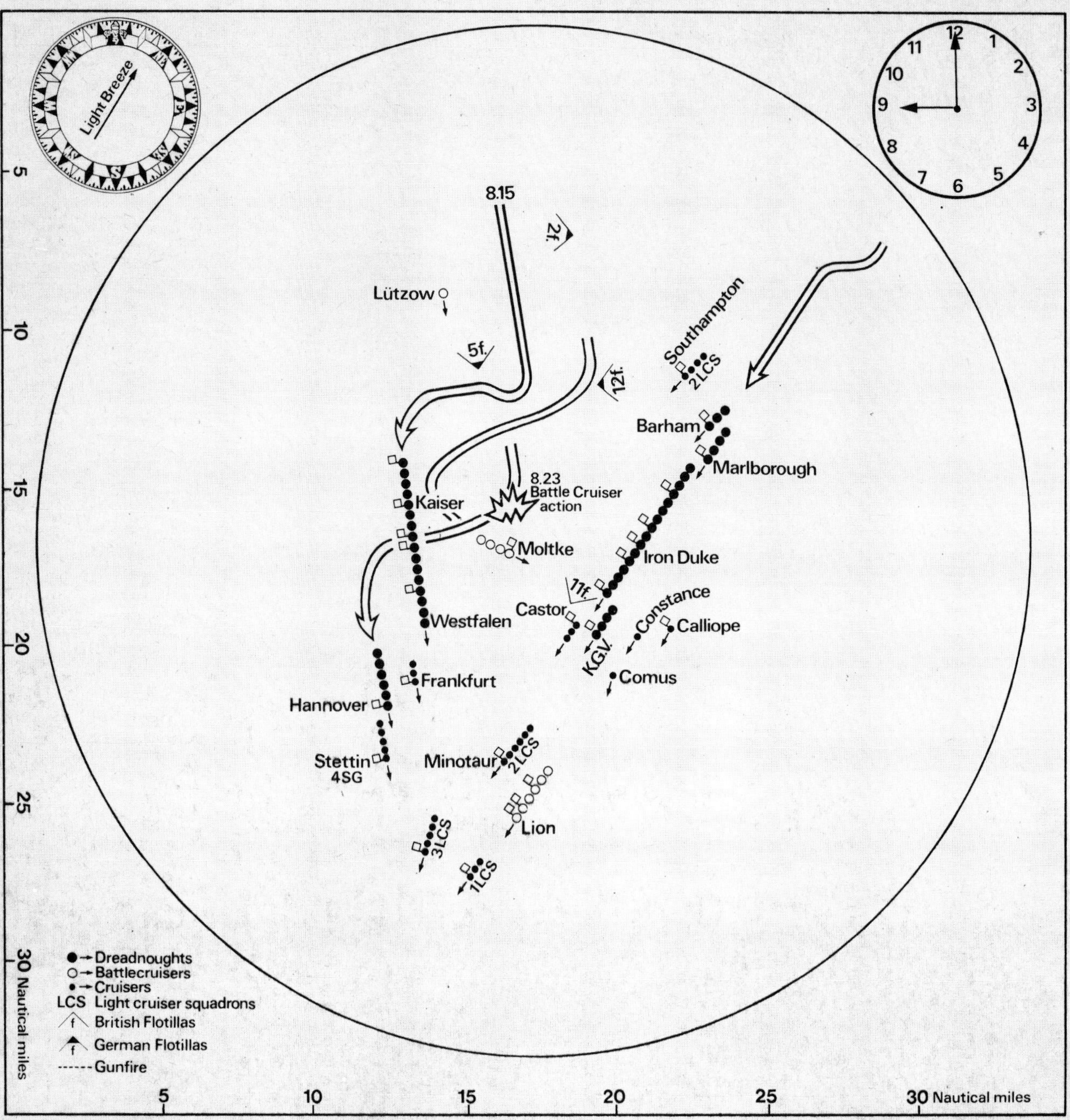

Light Breeze

11 12 1 2 3 4 5 6 7 8 9 10

8.15

2f.

Lützow

5f.

12f.

Southampton

2LCS

Barham

Marlborough

8.23
Battle Cruiser
action

Kaiser

Moltke

Iron Duke

11f.

Castor

Constance

Calliope

Westfalen

KGV.

Comus

Frankfurt

Hannover

Stettin
4SG

Minotaur

2LCS

Lion

3LCS

1LCS

Dreadnoughts
Battlecruisers
Cruisers
LCS Light cruiser squadrons
British Flotillas
German Flotillas
Gunfire

5 10 15 20 25 30 Nautical miles

5 10 15 20 25 30 Nautical miles

(Opposite) Shortly after 8 pm, with the High Seas Fleet edging on to a south-east course for home, the battlecruisers were back in action with Beatty. The remnants of Hipper's squadron, led by the *Moltke*, swerved away, covered by the pre-Dreadnought squadron (inset below) led by SMS *Hanover*. Just before 9 pm, courses converged again when less than 5 miles separated the *Westfalen* from the *King George V*'s squadron (below). But Admiral Jerram (inset), Jellicoe's deputy, refused to fire without orders.

8.28 URGENT. AM ENGAGING ENEMY'S CRUISERS MY POSITION LAT 56 DEG 47'N; LONG 6 DEG 25'E.

HMS Falmouth *to C-in-C.*

to fire the occasional shot . . . It was impossible to observe the splashes. The situation had once more become very uncomfortable. Then help came from the least expected quarter.

Admiral Mauve had courageously pulled his 2nd Squadron of pre-Dreadnoughts out of line and interposed his force between the damaged battlecruisers and the enemy fire.

Mauve's six old battleships lasted somewhat longer than the '5 minutes' that they were expected to stand up to the enemy fire. But at 8.35 pm after being repeatedly hit they were forced to withdraw. But their advance to within 8,000 yards of the British battlecruisers certainly saved the German battlecruisers, which under their cover and a smoke-screen had retreated to the other side of Scheer's battle line. Beatty ceased fire at 8.40 pm when visibility and poor light obscured targets. Nobody realized that this indecisive engagement was the last battle of the war between capital ships.

Whilst this encounter was taking place at the head of the German line, at the rear the *Southampton* and the 2nd Light Cruiser Squadron were beating off a final attack by the German 12th Torpedoboat Flotilla. Under Beatty's pressure Scheer was forced once again to turn to the south-west away from the attack. Minutes later at 8.45 pm the *Caroline* and *Royalist* of the 4th Light Cruiser Squadron, steaming two miles ahead of the *King George V*, sighted three enemy battleships in the twilight. They were in fact the leading pre-Dreadnoughts in Mauve's 1st Battle Squadron joining up again with the head of the enemy line. On the bridge of the *King George V* Jerram hesitated to open fire because he refused to accept that they were definitely German ships. In fact the *Caroline* and *Royalist* had made positive identification and fired their torpedoes, anticipating that Jerram would lead the 5th Battle Squadron into attack.

But Jerram displayed an appalling lack of initiative and decided to withhold his fire. In the 2nd Battle Squadron, which had also observed the ships, Admiral Leveson's flag-lieutenant urged him to take the initiative with the *Orion*: 'Sir, if you leave the line now and turn towards, your name will be as famous as Nelson's.' But Leveson, like so many of the senior commanders at Jutland, failed to seize the initiative open to him. After considering the suggestion he replied, 'We must follow the next ahead.' Once again, a failure to act on initiative by divisional commanders had robbed Jellicoe of his last opportunity to bring about an encounter in the closing minutes of daylight.

8.40 TAKE UP NIGHT STATIONS NO

C-in-C.

During the final hour of daylight before darkness finally closed in over the North Sea at 9.30 pm the Grand Fleet was well placed to cut off the High Seas Fleet and even force it into a final action before night. Less than ten miles separated the two fleets which were now both steaming south-west on a converging course. At nine o'clock Jellicoe at last had a fairly accurate picture, from reports of the clashes at the rear and van of the fleet, of the precise disposition of the enemy. But these engagements had also given Scheer a similar picture and, desperate to avoid action before he could escape under cover of darkness, he had turned his forces away again to the west. This robbed the British of their last chance of decisive action on 31 May. As Jellicoe later wrote to his wife, 'By this time we were between the enemy and his base, and if it had only been about 6 pm instead of nearly dark, and clear instead of thick, we should have had a second Trafalgar.' Just how close he had come to achieving the decisive battle was revealed later when it was discovered that less than five miles separated the *King George V* from the *Westfalen*, the leading ships in the two battle lines. That a clash had not taken place was due largely to the lack of initiative of Vice-Admiral Jerram when he failed to open fire on the enemy battleships reported by the *Caroline*. Now as darkness reduced visibility almost to zero the British Fleet looked forward to the following morning, which they firmly believed would bring them a second 'Glorious First of June'.

The British Commander-in-Chief, confident of having cut the enemy off from his line of retreat, now resolved to maintain this position during the night in order to bring the High Seas Fleet to action at dawn. In Jellicoe's mind there could be no question of a night battle: 'I rejected at once the idea of a night action between the heavy ships as leading to possible disaster owing, firstly, to the presence of torpedo craft in such large numbers and, secondly, to the impossibility of distinguishing between our own and enemy vessels. Further, the results of a night action under modern

Only some ten miles separated the Grand Fleet from the German ships as darkness fell (bottom). Jellicoe was determined to avoid a night action at all costs. Night firing exercises (below) had convinced the British C-in-C that the problems of gunnery direction and control of his huge Fleet would be unsurmountable during darkness; Scheer, on the other hand, was determined to exploit darkness to escape.

conditions must always be very largely a matter of pure chance.'

To bring about a decisive engagement at first light the British forces would have to keep contact during the five short hours of summer darkness and, most important, keep the Grand Fleet blocking Scheer's escape route. Jellicoe knew that Scheer must choose from three probable return routes. The first – and quickest – was to head for the Horns Reef light vessel and the coastal channel to the Jade; the second was to cut through the middle of the vast German Bight minefield. (The British had deliberately left a channel through the centre, and the High Seas Fleet had made their exit through a specially swept channel.) Scheer's final possibility was to skirt the minefield by going south along the Ems route – the longest way home.

Jellicoe calculated that the German Fleet would avoid the chance of action by heading for the most southerly and farthest passage, via the Dutch coast and the Ems. His views were confirmed when he received a signal from Beatty at 9.41 pm, 'Enemy

MAINTAIN COURSE IN DEFIANCE OF ALL ATTACKS BY THE ENEMY.

Night Order, Scheer to High Seas Fleet.

The German C-in-C's intention to head westward for the Horns Reef Channel was passed to every ship. In the steering position (right) the quartermasters responded to changes of course as Scheer's scouting cruisers probed Jellicoe's dispositions. As the hours of darkness wore on, Scheer's plan succeeded as he pushed his way through the weak destroyer screen at the rear of Jellicoe's battle line.

bearing N by W steering WSW.' The message was received nearly three-quarters of an hour after the event, by which time the Germans had turned back to the south-west. This was a vital factor in leading Jellicoe to the fatal conclusion, 'In view of the WSW course of the German Fleet at 9.41 pm and remembering our submarine patrol so frequently maintained off the Horns Reef, it appeared to me that Admiral Scheer might consider that he had the best chance of evading the Grand Fleet if he made for the Ems Route.' To cover the Horns Reef Jellicoe sent on the minelayer *Abdiel* to lay mines south of the submarine patrol line. Confident that he had blocked the northern escape route, Jellicoe then ordered a course which would concentrate his fleet off the middle of the minefield at 2 am, where he felt confident that he would be able to intercept Scheer at first light before he passed its southern tip into the Ems.

Jellicoe had made the wrong decision. Unknown to him, Scheer had decided to head 'at all costs' for the one route the British had left open apart from the submarines and the *Abdiel.* The main fleet was commanded by Scheer to make for the Horns Reef and 'to maintain this course in defiance of all attacks of the enemy'.

Jellicoe's miscalculation cost him his early advantage, and he was also fatally let down by the Admiralty and his own reconnaissance. Although intelligence reports came into the Admiralty during the night, and sporadic fighting broke out between many ships, no useful information reached the flagship of the C-in-C in a form which allowed him to deduce – until too late – that the Germans were heading for the Horns Reef.

At 9.17 pm on a signal from Jellicoe, 'Assume second organization. Form divisions in line ahead columns disposed abeam', the battle fleet took up its night cruising formations: four columns of battleships, a mile apart and in visual contact with one another. Admiral Jerram in *King George V* led the starboard column nearest the enemy; next came the column led by *Iron Duke* then the third column with *Colossus* and the fourth line led by the damaged *Marlborough* which lagged some four miles behind the others on the port quarter. In front steamed the 4th Light Cruiser Squadron probing ahead; Goodenough's 2nd Light Cruiser Squadron steered to the west to keep contact with the enemy flank. Some fifteen miles WSW, and ahead of the four columns, steamed Beatty with the battlecruisers on a more southerly course: 'My duty in this situation was to ensure that the enemy fleet could not regain its base by passing round the southern flank of our forces.' The battlecruisers would see no action during the night. However, when the *Lion* signalled to the *Princess Royal* by light 'Please give me challenge and reply now in force as they have been lost', two miles away the watching German 2nd and 4th Scouting Groups were able to read the recognition signals and pass valuable information around their Fleet. Good use was to be made of this information during the ensuing actions.

Jellicoe disposed his destroyer flotillas five miles astern of the four columns of the battle fleet. From port to starboard the 12th, 10th, 9th, 13th, 4th, and 11th Flotillas were deployed in depth. Their principal tasks were 'providing the battle fleet with a screen against attack by torpedo craft at night and also giving our flotillas an opportunity for attacking the enemy's heavy ships should they also be proceeding southwards with the object of regaining their bases.' The operational orders for the destroyers at night were insufficient and limited, and compared to the German practice of keeping their torpedo-boats continually informed of developments, Jellicoe left them very much on their own during the night actions.

In pitch darkness, the British Fleet steamed south at 17 knots in night formation. Less than eight miles away the High Seas Fleet was steaming one knot slower, on a parallel course, dropping back all the time, with Scheer waiting for his chance to cut across the Grand Fleet in the darkness. Leading the German line was the 1st Battle Squadron with the *Westfalen* at the head; next came the 3rd Squadron with the pre-Dreadnoughts of the 2nd Squadron bringing up the rear. Tacked on to the end of the line were the battlecruisers *Derfflinger* and *Von der Tann*, The badly damaged *Seydlitz* and *Moltke* had separated from the

main fleet and were limping along some distance to the east of it; a long way behind the *Lützow* was fighting a losing battle to stay afloat. The light cruisers of the 2nd Scouting Group were screening the van and the 4th Scouting Group, which included the detached *Elbing*, covered the flank nearest the enemy.

The faster speed of the Grand Fleet meant that shortly after 9.30 pm the British battlecruisers started to cut across the head of the High Seas Fleet; but neither side saw a thing. Fifteen minutes later Scheer calculated that the whole of the Grand Fleet was now ahead of him and that the time had come to alter course a few more degrees to the east to cut across their stern. He had earlier ordered the torpedoboat flotillas to cover his escape with a series of diversionary attacks on the British line. Unfortunately, things had started badly. At 9.30 pm Behncke's battleships opened fire on their own 7th Flotilla – without doing any damage. Then the torpedoboats, restricted to 18 knots to avoid detection by funnel sparks, reached the British lines long after the battleships had passed and ran straight into the destroyers which were positioned five miles astern.

The first of the night encounters occurred at 9.50 pm between the German 7th Flotilla and the British 4th Destroyer Flotilla. Four torpedoes were fired, but none found a target. Most of the German torpedoboats then passed well astern of the British and, failing to find them, they headed eastwards to the Horns Reef.

At about the same time a second encounter occurred. The German light cruisers *Frankfurt* and *Pillau* sighted the 11th Destroyer Flotilla, led by the *Castor*, heading to take up their positions astern of the fleet. The Germans fired two torpedoes, but wisely did not turn on their searchlights or open fire so they were able to change course and slip away without being noticed by the British. The *Castor* having reached the

(Opposite) Scheer's light cruisers probed the British line resulting in two short sharp engagements with the British destroyers (left) at the rear of the Grand Fleet. The High Seas Fleet succeeded in smashing through and crossed Jellicoe's track at midnight. Just before 2 pm Scheer encountered the last British destroyer flotilla barring his escape.

rear of the British columns, resumed her southerly course and at 9.45 pm sighted and challenged three ships. Because they replied with a partially correct recognition signal, the *Castor* closed to within 2,000 yards to investigate. Suddenly the British destroyer found itself in a blaze of light as the German light cruisers turned on their searchlights and opened up with all guns. *Castor* suffered numerous casualties from the German fire and in the heat of the action failed to make a wireless report. Half an hour afterwards a confused account was finally sent to Jellicoe, which omitted the vital information of her position and the course of the enemy.

The third encounter at 10.00 pm was an equally short and fiercely contested engagement, at a range of 800 yards when Goodenough's flagship, the *Southampton*, with the 2nd Light Cruiser Squadron sighted von Reuter's 4th Scouting Group. Suddenly the *Southampton* and *Dublin* found themselves criss-crossed by searchlights and under heavy fire. The *Southampton* suffered severe damage during the brief engagement.

But the Germans suffered too when the *Frauenlob* was hit by one of the *Southampton*'s torpedoes:

> The cruiser reeled over so far to port that the projectiles in the shell room were dislodged, and shells hitting the ship aft started a fire. But nothing could daunt the courage of her ship's company. Up to their waists in water the crew of No.4 gun, under Petty Officer Schmidt, continued to engage the enemy until fire and water put an end to the fighting.

In the confusion the *Stuttgart* was only just able to swerve clear as the damaged *Moltke* ploughed straight through the middle of the four surviving and damaged light cruisers.

Goodenough's Squadron was also lost for a time in a confused situation that resulted in the dispersal of his damaged ships. Jellicoe did not receive a report of the action until an hour afterwards. It arrived at a most unfortunate time. An Admiralty intelligence message of critical importance, 'German Battle Fleet ordered home at 9.14 pm. Battlecruisers in rear. Course S S E$\frac{3}{4}$E. Speed 16 knots,' had just been decoded and handed to him, nearly half an hour after it had been received by the *Iron Duke*'s cypher staff.

The course of the battle now hinged on Jellicoe's correct interpretation of this information which Room 40 had culled from three of Scheer's earlier wireless messages. The course it indicated, if plotted back to his known position at 9.00 pm – which Jellicoe knew reasonably accurately – would have shown clearly that the High Seas Fleet was heading for the Horns Reef. Jellicoe would then have immediately appreciated that the Germans were about to escape across his stern. He was then about six miles nearer the Horns Reef than the Germans and with several knots' superior speed he could still have changed course and cut Scheer off at any time during the following hour.

But Jellicoe had by now no confidence in Admiralty intelligence. An hour before, he had received a signal that put the position of the rear German ship eight miles south-west of his van – at a time when he knew from the fighting that they must have been well to the north-west. 'Which should I trust?' he wrote later. 'Reports from my own ships which had actually seen the enemy, or a report from the Admiralty which gave information as to their movements at a time over two hours earlier?'

In fact the Admiralty's message, by an almost criminal oversight, neglected to tell Jellicoe vital information that would have made Scheer's intentions absolutely clear – a signal intercepted at 9.06 pm in Room 40 and passed on to the Operations Room an hour later read: 'C-in-C to airship detachment: early morning reconnaissance at Horns Reef is urgently requested.' In the course of the next hour and a half no less than six more crucial signals were passed to the Operations Division in the Admiralty. Each contained information that, had it been wirelessed to Jellicoe, would have prompted him to alter course immediately for the Horns Reef in time to trap a significant portion of the High Seas Fleet. A signal received at 11.15 pm from the officer commanding the 1st Flotilla, ordered all the destroyers to assemble at the Horns Reef; and another at 11.50 pm gave the actual position of the German Fleet.

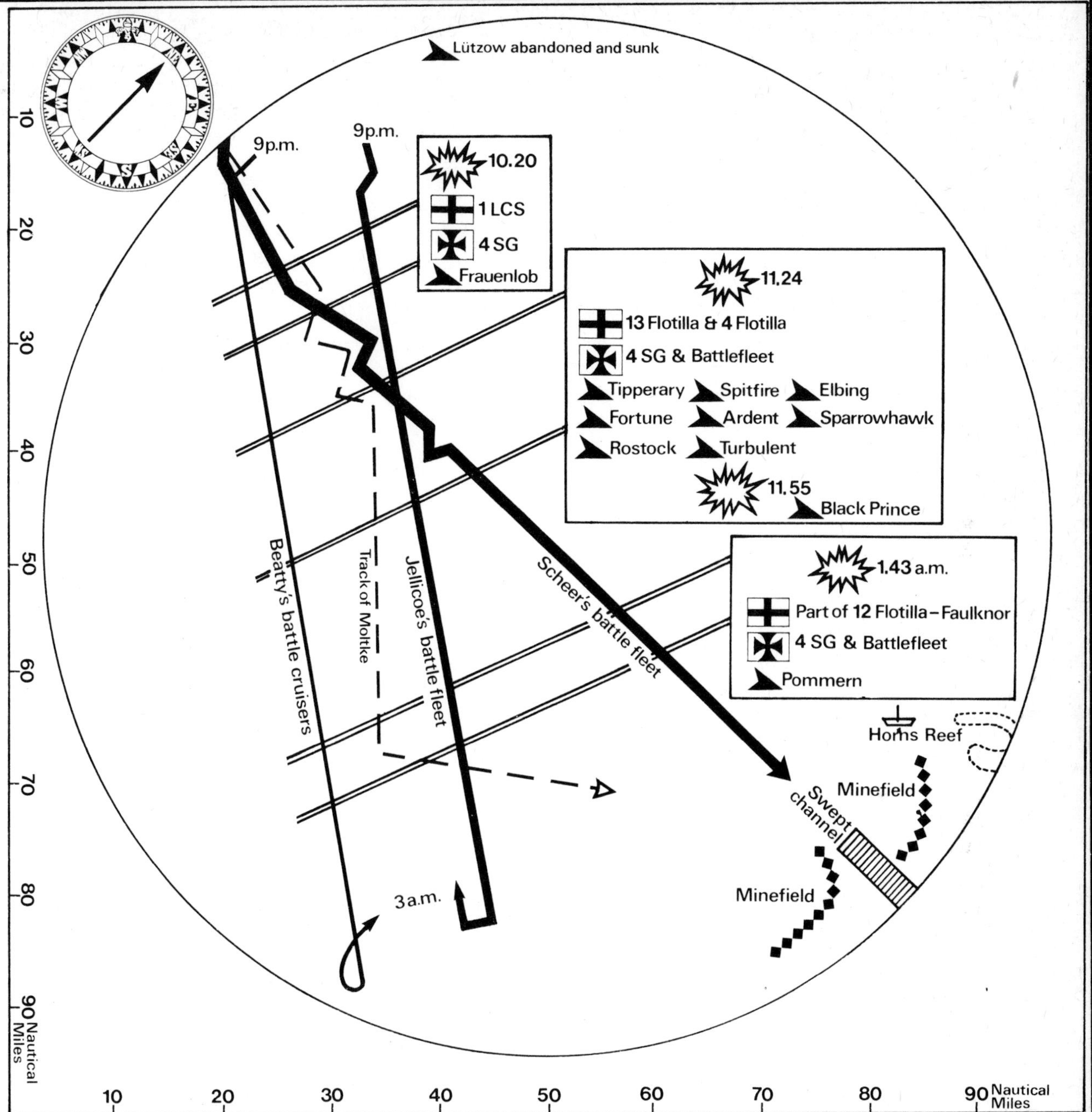

The fact that these signals were not sent was solely because that the Chief of Staff, Admiral Oliver, who conducted all operations virtually single-handed had decided to take a rest. Neither he nor anyone else expected any night action; consequently his relief officers failed to appreciate the significance of the situation or of the intelligence in their hands. The messages that could have changed the course of history were merely filed.

On the *Iron Duke*'s bridge just before midnight, Jellicoe was satisfied that the gunfire and flashes he could see astern were only attempts by the enemy light forces to penetrate his destroyer flotilla. This appeared to be confirmed by reports. He could not accept the accuracy of the Admiralty's message with its vital clues about the enemy's course. Shortly before midnight Jellicoe turned into the little shelter he had had constructed at the rear of the flagship's bridge for a few hours desperately-needed rest, to prepare himself for what he believed would be a decisive dawn.

There was to be no respite for the crews of the two fleets. On board the *Iron Duke*, 'in view of the prox-

The Admiralty were becoming concerned about Scheer's inflated claims. As the *Frauenlob* (right) was being sunk in a clash with Goodenough's light cruiser, the Admiralty failed to pass on vital wireless intelligence making clear Scheer's intention to break through to the Horns Reef which would bring it into contact with the 4th Destroyer Flotilla led by HMS *Spitfire* (below).

imity of heavy enemy ships, the hands remained at action stations, the guns' crews at their guns, but they were allowed to sleep in turn. Corned beef and biscuits were served out. Cocoa was provided from 9.30 pm onwards.' Whilst the Royal Navy kept awake on its traditional cocoa, made from dark slabs of rich chocolate and of such a thick consistency that 'a spoon would stand up in it', the Germans took their own sustenance. 'Because the battle had lasted so long, flour soup was handed out at midnight, and at 2 o'clock in the morning, coffee and corned beef.'

At 11.20 pm the biggest clash of the night began when the 4th Flotilla led by Captain Wintour in the *Tipperary* sighted shadowy shapes, and closed to within a 1,000 yards before making his challenge. He was met with a blaze of searchlights and shells from the *Frankfurt*, *Pillau* and *Elbing*: 'I thought it was one of our ships firing on us by mistake,' wrote the only surviving officer of the *Tipperary*, Sub-Lieutenant Willian Powlett.

But immediately afterwards the ship fired a salvo which hit us forward. I opened fire with the after guns. A shell then struck us in the steam-pipe, and I could see nothing but steam, but both our starboard torpedoes were fired . . . When the steam died away I found the ship was stationary and badly on fire forward. The enemy were not to be seen; nearly everybody amidships was either killed or wounded, the boxes of cartridges for the foreguns were exploding one after the other.

An hour later the *Tipperary* sank.

Following just behind in the wake of the *Tipperary* were the *Spitfire* and the *Broke*. Lieutenant-Commander Trelawney on the *Spitfire* wrote: 'I fired my after torpedo at the 2nd ship in the line which was a cruiser with four tall funnels. The torpedo struck her between the second funnel and the mainmast. She appeared to catch fire fore and aft simultaneously and heeled right over to starboard and undoubtedly sank.'

In fact the *Elbing*, which had the previous afternoon fired the first shot in the battle, staggered back towards the protection of her own battle line, only to be rammed by the pre-Dreadnought *Posen*, which crippled her still further, although she remained afloat a few hours longer.

After the attack Bödicker withdrew his surviving light cruisers, but the British destroyers of the 4th Flotilla then came under heavy fire from the battleships *Westfalen*, *Nassau* and *Rheinland* leading Scheer's battle fleet. Fortunately the battleships, which Trelawney mistook for cruisers, were erratic in their shooting as the destroyers dashed towards the giants with their guns blazing away:

> I fired a few rounds at the enemy searchlight, which went out, and then closed the *Tipperary* but immediately came in sight of two enemy cruisers close to, steering south-eastward. The nearer or more southern one altered course to ram me apparently. I therefore put my helm over hard-a-port and the two ships rammed each other, port to port, bow to bow . . . I consider I must have considerably damaged this cruiser [in fact the battleship *Nassau*] as 20 feet of the side plating was left on my forecastle . . . By the thickness of the coats of paint she would appear to have been a very new ship. The effect of this collision on the *Spitfire* was to completely demolish the bridge and searchlight platform; the mast and the foremast funnel were brought down, whaler, dingy and davits torn away. The cruiser also fired a large-calibre gun at point-blank range, the projectile passing through the starboard bridge screens without exploding . . . Just after getting clear of this cruiser an enemy battlecruiser grazed past our stern and I think she must have intended to ram us.

9.40 ENEMY CLAIM TO HAVE DESTROYED WARSPITE, QUEEN MARY, INDEFATIGABLE, TWO ARMOURED CRUISERS WITH FOUR FUNNELS, TWO SMALL CRUISERS AND 10 DESTROYERS. FALSE REPORTS WILL BE SHORTLY PROMULGATED REQUIRING PROMPT CONTRADICTION REPORT LOSSES ASCERTAINED AND VESSELS NOT ACCOUNTED FOR.

Admiralty to C-in-C.

'The ship stayed on alert all night and so was ready for action. Because we were so close to the enemy we could expect an attack at any time. The relief watch slept on deck whenever they had the chance.'
Seaman Stumpf SMS Helgoland.

With some 60 feet of her side plating missing the *Spitfire* could still manage six knots, so Trelawney extricated his damaged ship and 'with the remains of a chart patched together' began an agonizing journey back to the Tyne.

The remainder of the 4th Flotilla were gathered together by Commander Allen of the *Broke*, who had now assumed command. He headed south to try and regain contact with Jellicoe's ships. Once more, to their surprise, they ran into the head of the German line. Allen tried to bring his ship round . . .

> but the Germans had evidently been watching our movements and we were too late. Within a few seconds of our seeing his recognition signal, he switched on a blaze of searchlights straight into our eyes, and so great was the dazzling effect that it made us feel quite helpless. Then after another interval of a few seconds shells could be heard screaming over our heads and I vaguely remember seeing splashes in the water short of us and also hearing the sound of our 4-inch guns returning the fire of this German battleship, which afterwards we had strong reason to believe was the *Westfalen*. Then I remember feeling the ship give a lurch to one side as a salvo hit us, and hearing the sound of broken glass and debris flying around, after which the searchlights went out and we were once more in darkness.

Whilst the destroyers were heavily engaged with the head of the German battle line, the British armoured cruiser *Black Prince* blundered into the centre. Isolated since the late afternoon when the *Warrior* and *Defence* had been sunk, the *Black Prince* had been trying to regain station on the British line. The German battleships *Ostfriesland* and *Thüringen* opened up on the unfortunate British cruiser: 'In a few seconds she was on fire, and sank with a terrible explosion four minutes after the opening of fire. The destruction of this vessel,

The appalling failure of the British ships to make reports to their C-in-C particularly during the night was one of the principal factors that cost Jellicoe victory at Jutland. From 10.30 onwards a fierce battle raged between the destroyers and the head of Scheer's line pushing westwards – but incredibly no report reached the C-in-C until too late. Four British destroyers were sunk, the armoured cruiser HMS *Black Prince* (bottom) blown up and two German light cruisers SMS *Rostock* (below) and SMS *Elbing* sunk.

which was so near that the crew could be seen rushing backwards and forwards on the burning deck while the seachlights disclosed the flight of the heavy projectiles till they fell and exploded, was a grand but terrible sight.' There were no survivors from the holocaust.

The 4th Destroyer Flotilla finally met with success when a torpedo from the *Achates* struck the *Rostock*. According to the German report, 'both turbines stopped, the electric light failed and the steering gear broke down. The ship turned hard-a-starboard and collision with neighbouring ships was only just avoided.' The *Rostock* was taken in tow. Now the *Achates*' sister ships *Fortune* and *Ardent* paid dearly for this success. The Germans concentrated all their fire on the two small vessels. *Fortune* succumbed first, and then the *Ardent* was hit and sunk.

The heroic action of the 4th Flotilla might have had an important effect on the development of the battle if any of the British destroyer commanders had wirelessed the Commander-in-Chief what was happening.

In spite of the heroic efforts of the British destroyers (below) they were no match for the German battleships and the High Seas Fleet's night training. Incredibly, many of the British battle fleet saw the gunfire, some even spotted what were obviously enemy battleships, but not one of them opened fire or reported to the C-in-C. As Jellicoe drummed into his captains later: 'Never imagine that your commander sees what you see.'

It was a lost opportunity since the action cost Scheer valuable minutes and checked his escape. The action had been seen by the *Malaya* and the 5th Battle Squadron, which was less than four miles away. The Captain's report for 11.40 pm notes,

> what appeared to be an attack by our destroyers on some enemy big ships steering the same way as ours, two of which used searchlights. One of our destroyers with three funnels [*Tipperary*] was set on fire, but not before she had hit the second ship. This was seen by the column of smoke and also the explosion distinctly felt and heard. The leading ship of the enemy, which was seen by the flash of the explosion, had two masts, two funnels and a conspicuous crane (apparently Westfalen class).

10.50 MY POSITION COURSE AND SPEED
SOUTH 17 KNOTS. HAVE BEEN ENGAGED
BY ENEMY CRUISERS.

Commodore F to C-in-C.

'At once a most devastating fire was poured in on the *Ardent* from the two leading ships, who both had their searchlights on us. This bombardment continued for about five minutes, . . . after which period the ship was a total wreck and appeared to be sinking. I then sank the secret books, etc. . . . all our boats, carley floats etc., being smashed to bits. At this moment the enemy recommenced firing from point-blank range. I gave the order 'save yourselves'. – *Lieutenant Cmdr Marsden HMS* Ardent.

All the guns were trained on this ship, which was in fact the *Westfalen* leading Scheer's line; but Captain Boyle of the *Malaya* refused to give the order to fire since the ship ahead had not done so. The *Valiant* also momentarily sighted the action. There could be no doubt that they were enemy battleships, but *Valiant* did not open fire because Evan-Thomas, commanding the 5th Battle Squadron in the *Barham*, had not done so. Evan-Thomas did not open fire because he had received no orders and assumed that the ships ahead of him, including the *Iron Duke*, must have observed the action and had good reason for not firing. So the last chance to thwart Scheer's escape was missed. Not one of the engaged British ships nor the watching battleships reported the events to Jellicoe. Many years later at a tactical school presentation Jellicoe urged on those

present: 'Never imagine that your Commander-in-Chief sees what you see.'

The responsibility for the failure to keep the flagship and C-in-C posted on developments during the night was shared by other major British units. As early as 10.30 pm the *Thunderer* in the 2nd Battle Squadron had sighted the *Moltke* as she wandered into the British line in her lone efforts to push through to the east. Other ships in the squadron also sighted her, but no report was made to Jellicoe. The most extraordinary escape through the British line was that of the *Seydlitz* which blundered through the gap between the 2nd and the 5th Battle Squadrons at 11.45 pm. She was sighted by *Agincourt* whose captain wrote, 'I did not challenge her so as not to give our Division's position away. She altered course and steamed away.' *Seydlitz* passed less than a mile ahead of Evan-Thomas's powerful battleships, whose salvoes would have finished off the disabled battlecruiser in a few minutes. She was also sighted by the *Marlborough* and *Revenge* but no action was taken. The *Revenge* ordered that her 6-inch-gun crews should open fire, but their crews were all relaxing outside their turrets engrossed in the spectacle of the destroyer actions. By the time they were at their guns again the *Seydlitz* had vanished. The enemy battlecruiser was also spotted by the *Fearless* and 1st Destroyer Flotilla. But they held their fire: since no other ship had opened fire the destroyers did not want to reveal their position.

At 12.15 am on the morning of 1 June the leading ships of the High Seas Fleet were just three miles astern of the 5th Battle Squadron. Fifteen minutes later the fifth encounter of the night occurred when the German ships ran into the 9th, 10th and 13th Destroyer Flotillas eastward of the Battle Fleet. 'At 12.25 am we sighted a dark mass about 5 or 6 points

This wireless signal was never received by the *Iron Duke*, probably through German jamming. It marked the last chance for the Grand Fleet to interfere with Scheer's escape. Shortly afterwards, HMS *Faulknor* fired a torpedo that hit the pre-Dreadnought SMS *Pommern* (left), which vanished in a fireball.

1.56 URGENT. PRIORITY. ENEMY'S BATTLESHIP IN SIGHT. MY POSITION 10 MILES ASTERN OF 1ST BATTLE SQUADRON.

Captain 12 Destroyer Flotilla to C-in-C.

on our starboard bow, steering SE about 600 yards away,' wrote an officer on board the destroyer *Petard*:

> on looking at her closely we could see clearly large crane derricks silhouetted against the sky, and only German ships have these fittings. At the same time the German battleships switched on recognition lights, consisting of two red lights over a white one. As *Petard* had fired all her torpedoes in the day attack there was nothing we could do but get away, so we increased to full speed and altered course about a point to port to clear the enemy's stem. As soon as we had passed ahead of her she switched her foremost group of searchlights on us . . . we saw the flashes of the enemy's secondary armament being fired and on the bridge we felt the ship tremble slightly, and guessed we had been hit aft. They seemed to give us another salvo and then the second ship in the line – we could now see four – also joined in; the second salvo struck us further forward in the ship but luckily missed the bridge and the midship guns' crew. At this moment the foremost group of German searchlights were switched off us and trained round to port all together on to the *Turbulent* my next astern. Immediately afterwards . . . she was rammed and sunk by this leading German battleship . . . we escaped without any further incident.

If any of the three British flotillas had reported to the Commander-in-Chief the presence of the German ships, the *Marlborough*, which was less than five miles away, could have turned and blocked Scheer's escape. But now there was only one fragile barrier blocking the whole of the High Seas Fleet – Captain Stirling's 12th Destroyer Flotilla. According to one of Stirling's officers on the bridge of *Faulknor*,

> a division of battleships were sighted off our starboard bow, the *Faulknor* led her flotilla on to a parallel course and at about 1.55 am the battleships were again in sight on the starboard bow. Speed was at once increased to 25 knots and course altered, so that the ships were approaching at an angle of about 45 degrees. It was now apparent that they were Germans, but apparently they had not seen us yet, as there was no sign of searchlights or challenge. The Captain gave orders for the torpedoes to be fired as the sights came on, and at 2 am turned on to a parallel course. At 2.02 am the *Faulknor* fired her first torpedo, which probably passed ahead of the second enemy ship as the director officer fired rather too early and allowed too much for the enemy's speed. About two minutes later the second torpedo was fired, but almost simultaneously with this the Germans sighted our flotilla and all their battleships opened fire, together with the light cruisers astern of their line, who poured in particularly heavy fire upon us. The sea seemed to be alive with bursting shells and the air with the whistle of passing projectiles . . . Suddenly a huge explosion took place in the third German ship and with a deafening noise and shock she seemed to first of all open out then close together, then to go. The pre-Dreadnought *Pommern* vanished from sight in a fireball with all her crew. In the silence that followed a voice on our bridge was heard to say, 'Pity the poor devils, they ain't drawn their money's worth.' A heavy fire continued to be directed at us as the *Nessus* and *Onslaught* were hit.

Minutes later Admiral Mauve steamed past the spot: 'The wreck of the *Pommern* was about 1,000 metres away on a starboard side, but because of the darkness that still prevailed it was impossible to make out any details. It lay heavy on my heart to leave the wreck unaided and to fail to rescue friends that were still alive, but the situation was such that we could do nothing but hold on to our course.'

An exception to the generally poor reporting during the night action, *Faulknor*'s captain had transmitted three action reports on the engagement, but none got through to the flagship because of a combination of enemy jamming and poor transmission quality of the primitive radio apparatus then in use. It was the last time that Jellicoe could have changed course towards the Horns Reef where he could have stopped the tail end of Scheer's line getting through.

'ENEMY HAS R

Home from the Skagerrak The High Seas Fleet regained the safety of The Horns Reef Channel early in the morning of 1 June. Some German ships had taken such heavy punishment that they had great difficulty in reaching Wilhelmshaven, particularly the battlecruiser *Seydlitz* (below) flooded by 5,300 tons of water.

URNED TO HARBOUR'

Dawn was breaking when the light cruiser *Champion* leading the 13th Flotilla from the north-east heard the gunfire of the 12th Flotilla's last engagement. She raced towards the sound of the action at full speed in company with the destroyers *Obdurate* and *Moresby*, joined on the way by the *Marksman* and the *Maenad* which had become separated from the 12th Flotilla. At 2.30 am it was already getting light when the group sighted the last four enemy battleships. Only *Moresby* was able to fire a torpedo at the departing pre-Dreadnoughts which were bringing up the rear of Scheer's battle line. The torpedo found a mark, but not in one of the German battleships. The torpedo-boat *V4* was hit and sent to the bottom. Again no immediate report was made to Jellicoe, although by now it would have been too late for him to take any effective action as the 2nd Squadron, followed by the surviving battlecruisers *Derfflinger* and *Von der Tann* were making for the Horns Reef lightship, completing Scheer's remarkable escape. The *Lützow* had been finally abandoned in a sinking condition at 1:45 am. The destroyers which had taken off the *Lützow*'s crew were sighted by the light cruiser *Champion* at 3.30 am and she opened fire on them with her 6-inch guns. Then for an inexplicable reason she sheered off and left them to make for Wilhelmshaven unmolested. So ended the last of the night encounters which completed the fighting at Jutland.

The lost Trafalgar Scheer's fleet was jubilantly welcomed at Wilhelmshaven. 'The voices of thousands of people welcomed us, everywhere the flags hung out of windows and the bells of the churches rang for an hour.' But whilst the British studied hundreds of hand-written battle reports (below) to discover why they had missed victory, Scheer realized that severe battle damage like the gaping holes in the *Derfflinger* (below left) would keep his fleet confined to harbour for months.

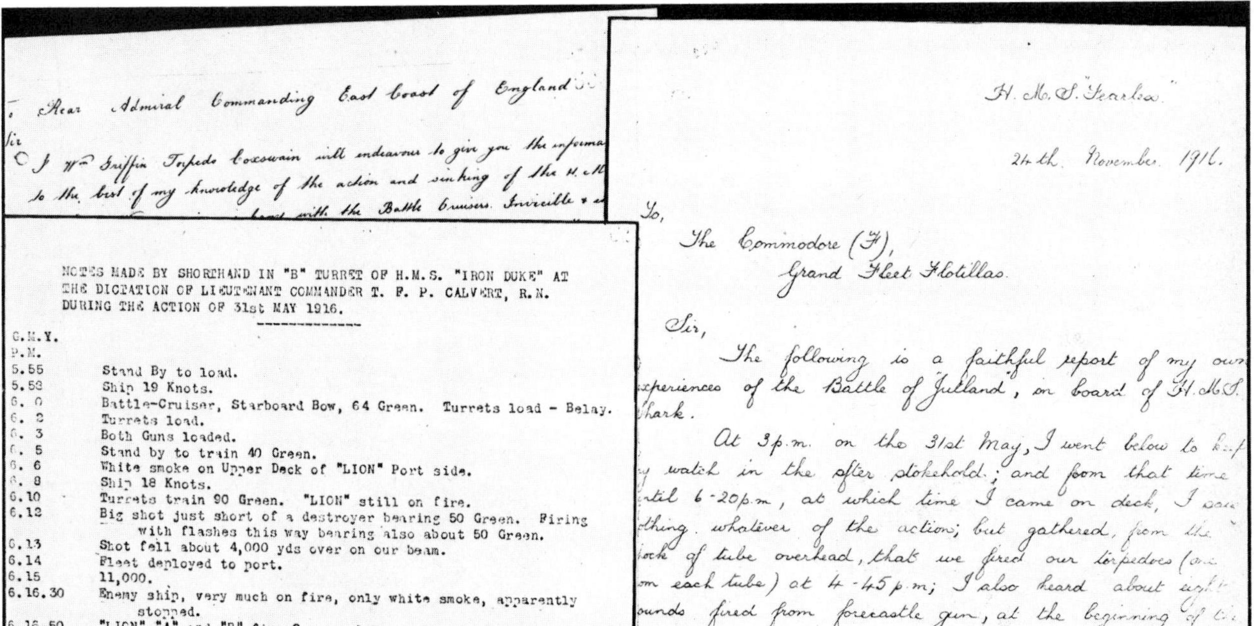

To Rear Admiral Commanding East Coast of England

Sir

I Wm Griffin Torpedo Coxswain will endeavour to give you the informa[tion]
to the best of my knowledge of the action and sinking of the H.M[S]
... with the Battle Cruisers. Invincible & ...

NOTES MADE BY SHORTHAND IN "B" TURRET OF H.M.S. "IRON DUKE" AT THE DICTATION OF LIEUTENANT COMMANDER T. F. P. CALVERT, R.N. DURING THE ACTION OF 31st MAY 1916.

G.M.Y.
P.M.

5.55	Stand By to load.
5.58	Ship 19 Knots.
6. 0	Battle-Cruiser, Starboard Bow, 64 Green. Turrets load - Belay.
6. 2	Turrets load.
6. 3	Both Guns loaded.
6. 5	Stand by to train 40 Green.
6. 6	White smoke on Upper Deck of "LION" Port side.
6. 8	Ship 18 Knots.
6.10	Turrets train 90 Green. "LION" still on fire.
6.12	Big shot just short of a destroyer bearing 50 Green. Firing with flashes this way bearing also about 50 Green.
6.13	Shot fell about 4,000 yds over on our beam.
6.14	Fleet deployed to port.
6.15	11,000.
6.16.30	Enemy ship, very much on fire, only white smoke, apparently stopped.
6.16.50	"LION" "A" and "B" fire 2 gun salvo

H.M.S. "Fearless".

24th November 1916.

To,

The Commodore (F),
Grand Fleet Flotillas.

Sir,

The following is a faithful report of my own [e]xperiences of the Battle of "Jutland", on board of H.M.S. [S]hark.

At 3 p.m. on the 31st May, I went below to k[eep] [m]y watch in the after stokehold; and from that time [u]ntil 6-20 p.m, at which time I came on deck, I saw [no]thing whatever of the action; but gathered, from the [kn]ock of tube overhead, that we fired our torpedoes (one [fro]m each tube) at 4-45 p.m; I also heard about eight [r]ounds fired from forecastle gun, at the beginning of the

The misty grey light of a North Sea dawn found Jellicoe on the *Iron Duke*'s bridge surveying the horizon and the prospect of renewing the action. He was still unaware that Scheer had given him the slip during the night and was now well to the west of the British Fleet and almost out of reach. Expectations were high on the battleship as the crew confidently waited for the C-in-C's flagship's signal to regroup the destroyers preparatory to reforming their line of battle. 'The visibility gave promise of a better day,' wrote one midshipman reflecting the confidence of the fleet. 'We had plenty of ammunition left and felt that, given the chance, we could make short work of what remained of the enemy. The guns had been loaded and we were ready to start again.' Shortly before 3 am the Grand Fleet reformed into its battle line and in accordance with Jellicoe's plan to close the Horns Reef if there had been no sighting at dawn, they steamed to the north. But it was too late. At 3.29 am the *Iron Duke* received a signal from the Admiralty which had intercepted reports of an hour earlier placing Scheer on a south-easterly course about 30 miles to the north-east of *Iron Duke* and only an hour's steaming-time from the safety of the Horns Reef. Immediately Jellicoe realized the situation – the High Seas Fleet would already be passing into the safety of the swept channel. 'This signal made it evident that by no possibility could I catch the enemy before he reached port, even if I disregarded the danger of following him through the minefields and allowing some error in the position assigned to the enemy.' Beatty who was still convinced that the enemy was still to the south asked for permission to make a sweep as late as 4.40 am but by then Jellicoe could only reluctantly signal 'Enemy has returned to harbour.'

As the sun came up the Grand Fleet was re-formed into cruising order of six columns to search northwards for any enemy stragglers and survivors among the desolate flotsam that littered the surface of the water. With sinking hearts the British accepted that this first of June would be anything but glorious.

Scheer had succeeded in escaping what must have been inevitable destruction since the German ships were in no condition to withstand another action. The battleships of Behncke's squadron had been damaged and were running short of ammunition; the *Lützow* had been sunk, *Derfflinger* and *Moltke* badly mauled and the *Von der Tann* had no turrets in action; *Seydlitz* was even more badly crippled and was slowly sinking by the bows. As Scheer reported: 'The ships in the van of the 3rd Squadron must also have lost in fighting value. Of the fast light cruisers only the *Frankfurt*, *Pillau* and *Regensburg* were at my disposal. Owing to bad visibility further scouting by airship could not be counted on. It was therefore hopeless to try and force a regular action on the enemy reported to the south.' But he was to suffer a final – if not very

Scars of Jutland The long journey home was particularly difficult for crippled British ships like the light cruiser HMS *Chester* (below) whose hull had been penetrated by German shells in several places. The destroyer *Spitfire* reached home two days after the battle. 'Mess tables, collision mats and stores were used to try and fill the gaping bow – but they were all washed in board again, time after time, as the wind and sea were now rising fast. . . . We began to get very anxious whether the fore boiler room bulk head would stand the strain.'

serious – blow when the *Ostfriesland* hit a mine laid three weeks earlier by the *Abdiel*. However, she was not seriously damaged and succeeded in making harbour that afternoon with the rest of the fleet.

The British Fleet had a much less joyful day. On board the *New Zealand*, while the ship's company sat and dozed at their stations, 'the only signs of the enemy were hundreds of their drowned bluejackets in their life-saving waistcoats, floating near the great smears of oil and wreckage that marked the grave of some ship, with large numbers of dead fish floating near these patches of wreckage apparently killed by the explosion.' The British ships had much further to go, and the North Sea weather proved capricious, with gale-force winds blowing up. It took some of the crippled ships, travelling at 2 or 3 knots, three days to reach the safety of harbour. The destroyer *Broke*, which had suffered extensive damage to her bows, could only make way by sailing stern first, and during the heavy seas which came up on 1 June she had to sail slowly towards the German coast for a time before she could get on to a homeward course.

The British Battlecruiser Fleet, moored at Rosyth immediately after Jutland, had suffered the greatest British casualties, mainly due to serious design faults such as the inadequacy of magazine protection which almost caused the loss of HMS *Lion* (below centre with HMS *Tiger* at Rosyth after the battle) when struck on Q turret (left). (Beatty's aggressive spirit in the battle however was contrasted in the Press with Jellicoe's caution in failing to annihilate the Germans.)

'One of the saddest days of my life.'
– *Beatty*.

Several ships were damaged to such an extent that their commanders wondered whether they were seaworthy enough to make the journey home. They had also lost navigation equipment, wireless and signals equipment. Sometimes damaged ships were towed in by a sister ship. *Onslow* was in the tow of *Defender* making a slow 3–4 knots, and *Acasta* was being brought home by *Nonsuch*. The *Warspite* limped towards the Forth and managed to avoid two German U-boat attacks. Lieutenant Bickmore remembered the atmosphere as they brought the great ship home.

> We got into Rosyth and we steamed up the Firth and under the Forth Bridge, still on fire in seven places, smoke belching out of us in all directions; all the permanent painting-party of the Forth Bridge saw us coming and they all came down off their ladders and cheered us in. We went straight into dock . . .

Bickmore was ordered to take a note to the captain of the *Queen Elizabeth* which had been refitting:

> I jumped over the side and I went on board the *Queen Elizabeth* . . . I handed over the message . . . and the captain sent for a bottle of champagne. I wolfed some of that down and he asked me to tell him all about it and then the commander came in and I was taken to the wardroom. The wardroom gave me whisky and I told them all about it. When I'd finished I was handed over to the gunroom and the gunroom gave me beer and I told them about it and then the warrant officers were lurking outside and they took me off and gave me rum. And by that time I didn't know what the story was like – probably quite incoherent I should think. After all I was only just eighteen.

In contrast to the Grand Fleet's mood of disappointment the Germans were almost amazed that they had returned with their fleet intact. They had at long last met the British and had survived to tell the tale. There was an atmosphere of jubilation. Scheer cracked open a bottle of champagne in celebration on the bridge of the *Friedrich der Grosse*. 'Meanwhile the crews on all our ships had attained full consciousness of the greatness of our successes against superior enemy forces, and loud and hearty cheers went up as they steamed past the flagship of their leader.' Scheer noted that most ships hardly seemed to have been involved in a battle at all as there were few marks from the heavy British fire. In fact there had been considerable internal damage to some of the ships. The *Seydlitz* was little more than a wreck, and it was six months before the *Derfflinger* could re-join the fleet. Other ships were despatched to repair yards. The *Grosser Kurfürst*, *Markgraf* and *Moltke* were sent to Hamburg, the *Seydlitz*, *Ostfriesland* and *Helgoland* remained at Wilhelmshaven and the *König* and *Derfflinger* were eventually sent to Kiel.

The loss of British prestige following German claims of a naval victory is cuttingly shown in a Simplicissimus cartoon, 'Home-coming from the Skagerrak' (inset). On 2 June Jellicoe reported to the Admiralty that *Iron Duke* (below) could lead a battle-ready fleet of twenty-four undamaged Dreadnoughts to sea at four hours' notice. Only ten were available to Scheer. The strategic balance was unchanged.

THE LOST VICTORY

'The spell of Trafalgar has been broken.'
– *The Kaiser, 5 June 1916.*

The paper war The Imperial Navy suppressed the true extent of German losses, and the Press built up (right) a false picture of a victory. Lukewarm Admiralty communiqués undermined the true achievement of Jutland, summed up by the *Pall Mall Gazette*:

The Germans cry aloud 'We've won!'
But surely 'tis a curious view
That those are conquerors who run
And those the vanquished who pursue.

The German Press was in no doubt about the outcome of the battle. The Imperial Naval Office had quickly issued a communiqué based on Scheer's report, in which the total number of British ships sunk was put at one super-Dreadnought (the *Warspite*), three battle-cruisers, two armoured cruisers, two light cruisers and thirteen destroyers. The release admitted the loss of the *Pommern* and *Wiesbaden* but deliberately suppressed the news of the sinking of the *Lützow* and the *Rostock*. The true Jutland figures favoured the Germans, but they were not as bad for the British as the Germans led the world to believe.

The British lost 14 ships totalling 111,000 tons, against 11 German sinkings of 62,000 tons. The details were:

	British	German
Battleships	–	*Pommern*
Battlecruisers	*Indefatigable*	*Lützow*
	Invincible	
	Queen Mary	
Cruisers	*Black Prince*	
	Defence	
	Warrior	
Light cruisers	–	*Elbing*
		Frauenlob
		Rostock
		Wiesbaden
Destroyers	*Ardent*	*S35*
	Fortune	*V4*
	Nestor	*V27*
	Nomad	*V29*
	Shark	*V48*
	Sparrowhawk	
	Tipperary	
	Turbulent	

In manpower the Germans lost far fewer men. The High Seas Fleet suffered 2,551 killed and 507 wounded, which represented 6.79 per cent of the total strength of ships' companies. The Grand Fleet lost 6,097 men killed and 510 wounded with 177 taken prisoner from the water. This was 8.84 per cent of ships' companies totalling 60,000 men. The Imperial Naval Office communiqué however made the results of the battle appear far more favourable to Germany.

The *Frankfurter Zeitung* of 2 June boldly broke the news of the German success under the headline. 'Great sea battle in the North Sea. Many English battleships destroyed and damaged. *Pommern*, *Wiesbaden* sunk; *Frauenlob* and some torpedoboats missing.' The *Berliner Tageblatt* wrote of 'the great sea victory over the British': and the *Vossiche Zeitung* carried banner headlines: 'German sea victory between Skagerrak and the Horns Reef'. There were celebrations all over Germany. Each army division sent congratulations to the fleet. Schoolchildren were given a holiday.

The Kaiser was overcome with emotion. He hastened down to Kiel to decorate the two victorious admirals and he addressed the crews, drawn up in attentive ranks alongside the berth of the fleet flagship, *Friedrich der Grosse*:

> The journey I have made today means very much to me. I would like to thank you all. Whilst our army has been fighting our enemies, bringing home many victories, our fleet had to wait until they eventually came. A brave leader led our fleet and commanded the courageous sailors. The superior English armada eventually appeared and our fleet was ready for battle. What happened? The English were beaten. You have started a new chapter in world history. I stand before you as your Highest Commander to thank you with all my heart.

In Britain the attitude was very different. On board his flagship, Jellicoe put his head in his hands and confessed, 'I missed one of the greatest opportunities a man ever had.' The frustration at having been so near and yet so far from a great victory had its effect on Beatty too. He was described by Chalmers on the *Lion*, the day after the battle: 'Tired and depressed, he sat down on the settee, and settling himself in a corner he closed his eyes. Unable to hide his disappointment at the result of the battle, he repeated in a weary voice, "There is something wrong with our ships"; then, opening his eyes and looking at the writer, he added, "and something wrong with our system."' Beatty also wrote to Jellicoe, 'It seems hard, terribly

The Daily News

A BEAUTIFUL PHOTOGRAVURE PICTURE OF LORD KITCHENER

HORNS REEF: HOW GERMANY IS FED WITH FALSE HOPES OF VICTORY.

If you love Jack

WRIGLEY'S SPEARMINT

W. J. HARRIS

Morgen-Ausgabe

Berliner Tageblatt

und Handels-Zeitung

Nach der Seeschlacht am Skagerrak.

DERFFLINGER ON FIRE AND SINKING.

British Battle Cruisers' Fight With Main German Fleet.

HOLDING THE ENEMY UNTIL JELLICOE CAME.

(From Our Special Correspondent.)

THE EAST COAST, Sunday.

It is becoming increasingly evident that when the full story of the naval battle

WHEN THE GERMANS TURNED & RAN.

hard, that after all this weary wait, after losing so many of our best friends, after a veritable nightmare of an afternoon, we should have been baulked. My heart aches with thinking about it and that our magnificent battle fleet should have been deprived at the eleventh hour of their reward.'

As the British sailors telegraphed home to reassure their wives and families that they had survived, and as battered warships limped into the east-coast ports, news spread that there had been a great North Sea battle. But the public's hopes were cruelly dashed on the morning of 3 June, when they read the Admiralty's first official statement on the battle. Balfour's statement, issued before Jellicoe's despatch had been received, read like a thinly disguised cover-up for a disastrous defeat:

> On the afternoon of Wednesday, 31 May a naval engagement took place off the coast of Jutland.
>
> The British ships on which the brunt of the fighting fell were the battlecruiser fleet and some cruisers and light cruisers supported by four fast battleships. Among those the losses were heavy.
>
> The German Battle Fleet, aided by low visibility, avoided prolonged action with our main forces and soon after these appeared on the scene the enemy returned to port, though not before receiving severe damage from our battleships.

The communiqué then continued with a list of known British losses but omitted to mention any specific German losses:

> The enemy's losses were serious. At least one battlecruiser was destroyed and one severely damaged; one battleship was reported sunk by our destroyers during a night attack; two light cruisers were disabled and probably sunk.
>
> The exact number of enemy destroyers disposed of during the action cannot be ascertained with any certainty, but it must have been large.

This was hardly the language to raise the spirits of the British people. There were sad scenes outside the Admiralty in Whitehall where an inquiry office had been set up. Anxious relatives waited for news. 'Police constables gave kindly and sympathetic help to the grief-stricken women, a task in which the London constable is at his best.' The reporters also told of the grim atmosphere in the naval towns:

> To Portsmouth Dockyard gate, down by historic Hard, a constant stream of men and women has gone to read a typewritten communiqué more tragic in its brevity than all descriptions of this great action. I stood in the crowd, ever a great one, and heard the words repeated, 'All lost, all lost', and saw women turn away with mournful faces but dry eyes, trying to realize what it meant.

In Chatham it was the same grim story. The *Daily Mail* reporter 'knocked at the house door of a little general store in the window of which there were many pictures of ships and greeting cards in many colours. Mrs Pritchard came to the door, a weary little woman

with smooth hair. "Yes I have two boys in the destroyer *Nomad*, all I have in the world – and now I think I am alone."'

Balfour issued two new communiqués on 3 and 4 June to correct the damage; the British claimed that the High Seas Fleet had lost two battleships, two battlecruisers, four light cruisers and nine destroyers, as well as a U-boat. It was also pointed out that the British had remained in command of the sea and that the Germans had fled behind the defensive minefields of the Bight.

The Germans now had to admit the loss of the *Lützow* and *Rostock*, and from the British side Jutland did not seem to be quite the defeat people had feared.

The incompetent handling of the Press release had severe repercussions on Britain's image abroad. British embassies were soon writing to London to vent their wrath on the Admiralty.

The British Government was most concerned about opinion in the greatest neutral of them all, the United States. The large German minority in the United States were served by the magazine, *Fatherland*, which proudly published a picture of Admiral Scheer, 'the victor of Skagerrak'. Its editorial was strident: 'If England continues to lose a few more naval fights such as the Skagerrak engagement, her importance as a naval power will have vanished and the trident fallen from her palsied hand will be firmly held by the Kaiser.' Other American papers accepted this version of the conflict, especially the Irish-American Press.

Yet the U-boat campaign had already deeply influenced American opinion, and in spite of the *Fatherland* and sympathetic newspapers, a favourable Press did exist for the Royal Navy. The New York *American* sardonically referred to the deadliest weapon of naval warfare – the typewriter:

> We can recall nothing in the annals of naval warfare to equal the supreme gallantry and skill with which the journalistic auxiliary naval reserve has demolished ship after ship of the Teutonic enemy during the past four days, and the astonishing success with which it has converted defeat into a glorious triumph without the loss of even so much as an inkpad.

The performance of the Germans at Jutland shook the Grand Fleet into a complete review of its efficiency and readiness for battle. The Admiralty immediately sought ways of rectifying the errors of Jutland for the next encounter. New anti-flash devices were fitted to the British ships and studies began for a new armour-piercing British shell. The Grand Fleet's lyddite armour-piercing shell had proved highly ineffective, with the projectiles exploding or breaking up on impact rather than penetrating a ship's vitals before detonation. There were studies of signals and communication procedures. The battlecruiser fleet asked for a whole series of improvements, ranging from better torpedo spotting and better positions for the director systems to the use of aircraft.

But the fleet could not escape the charge that it had failed to win a Nelsonian victory, although the Grand Fleet had kept the High Seas Fleet in check. German

Tethered Tiger Unwilling to risk the High Seas Fleet once more, the Kaiser accepted Scheer's advice and finally abandoned his objection to unrestricted U-boat warfare as a way to break the British blockade. In spite of morale-boosting visits to Wilhelmshaven (left) the morale of the inactive High Seas Fleet began to crack.

battle squadrons would not penetrate far into the North Sea if they expected to be trapped by a superior British force, as at Jutland. The tight blockade of Germany continued and Britain retained command of the sea and the all-important communications with Europe, the United States and the world. Ironically, it was left to Scheer to admit the impracticality of Germany's attempt to decide to win the war through a great fleet action. In a report to the Emperor he stated:

> There can be no doubt that even the most successful outcome of a fleet action in this war will not force England to make peace. The disadvantages of our military geographical position in relation to that of the British Isles, and the enemy's great material superiority cannot be compensated for by our fleet to the extent where we shall be able to overcome the blockade or the British Isles themselves – not even if the U-boats are made fully available for purely naval operations.
>
> A victorious end to the war within a reasonable time can only be achieved through the defeat of British economic life – that is, by using the U-boats against British trade.

Scheer went on to urge the Kaiser to avoid all half measures and to launch all-out U-boat warfare. The Tirpitz doctrine had at last been rejected, ironically by the only German admiral to stand up to the full might of the British Battle Fleet in the North Sea.

The High Seas Fleet emerged only three more times between Jutland and the end of the War. German naval strategy was concentrated on U-boat warfare. Winston Churchill, speaking in February 1917, summed up the German switch in strategy:

> All that great fleet which was the product of successive German Navy Laws and grew year-by-year under our eyes, against which we used to measure ourselves so carefully, so anxiously, with just this or that percentage of margin of superiority in every class of vessel – all that great fleet, and all the preparations of a secret and elaborate character which they had made in every part of the world for the levying of aggressive war by sea, have been effectively frustrated, and our chief and almost sole anxiety at the present time arises not from the ships of the German Fleet as we knew it before the War, but from vessels scarcely one of which was in existence at the declaration of war, and from the adoption of methods of warfare which before this war were considered by the best judges incredible or almost incredible that any civilized belligerent would adopt or that neutral nations would endure.

The general British propaganda line, that the German Fleet never came out again after Jutland during the First World War, became incorrectly accepted as a historical truth. In fact Scheer put his original Jutland plan into operation on 19 August 1916. On this sortie, Zeppelins and U-boats formed reconnaissance lines to warn of the approach of the Grand Fleet, whilst Scheer's fleet demonstrated to the British that Germany was by no means defeated at sea by taking his force north to bombard Sunderland.

This time, however, the British, having analysed the lessons of Jutland, were determined to avoid all mistakes. Warned by intercepted signals, Jellicoe was at sea in overwhelming strength before the Germans left the Jade at 9 pm. The Grand Fleet made an early rendezvous with Beatty's battlecruiser fleet from the Forth and the combined force steamed towards the Germans. The battlecruisers operated much closer to the Grand Fleet than at Jutland, only thirty miles separating them.

But fate was to rob the British of an opportunity to re-fight Jutland. By chance Scheer had turned away a short time before, and the second Jutland was narrowly missed.

On 6 October 1916, submarine attacks were started again in accordance with prize rules. The role of the High Seas Fleet was changed from being an aggressive contender for domination of the North Sea to a supporting force for the U-boat campaign. Once again, after scenting the possibility of victory over the world's greatest sea power, the German Navy now returned to a policy of sitting in Wilhelmshaven, unable to affect the course of the War, whilst the U-boat commanders were given the responsibility for winning the war at sea. Stalemate developed. Scheer made another foray on 18 October 1916, but the Grand Fleet, although ordered to raise steam, did not venture out and Scheer returned uneventfully to base.

The morale of the High Seas Fleet, which had been so high after Jutland, now began to collapse disastrously. With the ships lying at anchor in the forbidding location of Wilhelmshaven, monotony became a serious problem which Scheer's officers did little to relieve. They still showed their *Kastengeist* (caste spirit) by treating their crews with harsh discipline.

Richard Stumpf on board the *Helgoland* reflected the mood between decks: 'Since we have such limited contact with the actual war we wage a sort of internal war among ourselves on the ship.' The fleet's diet deteriorated and by the 'turnip' winter of 1917 the sailors were subjected to a dreadful diet of dumplings and *Drahtverhau* (a stew which, according to Stumpf, contained 75 per cent water, a morsel of meat and a few vegetables). The officers ate far better meals from their own galleys and on some ships had an allowance of eight bottles of wine a week.

In August 1917 there was a mutiny on board the *Prinzregent Luitpold*, mainly caused by appalling food. Special protest committees were formed and there was a march off the ship. The authorities, fearful of the spread of revolution from Russia, suppressed the mutiny. Scheer had two of the ringleaders shot.

The tension continued even though the Germans were achieving success with their unrestricted U-boat warfare. In the second quarter of 1917 U-boats were sinking an alarming number of ships, totalling 2.2 million tons, almost four times the amount of shipping under construction. Over six million tons were sunk by the year's end. Only the adoption of the convoy system brought a decline in these catastrophic losses.

Scheer's enthusiasm for all-out U-boat warfare which he hoped would strangle Britain into submission, although it narrowly failed, also brought about the downfall of Germany. The ruthless sinkings by the U-boats brought the United States into the War, with its immense military potential. An American battle squadron was sent to serve with the British Grand Fleet, which was moved south to Rosyth.

It was not until April 1918 that the High Seas Fleet embarked upon another sortie, when Scheer took his forces north to the latitude of the Norwegian coast to attack the northern convoy routes. Luck was not on his side and he had to turn back when the *Moltke* lost a propellor and flooded her engine-room.

With the Allied defeat of the U-boats in 1918, Scheer's thoughts turned towards mounting a surface offensive, as a last-ditch attempt to give Germany a bargaining counter in any peace negotiations. He concluded:

> It is impossible for the fleet to remain inactive in any final battle that may sooner or later precede an armistice. The fleet must be committed. Even if it is not to be expected that this would decisively influence the course of events, it is still, from the moral point of view, a question of the honour and existence of the Navy to have done its utmost in the last battle.

The naval officer corps deeply disapproved of the armistice negotiations. In October 1918, Scheer and Hipper planned to emulate the Dutch attack on the Medway during the peace negotiations at Breda in 1667. In this last attack, which the crews called 'the Admiral's death ride', light forces would attack warships and traffic off the Flanders' coast and in the Thames Estuary, with the battle fleet in support. As the Grand Fleet came south, lines of U-boats would be stationed ready to fire their torpedoes at every British vessel within range. Hipper would then meet Beatty in a huge final fight to the finish in the southern part of the North Sea.

The crews of the battle squadrons were horrified when they heard rumours of the plan. They had already had enough of the War and knew that peace negotiations were taking place.

In the last days of October 1918, as the fleet gathered, the disaffected sailors decided to act. Ship after ship refused to sail in accordance with Hipper's orders, including some of the most famous vessels in the High

Funeral for a Fleet The High Seas Fleet, reduced to the role of supporting the U-boat campaign, spent most of its time in harbour. Its morale broken by inactivity, and revolution, it sailed to surrender on 21 November 1918. It was a moment of sober triumph in the British Fleet as their old enemies hauled down their flag. SMS *Baden* (below) was one of the new German super-Dreadnoughts that had joined the High Seas Fleet after Jutland.

Seas Fleet, the *Von der Tann*, *König* and *Kronprinz Wilhelm*. In spite of Scheer's pressure on Hipper to deal severely with the mutineers, Hipper could make no other decision than to call off the 'death-ride'. The Fleet was dispersed to the Elbe, Kiel and Wilhelmshaven. Soon the red flag was to appear over the fleet instead of the imperial eagle.

The mutiny at Wilhelmshaven and Kiel was the spark which destroyed the internal unity of the German Empire. Civil disturbance and revolution spread throughout Germany. British conditions for the ceasefire were harsh indeed. On 11 November, when the armistice came into effect, Germany was on the verge of civil dissension and chaos.

British conditions for the ceasefire were particularly concerned with the German Navy. Lloyd George's Government accepted the Admiralty's case that two of Germany's three battle squadrons should be interned, together with all her five battlecruisers. All U-boats were to be given up. A delegation was sent, with the approval of the Revolutionary Sailors' Council, to the Firth of Forth in order to negotiate the arrival of the German ships.

At dawn on 21 November 1918, 370 ships of the Grand Fleet sailed on their last great mission, Operation ZZ, to escort the German Navy to its last anchorage. The British were determined to savour their victory in the twenty-year struggle. Forty capital ships steamed out in two long lines six miles apart. The guns were all manned but pointing fore and aft. On the bridge of the *Queen Elizabeth* stood Admiral Beatty, his peaked cap tilted at its usual rakish angle. All eyes were fixed on the horizon where shortly after 9.30 am the grey shapes of the German

Final reckoning On 21 November 1918 the Armistice negotiations achieved what the Grand Fleet had been unable to realize – the end of the High Seas Fleet. Detailed instructions were issued to the German ships being ceremonially interned by the Royal Navy (right). Beatty, now C-in-C Grand Fleet, urged the Prime Minister 'History will never acquit us if we miss the present opportunity of reducing effectively the menace to our sea power'. The *Riskflotte* finally died on 21 June 1919 when the disarmed ships were scuttled by their defiant crews in Scapa Flow.

Fleet were discernible through the haze. Nine battleships, five battlecruisers, seven light cruisers and 49 destroyers.

Admiral Ruge, then a junior officer on a torpedoboat, described the scene from the German side:

> There they came in the poor light of a grey November morning and surrounded us on all sides – squadron upon squadron, flotilla upon flotilla. In addition to the forty British capital ships, there were almost as many cruisers, 160 destroyers, an American squadron, a French ship and also aircraft and small non-rigid airships. Everywhere the crews stood by, their guns ready for action, equipped with gasmasks and flameproof asbestos helmets. If the situation was depressing for us, the deployment of such overwhelming strength looked like grudging recognition of the former powers of the High Seas Fleet . . .

The British, as they watched the superb ships of their enemies sailing through their lines ready to be escorted to their anchorage in Scapa Flow, expressed their own feelings of sadness that such a proud fleet should be brought to ignominious surrender. One officer wrote, 'I must confess it was a pitiful and morbid sight which was somewhat distasteful. I felt rather as if I was one of a crowd such as used to assemble for the funeral of some very sordid person who had been murdered, in pre-War days.'

The Germans were shepherded into their anchorage at Inchkeith. At 11 am Beatty signalled – 'The German Flag will be hauled down at sunset today, Thursday, and will not be hoisted again without permission.'

It was not until May 1919 that the High Seas Fleet interned in Scapa Flow discovered the Allied intentions, as laid before the German delegation at Versailles. The entire fleet at Scapa would be handed over to the victorious Allies, with Britain getting the largest share, 70 per cent. Germany would be allowed a minute navy of just 15,000 men and could maintain a small fleet of six vessels of 10,000 tons, six cruisers of 6,000 tons and a few destroyers and torpedoboats. Submarines or aircraft were strictly forbidden. The German sailors were deeply shocked by the uncompromising nature of the Treaty, which placed war guilt firmly on German shoulders and partitioned parts of the Reich. The peace conditions were so humiliating that the German Government considered whether they could possibly accept them. In the long delay whilst they considered their position, the ships at Scapa Flow began to prepare for a resumption of hostilities, even in their disarmed state. Misunderstanding the final position of the German Government, and taking advantage of the absence of Royal Navy guardships on exercises, Vice-Admiral von Reuter, commanding the Germans at Scapa Flow, issued orders for the High Seas Fleet to be scuttled.

Ruge described these last dramatic moments:

> The crews opened the valves and smashed pipes which had already been earmarked. They opened cabin doors, portholes and hatch covers. The anchor was thrown overboard and the capstan disabled. The British raced to the German anchorage but the scuttling had gone too far to be stopped.
>
> While we were disembarking the *Friedrich der Grosse*, Scheer's flagship at the battle of Jutland, was the first to sink at about 12.15 . . . The few officers had prepared her scuttling in secret so well that she sank in barely half an hour.
>
> The *König Albert* and the *Moltke* followed, and the *Seydlitz*, the champion of the fleet, which of all ships among friend and foe had suffered the heaviest battle casualties, turned on her side . . . A few minutes later the *Von der Tann* disappeared. She had won fame at the battle of Jutland, when, with a dozen salvoes from her heavy guns, she had destroyed the battlecruiser *Indefatigable*, a ship of the same size but more heavily armed. Half an hour later the fate of the *Derfflinger*, 'the iron dog', was settled. With the magnificent sweep of her 200-metre-long upper deck and her mighty funnel, she was the most beautiful ship in the fleet.

Precious little remained of the Kaiser's fleet and the German naval challenge except scrap-iron at the bottom of Scapa Flow.

"Der Tag."

Diagram of Surrender of German Fleet.

21st November, 1918.

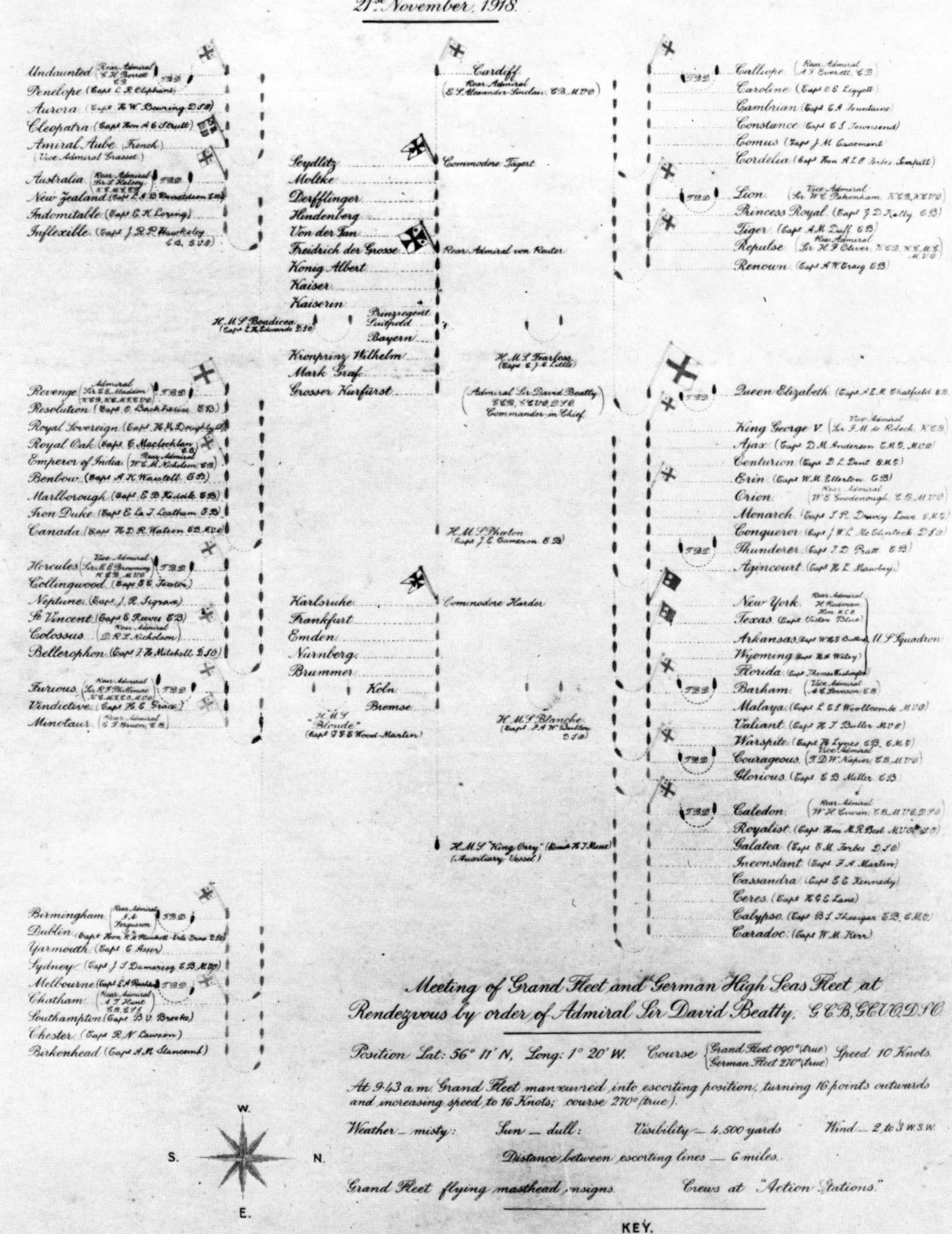

KEY.

Battleships	–	Blue.
Battle-cruisers	–	Red.
Cruisers	–	Green.
Aircraft Vessels	–	Shaded Black.
Destroyers	–	Black.

Saml A. Brooks, R.N.
Clarence H. Burd

63 (DESTROYERS) & TORPEDOBOATS ◢ ships sunk

9 LIGHT CRUISERS

4th Scouting Group

2nd Scouting Group

5 BATTLE CRUISERS

1st Scouting Group

Derfflinger
Lützow
Von der Tann
Moltke
Seydlitz

22 DREADNOUGHTS

2nd Sqdn.
3rd Div.: Pommern, Hessen, Deutschland
4th Div.: Schleswig Holstein, Schlesien, Hannover

1st Sqdn.
1st Div.: Oldenburg, Helgoland, Thüringen, Ostfriesland
2nd Div.: Westfalen, Nassau, Rheinland, Posen

3rd Sqdn.
5th Div.: Markgraf, Kronprinz Wilhelm, Grosser Kurfürst, König
6th Div.: Friedrich der Grosse, Prinzregent Luitpold, Kaiserin, Kaiser

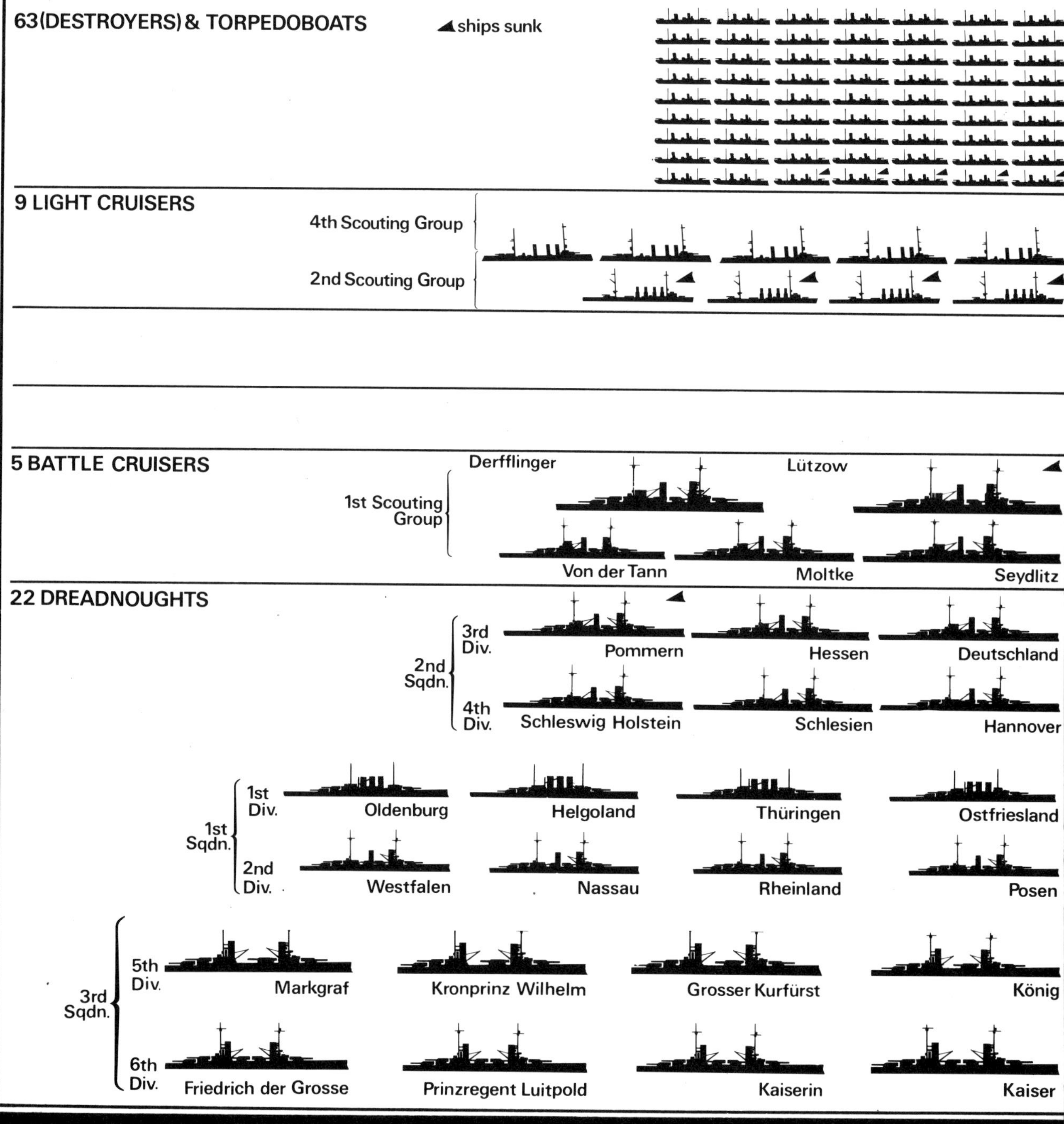

The Battle Fleets

THE GRAND FLEET

Admiral Sir John Jellicoe

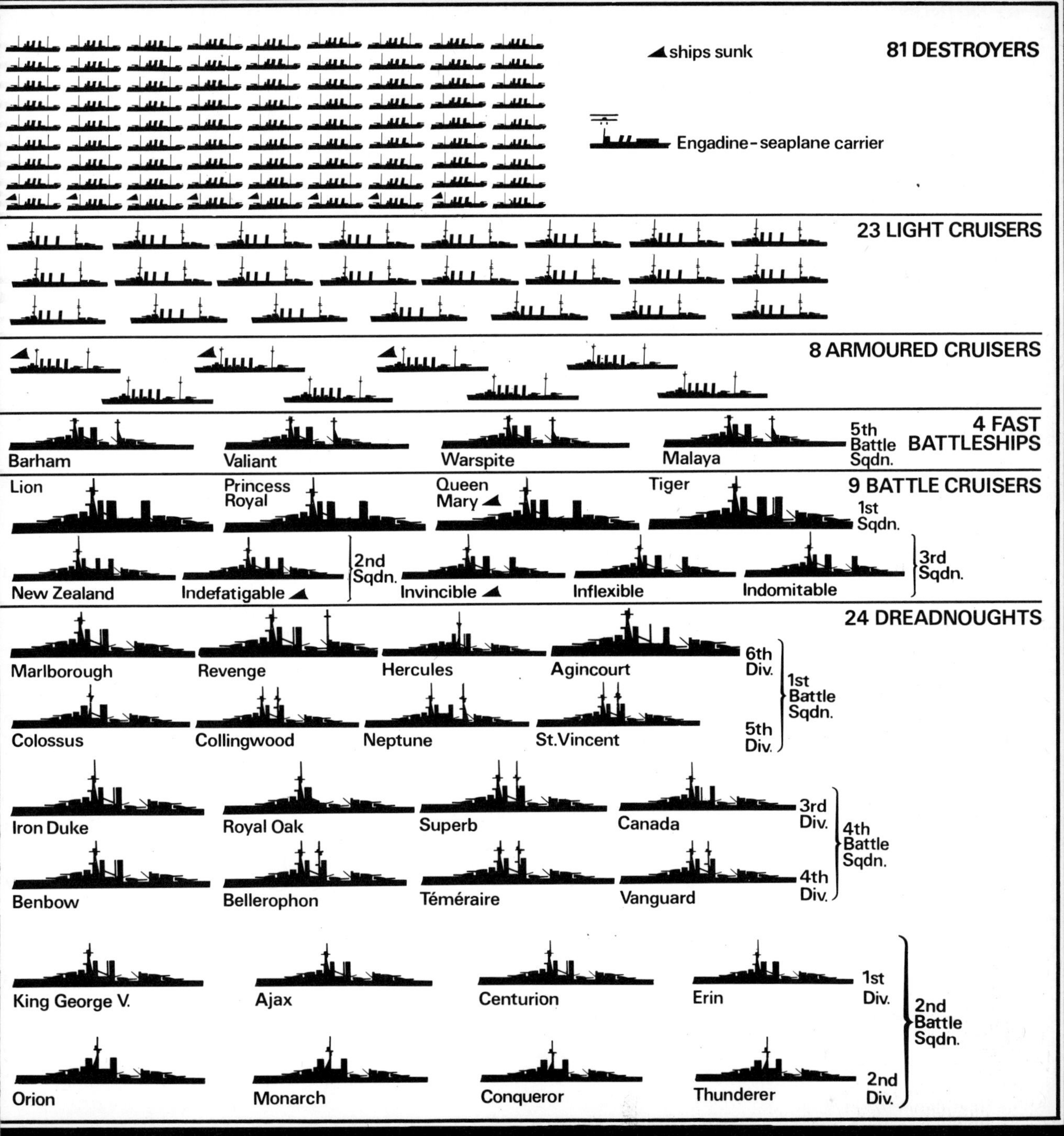

◢ ships sunk

81 DESTROYERS

Engadine - seaplane carrier

23 LIGHT CRUISERS

8 ARMOURED CRUISERS

4 FAST BATTLESHIPS — 5th Battle Sqdn.

Barham, Valiant, Warspite, Malaya

9 BATTLE CRUISERS

1st Sqdn.: Lion, Princess Royal, Queen Mary ◢, Tiger

2nd Sqdn.: New Zealand, Indefatigable ◢

3rd Sqdn.: Invincible ◢, Inflexible, Indomitable

24 DREADNOUGHTS

1st Battle Sqdn.

6th Div.: Marlborough, Revenge, Hercules, Agincourt

5th Div.: Colossus, Collingwood, Neptune, St.Vincent

4th Battle Sqdn.

3rd Div.: Iron Duke, Royal Oak, Superb, Canada

4th Div.: Benbow, Bellerophon, Téméraire, Vanguard

2nd Battle Sqdn.

1st Div.: King George V., Ajax, Centurion, Erin

2nd Div.: Orion, Monarch, Conqueror, Thunderer

Appendix Two

Organization of The High Seas Fleet

BATTLESHIPS

(in order from van to rear)

3rd SQUADRON
5th Division
König (Flagship of Rear-Admiral Paul Behncke)
Grosser Kurfürst
Kronprinz Wilhelm
Markgraf
6th Division
Kaiser (Flagship of Rear-Admiral Hermann Nordmann)
Kaiserin
Prinzregent Luitpold
Friedrich der Grosse[1] (Fleet Flagship of Vice-Admiral Reinhard Scheer)

1st SQUADRON
1st Division
Ostfriesland (Flagship of Vice-Admiral E. Schmidt)
Thüringen
Helgoland
Oldenburg
2nd Division
Posen (Flagship of Rear-Admiral Walter Engelhardt)
Rheinland
Nassau
Westfalen

2nd SQUADRON
3rd Division
Deutschland (Flagship of Rear-Admiral Franz Mauve)
Hessen
Pommern
4th Division
Hannover (Flagship of Rear-Admiral F. von Dalwigk zu Lichtenfels)
Schlesien
Schleswig-Holstein

CRUISERS

1st Scouting Group
(Battlecruisers)
Lützow (Flagship of Vice-Admiral Franz Hipper)
Derfflinger
Seydlitz
Moltke
Von der Tann

[1] Not in either the squadronal or the divisional organization.

2nd Scouting Group
(Light Cruisers)
Frankfurt (Flagship of Rear-Admiral Friedrich Boedicker)
Wiesbaden
Pillau
Elbing
4th Scouting Group
(Light Cruisers)
Stettin (*Broad pendant* of Commodore Ludwig von Reuter)
München
Hamburg
Frauenlob
Stuttgart

DESTROYER FLOTILLAS

Rostock (L.C.), 1st Leader of Torpedoboat Forces (*Broad pendant* of Commodore Andreas Michelsen)
First Half of 1st Flotilla (4 boats)
3rd Flotilla (7 boats)
5th Flotilla (11 boats)
7th Flotilla (9 boats)
Regensburg (L.C.), 2nd Leader of Torpedoboat Forces (*Broad pendant* of Commodore Paul Heinrich)
2nd Flotilla (10 boats)
6th Flotilla (9 boats)
9th Flotilla (11 boats)

Note. – Each flotilla consisted of 11 destroyers, and was divided up into two half-flotillas, the 1st Flotilla consisting of the 1st and 2nd Half-Flotillas, the 2nd Flotilla consisting of the 3rd and 4th Half-Flotillas, and so on.

Organization of The Grand Fleet

THE BATTLE FLEET

(in order from van to rear when deployed)

2nd BATTLE SQUADRON
1st Division
King George V (Flagship of Vice-Admiral Sir Martyn Jerram)
Ajax
Centurion
Erin
2nd Division
Orion (Flagship of Rear-Admiral A. C. Leveson)
Monarch
Conqueror
Thunderer

4th BATTLE SQUADRON
3rd Division
Iron Duke (Fleet Flagship of Admiral Sir John Jellicoe)
Royal Oak
Superb (Flagship of Rear-Admiral A. L. Duff)
Canada
4th Division
Benbow (Flagship of Vice-Admiral Sir Doveton Sturdee)
Bellerophon
Téméraire
Vanguard

1st BATTLE SQUADRON
6th Division
Marlborough (Flagship of Vice-Admiral Sir Cecil Burney)
Revenge
Hercules
Agincourt
5th Division
Colossus (Flagship of Rear-Admiral E. F. A. Gaunt)
Collingwood
Neptune
St. Vincent

Attached Light Cruisers[1]
Active
Bellona
Blanche
Boadicea
Canterbury
Chester
Attached
Abdiel (M.L.)
Oak (Destroyer Tender to Fleet Flagship)

BATTLE CRUISERS

3rd BATTLECRUISER SQUADRON
Invincible (Flagship of Rear-Admiral the Hon. H. L. A. Hood)
Inflexible

[1] Primarily for repeating visual signals between battle-fleet units.

Indomitable

ARMOURED CRUISERS

1st CRUISER SQUADRON

Defence (Flagship of Rear-Admiral Sir Robert Arbuthnot)
Warrior
Duke of Edinburgh
Black Prince

2nd CRUISER SQUADRON

Minotaur (Flagship of Rear-Admiral H. L. Heath)
Hampshire
Cochrane
Shannon

LIGHT CRUISERS

4th LIGHT CRUISER SQUADRON

Calliope (Commodore C. E. Le Mesurier)
Constance
Caroline
Royalist
Comus

DESTROYER FLOTILLAS

(Flot. L.: Flotilla Leader)

4th
Tipperary (Flot. L.; Captain C. J. Wintour)
Acasta
Achates
Ambuscade
Ardent
Broke (Flot. L.)
Christopher
Contest
Fortune
Garland
Hardy
Midge
Ophelia
Owl
Porpoise
Shark
Sparrowhawk
Spitfire
Unity
11th
Castor (L.C.; Commodore J. R. P. Hawksley)
Kempenfelt (Flot. L.)
Magic
Mandate
Manners
Marne
Martial
Michael
Milbrook
Minion
Mons
Moon
Morning Star
Mounsey
Mystic
Ossory
12th
Faulknor (Flot. L.; Captain A. J. B. Stirling)
Maenad
Marksman (Flot. L.)
Marvel
Mary Rose
Menace
Mindful
Mischief
Munster
Narwhal
Nessus
Noble
Nonsuch
Obedient
Onslaught
Opal

THE BATTLE-CRUISER FLEET

BATTLECRUISERS

(in order from van to rear)

Lion (Flagship of Vice-Admiral Sir David Beatty)

1st BATTLECRUISER SQUADRON

Princess Royal (Flagship of Rear-Admiral O. de Brock)
Queen Mary
Tiger

2nd BATTLECRUISER SQUADRON

New Zealand (Flagship of Rear-Admiral W. C. Pakenham)
Indefatigable

FAST BATTLESHIPS

5th BATTLE SQUADRON

Barham (Flagship of Rear-Admiral Hugh Evan-Thomas)
Valiant
Warspite
Malaya

LIGHT CRUISERS

1st LIGHT CRUISER SQUADRON

Galatea (Commodore E. S. Alexander-Sinclair)
Phaeton
Inconstant
Cordelia

2nd LIGHT CRUISER SQUADRON

Southampton (Commodore W. E. Goodenough)
Birmingham
Nottingham
Dublin

3rd LIGHT CRUISER SQUADRON

Falmouth (Flagship of Rear-Admiral T. D. W. Napier)
Yarmouth
Birkenhead
Gloucester

DESTROYER FLOTILLAS

1st
Fearless (L.C.; Captain D. C. Roper)
Acheron
Ariel
Attack
Badger
Defender
Goshawk
Hydra
Lapwing
Lizard
9th and 10th (combined)
9th
Lydiard (Commander M. L. Goldsmith)
Landrail
Laurel
Liberty
10th
Moorsom
Morris
Termagent
Turbulent
13th
Champion (L.C.; Captain J. U. Farie)
Moresby
Narborough
Nerissa
Nestor
Nicator
Nomad
Obdurate
Onslow
Pelican
Petard
Seaplane Carrier
Engadine

THE BATTLE THAT SHOULD NOT

The Lost Trafalgar

Within three days of the last shot being fired in the Battle of Jutland a full scale series of inquiries was ordered by the Admiralty into every aspect of the action. Committees were set up to review strategy, tactics, intelligence, communications and above all materiel. The inquest sought the answer to one vital question: why had the Grand Fleet, with its superior numbers and overwhelming gunpower been unable to achieve a second Trafalgar? Recriminations as to who was to blame for losing such an opportunity split the Royal Navy into factions until the outbreak of the Second World War. The debate centred largely on the actions of Beatty and Jellicoe. The Beatty camp maintained that an over-cautious Jellicoe had not exploited Beatty's skilful delivery of the High Seas Fleet into the jaws of the Grand Fleet. The C-in-C's protagonists charged that Beatty failed to keep Jellicoe informed of the movement and disposition of the Germans and that his impetuous charge on sighting Hipper, together with signalling failures, had failed to bring the 5th Battle Squadron into action at the decisive point.

31 May: Indecisive Confrontation

In the sound and fury, the central issue was rarely examined. This, in our view, is: could any Admiral, British or German – even Nelson himself – have fought Jutland to a decisive conclusion given the circumstances of uncertain visibility and weather; the limitations of materiel and communications and the overriding strategic dictates of the war?

In the first phase of the battle on 31 May, the Germans sought a decisive action with Beatty's battle-cruisers, in pursuit of their plan to destroy a part of the British Fleet. Following Hipper's brilliant decoy of Beatty's forces on to the guns of the German Battle Fleet, the British commander skilfully turned the tables and, in spite of heavy losses, lured Scheer's High Seas Fleet into Jellicoe's battle line.

Once Scheer realized that he was confronting the full might of the enemy – which had never figured in his tactical and strategic plan – he turned away to avoid destruction by the overwhelming British firepower (although minutes later, perhaps anxious to avoid the stigma of retreat, Scheer turned once more towards Jellicoe's line before being forced to withdraw).

Jellicoe, bound to his cautious tactics which discounted the option of pursuing a retreating enemy, was not in a position to fight a decisive action in the remaining hours of daylight. Moreover, if Jellicoe had accepted the risk of pursuing Scheer through the smoke screens and anticipated mine and torpedo attacks, his battle fleet lacked the speed to bring its full weight to bear against the Germans once again. In any event, failing visibility, inadequate reconnaissance and uncertain communications between the British ships would have militated against a decisive Fleet action in the last hours of daylight.

Had Jellicoe managed to bring Scheer to an extended battle, it should be remembered that the Germans had achieved a far higher degree of success than the Grand Fleet in the daylight gunnery actions of 31 May. Although each side scored approximately the same percentage of hits, the British failed to sink a comparable number of Scheer's warships. As the *Seydlitz* revealed, after surviving twenty-one hits by heavy shell, ship-for-ship the High Seas Fleet was far stronger than the British. Internal sub-division, damage control, and the anti-flash protection installed after Dogger Bank went a long way towards fulfilling Tirpitz's dictum of making German ships 'unsinkable'. Furthermore the Grand Fleet's anticipated advantage in superior gun-power, bought at the expense of lighter protection, was sadly thrown away because of the poor quality of British shells. At the oblique impact produced by the very long gunnery ranges, the sensitive explosive and weak fuses of the British ammunition exploded before penetrating the German side armour. According to Admiralty experts, efficient armour piercing shell, with which the Fleet was supplied after Jutland, could have sunk at least six German capital ships.

1 June: The Empty Dawn

If the action on 31 May was inconclusive, could the Royal Navy have achieved a second Glorious First of June the next day? As darkness closed in, the British had the immense advantage of being between Scheer

AVE BEEN FOUGHT?

and his bases. Even though the German admiral was unwilling to risk battle, all other things being equal and provided the Grand Fleet could maintain its position – Scheer was trapped. That night, a Fleet action seemed inevitable the next day. What went wrong?

Jellicoe's night dispositions proved insufficient to keep track of the precise course of the High Seas Fleet. This was compounded by the British Fleet's aversion to night fighting. Lacking star-shell and an efficient night signalling system, British ships were ill-equipped and untrained for fighting in darkness. Even when they brushed with Scheer's forces during the hours of darkness, the British captains failed to report the action to the C-in-C. Incredible lapses in signalling vital information occurred, not once, but many times during the night.

Deprived of this essential information and having made the wrong assumption on Scheer's route for home, Jellicoe was unable to reconcile Admiralty intelligence signals with what he believed the situation to be. Moreover, information deciphered by the Admiralty which would have made it clear that the High Seas Fleet was stealing across the rear of the Grand Fleet was not transmitted to Jellicoe in time for him to take action. This chain of errors and misjudgements, combined with Scheer's determination to push through to his bases, meant that by dawn on 1 June the Germans had effected their escape.

Churchill's Mistake

Many of the Grand Fleet's shortcomings at Jutland might have been overcome, had the lessons of the Dogger Bank action been properly evaluated. In 1915, a review of the conduct of the Dogger Bank battle was refused by the First Lord, Winston Churchill. This was a mistake. The Dogger Bank battle had revealed the poor gunnery performance of the battlecruisers, their vulnerability to damage, and mismanagement of signalling and communication. Even the 'turn away' from suspected submarine attack, which had been instrumental in assisting the German battlecruisers to escape, might have been reconsidered as a result of an analysis of the action. Battlecruiser losses at Jutland might also have been averted had anti-flash precautions been installed following the damage inflicted on British ships at Dogger Bank and the Falkland Islands. But Churchill's understandable motive for refusing the demand for an inquiry was his determination to ensure that the Navy's much-needed victory should not be tarnished. As he wrote: 'The victory of the Dogger Bank brought for the time being abruptly to an end the adverse movement against my administration of the Admiralty.'

The Unmanageable Deterrent

Yet even if the errors and inadequacies which had been revealed in the British Fleet had been remedied and Jellicoe had succeeded in bringing the Germans to battle on 1 June, could a decisive result have been achieved by two dreadnought battle fleets? Were the means of command and communication then in existence sufficient to allow the two commanders to control their long battle lines, squadrons and flotillas at high speed over vast areas in uncertain visibility? Could they, in the confusion of battle, have concentrated their forces long enough to achieve a truly decisive result? The dreadnought technology and tactics which had been forced at a frantic pace before the war, may well have outstripped the human capability to control it.

The Grand Fleet achieved its strategic purpose simply by being in Scapa Flow, supporting the blockade and presenting a threat to the inferior German force, which dare not confront it in a head-on clash. In this sense, even though the public clamoured for a long-awaited naval victory, the Battle of Jutland was unnecessary for both sides. The British did not need to force a battle; the Germans could not risk one.

For all Admiral Scheer's belief that the Royal Navy's dominance could be ended by a series of actions with inferior units of the Grand Fleet, Jutland proved his thinking to be fallacious. The only successful strategy for the Germans might well have been for them to borrow Fisher's concept of a 'bolt from the blue' – to 'Copenhagen the Grand Fleet' with a pre-emptive strike by torpedoboats and submarines, before the outbreak of war. It was just this tactic which was ruthlessly applied by another inferior naval-power twenty-five years later, when Japanese carrier planes attacked the American fleet at Pearl Harbor.

BIBLIOGRAPHY

ADMIRALTY, British
Jutland Despatches
Narrative of the Battle of Jutland
Record of the Battle of Jutland; prepared by Captain J. E. T. Harper

BACON, Admiral Sir R. H.
The Life of John Rushworth Earl Jellicoe

BALFOUR, Michael
The Kaiser and His Times

CHALMERS, Rear-Admiral W. S.
The Life and Letters of David Beatty, Admiral of the Fleet

CHATFIELD, Admiral of the Fleet, Lord
The Navy and Defence

CHURCHILL, Winston S.
The World Crisis, 1914–1918

CORBETT, Julian, and NEWBOLT, Henry
Naval Operations, 1914–1918

DREYER, Admiral Sir Frederic
The Sea Heritage

FAWCETT, H. W., and HOOPER, G. W. W.
The Fighting at Jutland

FISCHER, Fritz
Griff nach der Weltmacht
World Power or Decline

FREIWALD, Ludwig
Last Days of the German Fleet

FROST, Commander H., USN
The Battle of Jutland

GEBESCHUS, K.
Doggerbank

GIBSON, Langhorne, and HARPER, Vice-Admiral J. E. T.
The Riddle of Jutland

HARPER, Vice-Admiral J. E. T.
The Truth about Jutland

HASE, Commander G. von
Kiel and Jutland

HERWIG, H. H.
The German Naval Officer Corps

HISLAM, P. A.
The Admiralty of the Atlantic

HORN, Daniel
War, Mutiny and Revolution in the German Navy

JAMESON, Rear-Admiral Sir William
The Fleet that Jack Built

JELLICOE, Admiral Viscount John R.
The Grand Fleet, 1914–1916: Its Creation, Development and Work

KEMP, Lieutenant-Commander P. K.
The Papers of Admiral Sir John Fisher (*Navy Records Society*)

MACINTYRE, Captain Donald
Jutland

MARDER, A. J.
Fear God and Dread Nought
From the Dreadnought to Scapa Flow

MORRIS, A. J. (Editor)
Radicals Against War

MOUNTBATTEN, The Earl of Burma, Admiral of the Fleet
The Battle of Jutland (*remarks written in 1967, 51 years after the battle*)

NAVY RECORDS SOCIETY
The Jellicoe Papers

RITTER, Gerhard
Staatskunst und Kriegshandwerk, Das Problem des 'Militarismus' in Deutschland

RÜGE, Friedrich
Scapa Flow 1919

SCHEER, Admiral Reinhard
Germany's High Seas Fleet in the World War

SCHOFFELIUS, H., and DEIST, W.
Marine und Marinepolitik im Kaiserlichen Deutschland, 1871–1914 (*Seminar*)

STEINBERG, Jonathan
Yesterday's Deterrent

STUMPF
The Private War of Seaman . . .

TIRPITZ, Grand Admiral von
My Memoirs

WALDEYER-HARTZ, Hugo von
Admiral von Hipper

WOODWARD, C. L.
Great Britain and the German Navy

Articles

HAGGIE, Paul
'The Royal Navy and War Planning in the Fisher Era' – Journal of Contemporary History, Vol. 8 No. 3 (July 1973)

JORDAN, Gerald H. S.
'Pensions not Dreadnoughts' – Edwardian Radicalism 1900–1914 (Ed. A. J. A. Morris)

ROSKILL, S. W.
'The Dismissal of Admiral Jellicoe' – Journal of Contemporary History, Vol. 1 No. 4 (1966)

STEINBERG, Jonathan
'The Copenhagen Complex' – Journal of Contemporary History, Vol. 1 No. 3
'The Novelle of 1908' – Transactions of the Royal Historical Society (5th series, Vol. 21)
'The Kaiser's Navy and German Society' – Past and Present 28

WOODWARD, David
'Mutiny at Wilhelmshaven' – History Today, Vol. XVII No. 11

INDEX

The B

HIGH SEAS FLEET

Admiral Reinhard Scheer

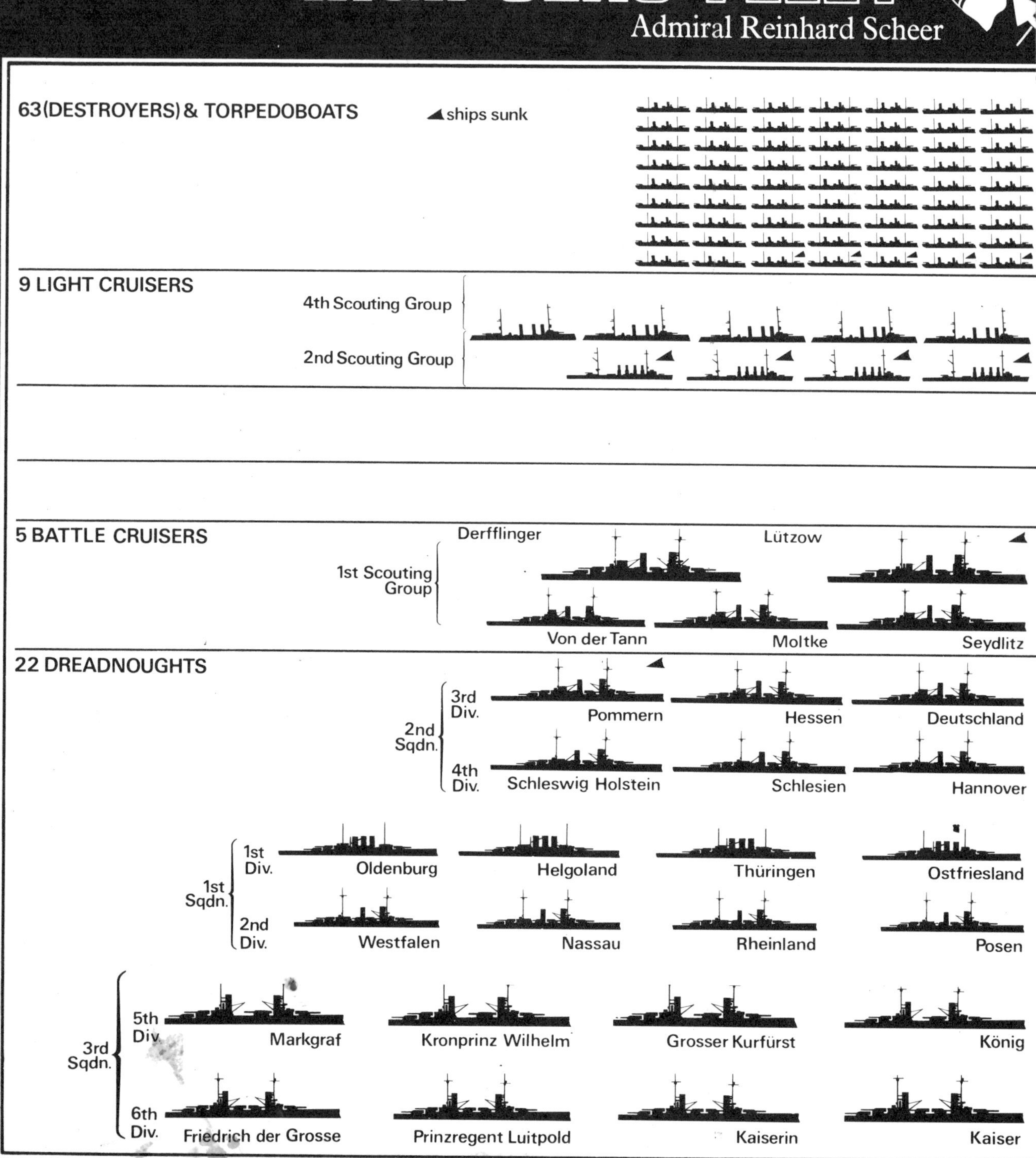